AL-MAJALLA AL AHKAM AL ADALIYYAH
(The Ottoman Courts Manual (Hanafi))

AL-MAJALLA AL AHKAM AL ADALIYYAH
(The Ottoman Courts Manual (Hanafi))

INTRODUCTION.

Part I Definition and Classification of Islamic Jurisprudence

- 1. The science of Islamic jurisprudence consists of a knowledge of the precepts of the Divine Legislator in their relation to human affairs.

The questions of Islamic jurisprudence either concern the next world, being known as rules relating to worship, or to this world, being divided into sections dealing with domestic relations, civil obligations and punishments. Thus Allah decreed the continuation of the world until the appointed time. This, however, can only occur by mankind being perpetuated which is dependent upon marriage of male and female with a view to procreation. Moreover, the continuation of the human species is assured by individuals association together. Man, however, is view of the weakness of his nature is dependent upon food, clothing, housing and the industries for his subsistence. In other words, in view of the fact that man is a civilised being, he cannot live in >itude like the other animals, but is in need of co-operation and association in work with his fellow men in order to live in a state of civilisation. Every person, however, asks for the things which he likes and avoids things which are disagreeable to him. As a result, it has been necessary to establish laws of a nature likely to maintain order and justice as regards marriage, mutual help and social relations, which are the basis of all civilisation.

The first division of Islamic jurisprudence is the section dealing with domestic relations. The second is the section dealing with civil obligations. In view of the fact that the continuance of civilisation on this basis necessitates the drawing up of certain matters relating to punishments, the third section of Islamic jurisprudence deals with punishments.

As regards the section dealing with civil obligations, the questions which are of the most frequent occurrence have been collected together from reliable works and set out in this Code in the form of Books. These Books have been divided into Chapters and the Chapters into Sections. The questions of detail which will be applied in the courts are those questions which are set out in the following Chapters and Sections. Islamic jurists. however, have grouped questions of Islamic jurisprudence under certain general rules, each one of which embraces a large number of questions and which, in the treatises on Islamic jurisprudence, are taken as justification to prove these questions. The preliminary study of these rules facilitates the comprehension of the questions and serves to fix them in the mind. Consequently, ninety nine rules of Islamic jurisprudence have been collected together as follows, before commencing on the main work and form part II.

Although a few of them, taken alone, admit of certain exceptions their general application is in no way invalidated thereby, since they are closely interrelated.

PART II. MAXIMS OF ISLAMIC JURISPRUDENCE.

- 2. A matter is determined according to intention; that is to say, the effect to be given to any particular transaction must conform to the object of such transaction.
- 3. In contracts effect is given to intention and meaning and not to words and phrases. Consequently, a contract for sale subject to a right of redemption has the force of a pledge.
- 4. Certainty is not dispelled by doubt.
- 5. It is a fundamental principle that a thing shall remain as it was originally.
- 6. Things which have been in existence from time immemorial shall be left as they were.
- 7. Injury cannot exist from time immemorial.
- 8. Freedom from liability is a fundamental principle. Therefore, if one person destroys the property of another, and a dispute arises as to the amount thereof, the statement of the person causing such destruction shall be heard, and the onus of the proof as to any amount in excess thereof is upon the owner of such property.
- 9. Non-existence is a fundamental principle which applies to all rights which may subsequently accrue. Example:- In a case of partnership of capital and labour, a dispute arises as to whether profit has been made or not. The statement of the person supplying the labour is heard, and the owner of the capital must prove that profit has in fact been made, since the fundamental principle is the non-existence of the profit.
- 10. Judgement shall be given in respect to any matter which has been proved at any particular time, unless the contrary is proved.

  Consequently, if it is proved at any particular time that a particular thing is owned by a particular person in absolute ownership, the ownership thereof shall be held to be valid unless circumstances arise which invalidate such ownership.
- 11. It is a fundamental principle that any new occurrence shall be regarded as happening at the time nearest to the present. That is to say, if a dispute arises regarding the cause of some new event and the time at which it occurred, such event shall be considered with reference to the time nearest to the present, unless it is proved that it relates to some remoter period.
- 12. It is a fundamental principle that words shall be construed literally.
- 13. No attention shall be paid to inferences in the face of obvious facts.
- 14. Where the text is clear, there is no room for interpretation.
- 15. A matter which has been proved contrary to legal analogy cannot be cited by way of analogy in respect to any other matter.
- 16. One legal interpretation does not destroy another.
- 17. Difficulty begets facility; that is to say, difficulty is the cause of facility and in time of hardship

consideration must be shown. Very many subjects of Islamic jurisprudence, such as loans, transfer of debts and interdiction are derived from this principle, and the latitude and indulgence shown by Islamic jurists in their rulings are all based upon this rule.

- 18. Latitude should be afforded in the case of difficulty, that is to say, upon the appearance of hardship in any particular matter, latitude and indulgence must be shown.

- 19. Injury may not be met by injury.

- 20. Injury is removed.

- 21. Necessity renders prohibited things permissible

- 22. Necessity is estimated by the extent thereof.

- 23. A thing which is permissible by reason of the existence of some excuse thereof, ceases to be permissible with the disappearance of that excuse.

- 24. When a prohibition is removed, the thing to which such prohibition attaches reverts to its former status of legality.

- 25. An injury cannot be removed by the commission of a similar injury.

- 26. A private injury is tolerated in order to ward off a public injury. The prohibition from practice of an incompetent physician is derived from this principle.

- 27. Severe injury is removed by lesser injury.

- 28. In the presence of two evils, the greater is avoided by the commission of the lesser.

- 29. The lesser of the two evils is preferred.

- 30. Repelling an evil is preferable to securing a benefit.

- 31. Injury is removed as far as possible.

- 32. Any want, whether of a public or private nature, is so dealt with as to meet the exigencies of the case. The validity of sale subject to a right of redemption is of this nature. The inhabitants of Bokhara having fallen badly into debt, this procedure was put into operation in order to meet the exigencies of the case.

- 33. Necessity does not invalidate the right of another. Consequently, if a hungry person eats bread belonging to another, such person must later pay the value thereof.

- 34. A thing which may not be taken may also not be given.

- 35. It is forbidden to request the performance of a prohibited act.

- 36. Custom is an arbitrator; that is to say, custom, whether public or private, may be invoked to justify the giving of judgement.

- 37. Public usage is conclusive evidence and action must be taken in accordance therewith.

- 38. A thing which it is customary to regard as impossible is considered to be impossible in fact.

- 39. It is an accepted fact that the terms of law vary with the change in the times.

- 40. In the presence of custom no regard is paid to the literal meaning of a thing.

- 41. Effect is only given to custom where it is of regular occurrence or when universally prevailing.

- 42. Effect is given to what is of common occurrence; not to what happens infrequently.

- 43. A matter recognised by custom is regarded as though it were a contractual obligation.

- 44. A matter recognised by merchants is regarded as being a contractual obligation between them.

- 45. A matter established by custom is like a matter established by law.

- 46. When prohibition and necessity conflict, preference is given to the prohibition.

  Consequently, a person may not sell to another a thing which he has given to his creditor as security for debt.

- 47. An accessory which is attached to an object in fact is also attached to it is law. Consequently, when a pregnant animal is sold, the young in its womb is sold with it.

- 48. An accessory to an object cannot be dealt with separately.yvT A Example: The young in an animal's womb cannot be sold separately.

- 49. The owner of a thing held in absolute ownership is also the owner of the things indispensable to the enjoyment of such thing.yvT K Example: A person who buys a house is also owner of the road leading to it.

- 50. If the principle fails, the accessory also fails.

- 51. A thing which fails is not restored; that is to say, that which goes does not return.

- 52. When a thing becomes void, the thing contained in it also becomes void.

- 53. When the original undertaking cannot be carried out, the equivalent thereof is carried out.

- 54. A thing which is not permissible in itself, may be permissible as an accessory. Example:- It is not permissible for purchaser to make the vendor his agent to receive the thing sold; but it he gives a sack to the vendor to measure and put therein the provisions which he has brought and the vendor puts the provisions into the sack, the purchaser thereby receives them impliedly and as an accessory.

- 55. A thing which is not permissible at the outset may become permissible at some later period. Example:- The disposal of a share of undivided jointly owned property by way of gift is invalid, but if a person entitled to a share of undivided jointly owned property which has been bestowed by way of gift appears and takes possession thereof, the gift does not become the property of the recipient of the gift.

- 56. Continuance is easier than commencement.

- 57. A gift becomes absolute only when delivery thereof is taken. Example:- A person bestows a thing upon another person by way of gift. Such gift is not binding until delivery thereof has been taken.

- 58. The exercise of control over subjects is dependent upon the public welfare.

- 59. Private guardianship is more effective than public guardianship. Example:- The guardianship exercised by the trustee of a pious foundation is more effective than the guardianship of the court.

- 60. A word should be construed as having some meaning, rather than passed over in silence. That is to say, if any particular meaning can be attributed to a word, it may not be passed over as devoid of meaning.

- 61. When the literal meaning cannot be applied, the metaphorical sense may be used.

- 62. If no meaning can be attached to a word it is disregarded altogether. That is to say, if a word cannot be construed in either a literal or metaphorical sense it is passed over in silence as being devoid of meaning.

- 63. A reference to part of an indivisible thing is regarded as a reference to the whole.

- 64. The absolute is construed in its absolute sense, provided that there is no proof of a restricted meaning either in the text of the law or by implication.

- 65. A description with reference to a thing present is of no effect, but the contrary is the case if such thing is not present. Example:- When a vendor who is about to sell a grey horse, such grey horse being present at the meeting where the sale took place, states that he is selling a brown horse for so many thousand piastres, his offer is held to be good and the word brown is of no effect. But if he sells a grey horse which is not present and he describes it as brown, the description is held to be good but the sale is not concluded.

- 66. A question is considered to have been repeated in the answer. That is to say, in the event of a question being answered in the affirmative, the person answering the question is considered to have repeated the question.

- 67. No statement is imputed to a man who keeps silence, but silence is tantamount to a statement where there is an absolute necessity for speech. That is to say, it may not be said that a person who keeps silence has made such and such a statement, but if he keeps silence where he ought to have made a statement, such silence is regarded as an admission and statement.

- 68. In obscure matters the proof of a thing stands in the place of such thing. That is to say, obscure matters concerning which it is hard to discover the truth are judged according to the obvious proof concerning them.

- 69. Correspondence takes the place of an exchange of conversation.

- 70. The sign of a dumb person which are generally recognised take the place of a statement by word of mouth.

- 71. The word of an interpreter is accepted in every respect.

- 72. No validity is attached to conjecture which is obviously tainted by error.

- 73. Probability, even though based upon evidence, is not proof. Example:- If a person admits while suffering from mortal sickness that he owes a certain sum of money to one of his heirs, such admission is not a proof unless confirmed by the other heirs, since the probability of such person defrauding the other heirs of their property is based upon the mortal sickness . If the statement, however, is made while in a state of good health, such admission is considered to be valid. The probability is that case is mere supposition and consequently there is no objection to the validity of the admission.

- 74. No weight is attached to mere supposition.

- 75. A thing established by proof is equivalent to a thing established by ocular inspection.

- 76. EVIDENCE IS FOR HIM WHO AFFIRMS; THE OATH FOR HIM WHO DENIES.

- 77. The object of evidence is to prove what is contrary to appearance; the object of the oath is to ensure the continuance of the original state.

- 78. Evidence is proof affecting third person; admission is proof affecting the person making such admission only.

- 79. A person is bound by his own admission.

- 80. Contradiction and proof are incompatible; but this does not invalidate a judgement given against the person contradicting. Example:- Witnesses contradict themselves by going back upon the evidence they have given. Such evidence is not proof; but if the court has already given judgement based upon the original evidence, such judgement may not be set aside, but the witnesses must pay the value of the subject matter of the judgement to the persons against whom judgement has been given.

- 81. Failure to establish the principle claim does not imply failure to establish a claim subsidiary thereto. Example:- A person states that A owes a sum of money to B and that he has the surety of A. Such person will be obliged to pay the sum in question if A repudiates the debt and B demands payment.

- 82. If the validity of a condition is established, the validity of anything dependent thereon must also be established.

- 83. A condition must be observed as far as possible.

- 84. Any promise dependent upon a condition is irrevocable upon such condition being fulfilled. Example:- A person tells A to sell a certain thing to B and informs A he will pay him in the event of B failing to do so, and B does in fact fail so to do. The person making the promise is obliged to pay the money.

- 85. The enjoyment of a thing is the compensating factor for any liability attaching thereto; that is to say, in the event of a thing being destroyed, the person to whom such thing belongs must suffer the loss and conversely may enjoy any advantages attaching thereto. Example:- An animal is returned by reason of an option for defect. The vendor may not charge any fee on account of the use of the animal, because if it had been fallen upon the purchaser.

- 86. Remuneration and liability to make good loss do not run together.

- 87. Disadvantage is an obligation accompanying enjoyment. That is to say, a person who enjoys a thing must submit to the disadvantages attaching thereto.

- 88. The burden is in proportion to the benefit and the benefit to the burden.

- 89. The responsibility for an act falls upon the author thereof; it does not fall upon the person ordering such act to be performed, provided that such person does not compel the commission thereof.

- 90. If a person performs any act personally and is implicated therein with the person who is the cause thereof, the person performing such act is responsible thereof. Example:- A digs a well in the public highway and B causes C's animal to fall therein and to be destroyed. B is responsible thereof and no liability rests with the person who dug the well.

- 91. An act allowed by law cannot be made the subject of a claim to compensation. Example:- An animal belonging to A falls into a well which B has dug on his own property held in absolute ownership and such animal is destroyed . No compensation can be claimed.

- 92. A person who performs an act, even though not intentionally, is liable to make good any loss caused thereby.

- 93. A person who is the cause of an act being performed is not liable to make good any loss caused by such act unless he has acted intentionally.

- 94. No liability attaches in connection with offences of or damage caused by animals of their own accord.

- 95. Any order given for dealing with the property of any other person held in absolute ownership is void.

- 96. No person may deal with the property of another held in absolute ownership without such person's permission.

- 97. No person may take another person's property without some legal reason.
- 98. Any change is the cause of the ownership of a thing held in absolute ownership is equivalent to a change in that thing itself.
- 99. Any person who hastens the accomplishment of a thing before its due time, is punished by being deprived thereof.
- 100. If any person seeks to disavow any act performed by himself, such attempt is entirely disregarded.

AL-MAJALLA AL AHKAM AL ADALIYYAH
(The Ottoman Courts Manual (Hanafi))

BOOK 1. SALE.

INTRODUCTION

TERM OF ISLAMIC JURISPRUDENCE RELATING TO SALE.

- 101. Offer is the statement made in the first place with a view to making a disposition of property and such disposition is proved thereby.

- 102. Acceptance is the statement made in the second place with a view to making a disposition of property. The contract becomes completed thereby.

- 103. Contract is what the parties bind themselves and undertake to do with reference to a particular matter. It is composed of the combination of offer and acceptance.

- 104. The conclusion of a contract consists of connecting offer and acceptance together legally in such a manner that the result may be perfectly clear.

- 105. Sale consists of exchanging property for property. It may be concluded or non-concluded.

- 106. A concluded sale is a sale in which there is a concluded contract. Such sales are divided into valid, voidable, executory, and conditional.

- 107. A non-concluded sale is a :
  (1) It is a thing the benefit of which is lawful to enjoy;
  (2) The other is acquired property.

  Example:- A fish while in the sea is not of any specific value. When it is caught and taken, it becomes property of some specific value.

- 108. A valid sale, or a sale which is permitted, is a sale which is lawful both in itself and as regards matters incidental thereto.

- 109. A voidable sale is a sale which, while valid in itself, is invalid as regards matters incidental thereto. That is to say, it is a concluded sale in itself, but is illegal as regards certain external particulars.(See chapter Vll.)

- 110. A void sale is a sale which is invalid in itself.

- 111. A conditional sale is a sale which is dependent upon the rights of some third party, such as a sale by an unauthorised person.

- 112. An unauthorised person is a person who, without any legal permission, deals with the property of some other person.

- 113. An executory sale is a sale not dependent upon the right of any third person. Such sales are divided into irrevocable and revocable sales.

- 114. An irrevocable sale is an executory sale to which no option is attached .

- 115. A revocable sale is an executory sale to which an option is attached.

- 116. An option means having the power to choose, as will be explained in the relevant chapter.

- 117. An absolute sale is a final sale.

- 118. A sale subject to a right of redemption is a sale in which one person sells property to another for a certain sum of money, subject to the right of redeeming such property, upon the price thereof being returned. Such a sale is considered to be permissible in view of the fact that the purchaser has a right to enjoyment of the property sold. It is also in the nature of a voidable sale inasmuch as the two parties have the right of cancelling the sale. Again, it is in the nature of pledge, in view of the fact that the purchaser cannot sell the property sold to any third party.

- 119. A sale with a right of usufruct is a sale subject to a right of redemption, the vendor having a right to take the property sold on hire.

- 120. Sales are also divided into four categories with reference to the thing sold:
  1) Sale of property to another person for a price. This is the commonest category of sale and is consequently specifically called sale;
  2)Sale by exchange of money for money;
  3) Sale by barter; $ Sale by immediate payment against future delivery.

- 121. Exchange of money for money consists of selling cash for cash.

- 122. Sale by barter consists of exchanging one specific object for some other specific object, that is to say, of exchanging property for property other than money.

- 123. Sale by immediate payment against future delivery consists of paying in advance for something to be delivered later, that is to say, to purchase something with money paid in advance, thereby giving credit.

- 124. A contract for manufacture and sale consists of making a contract with any skilled person for the manufacture of any thing. The person making the article is called the manufacturer; the person causing the article to be made is called the contractor for manufacture, and the object made is called the manufactured article.

- 125. Property held in absolute ownership is anything owned absolutely be man and may consist either of some specific object or of an interest therein.

- 126. Property consists of something desired by human nature and which can be put aside against time of necessity. It comprises movable and immovable property.

- 127. Property of some specific value is spoken of in two senses.
  (1) It is a thing the benefit of which is lawful to enjoy;
  (2) The other is acquired property.
  Example:- A fish while in the sea is not of any specific value. When it is caught and taken, it becomes property of some specific value.

- 128. Movable property consists of property which can be transferred from one place to another. This includes cash, merchandise, animals, things estimated by measure of capacity and things estimated by weight.

- 129. Immovable property consists of property such as houses and land which are called real property and which cannot be transferred to another place.

- 130. Cash consists of gold and silver coins.

- 131. Merchandise consists of things such as goods and piece-goods other than cash, animals, things estimated by measure of capacity and things estimated by weight.
- 132. Things estimated by quantity are those things the amount of which is determined by any measure of capacity or of weight, or of number, or of length.
- 133. These articles repeat the measures of capacity etc. given in Articles 131 and 132 above.
- 134. These articles repeat the measures of capacity etc. given in Articles 131 and 132 above.
- 135. These articles repeat the measures of capacity etc. given in Articles 131 and 132 above.
- 136. These articles repeat the measures of capacity etc. given in Articles 131 and 132 above.
- 137. The expression 'possessing defined boundaries' refer to real property the boundaries and limits of which can be fixed.
- 138. undivided jointly owned property is property which contains undivided jointly owned shares.
- 139. An undivided jointly owned share is a share which extends to and includes every part of the jointly owned property.
- 140. By a particular species of thing is meant a thing in respect to which there is no disproportionate difference in so far as the component elements thereof are concerned.
- 141. A wholesale contract is a contract for sale en bloc.
- 142. Right of way is the right of passing over real property held in absolute ownership belonging to another.
- 143. The right of taking water is the right of taking a clearly defined and ascertained share of water from a river.
- 144. The right of flow is the right of discharging water and of letting water drip from a house to some place outside.
- 145. A common article is a thing the like of which can be found in the market without any difference of price.
- 146. A rare article is an article the like of which cannot be found in the market, or, if it can be found, is different in price.
- 147. Articles measured by enumeration and which closely resemble each other are those things in respect to which there is no difference as regards the price of each particular object. They are all in the nature of common articles.
- 148. Articles measured by enumeration and which are dissimilar from each other are those things is respect to which a difference in price exists as regards each particular article. They are all regarded as rare articles.
- 149. The fundamental basis or essence of sale consists of one piece of property being exchanged for another. Offer and acceptance are also referred to as the fundamental basis of sale, since they imply exchange.
- 150. The subject of sale is the thing sold.
- 151. The thing sold is the property disposed of, that is, the specific object specified at the sale and which constitutes the original object thereof, because enjoyment can only be had of specific objects, price being the means of exchanging property.
- 152. The price is the amount to be paid for the article sold, and entails liability to make payment.

- 153. The fixed price is a price mutually named and agreed upon by the two contracting parties whether corresponding to the real value of whether more or less.

- 154 . The value is the real price of an article.

- 155. A priced article is a thing which is sold for a price.

- 156. A postponement of payment consists of putting off a debt to a definite date.

- 157. Payment by instalments consists of a postponement of payment of a debt in order that it may be paid at deferent and definite periods.

- 158. A debt is the thing which is proved to be owing.

Examples:-
(1). A certain sum of money lend to A and owed by him;
(2). A sum of money not immediately available;

- 159. A specific object is any which is definite and identified.

Examples:- A house; a horse; a chair; a heap of corn in existence; a sum of money. All these are specific.

- 160. The vendor is a person who sells property.

- 161. The purchaser is a person who buys.

- 162.The two parties to the sales are the vendor and the purchaser. They are also called the two contracting parties.

- 163. Rescission is setting aside and stopping a contract of sale.

- 164. Deceit is cheating.

- 165. Flagrant misrepresentation is representation which is practised with regard to no less than one twentieth in the case of merchandise; one tenth in the case of animals; and one fifth in the case of real property.

- 166. Time immemorial refers to that thing the origin of which is unknown to any person.

CHAPTER I. THE CONTRACT OF SALE.

SECTION I. FUNDAMENTAL BASIS OF SALE.

- 167. Sale is concluded by offer and acceptance.

- 168. In sale, offer and acceptance is made by the use of words commonly employed in the particular locality in making a contract of sale.(*) (An explanation of a turkish word is not translated here as being of no significance to the English reader.)

- 169. The past tense is usually employed in offer and acceptance.

Example:-
(1). A vendor informs a purchaser that he has sold him a certain thing for one hundred piastres and the purchaser states that he has purchased it; or the purchaser states that he has bought a certain thing and the vendor afterwards states that he has sold such thing. The sale is concluded. In the first case the offer consists of the words "I have sold " and the acceptance of the words " I have purchased". In the second case the words " i have purchased" constitute the offer and the words "I

have sold " the acceptance.

(2). The vendor, instead of stating that he has sold, states that he has given a person something or has transferred the property in it to him, and the purchaser instead of stating that he has purchased states that he has agreed thereto or has accepted. A valid contract of sale is concluded.

- 170. A contract of sale may be concluded by employing the futurist tense if it imports the present: but if the future is meant, no sale is concluded.

- 171. If the future tense is used is the sense of a mere promise, such as the statement " I will buy" or " I will sell" no sale is concluded.

- 172. No sale is concluded by the use of the imperative mood, such as the expression"sell" or "Buy". But when the present tense is necessarily meant a sale may also by concluded by the use of the imperative mood.

  Example:- A purchaser says to a vendor: " Sell me this article for so much money." No sale is concluded. But if the vendor says: "Take this article for so much money" and the purchaser replies saying : "I have taken it"; or if the purchaser says "I have taken it", and the vendor says, " take it" or " you may enjoy the benefit of it," a valid sale is concluded, the expressions 2take" or" enjoy the benefit of it" being equivalent to " I have sold" and " take it".

- 173. Offer and acceptance may be made by writing as well as by word of mouth.

- 174. A dumb person may make a valid contract of sale by making use of generally recognised signs.

- 175. The fundamental object of offer and acceptance being the mutual agreement of the parties, a sale may also be concluded by any conduct of the parties which is evidence of offer and acceptance. This is called sale by conduct of the parties.

  Examples:-
  (1) A purchaser without bargaining and without making any statement gives money to a baker and the baker delivers bread to the purchaser. A contract of sale is concluded.

  (2) A purchaser tenders money and takes a melon. The vendor remains silent. A contract of sale is concluded.

  (3) A purchaser wishes to buy corn. With this object in view he tenders five pounds to a corn merchant asking the latter to tell him at what price he sells corn. The corn merchant replies that he sells corn at one pound per kile. The purchaser thereupon remains silent, and later asks for the corn and the corn merchant states that on the following day he will deliver it to him. In this case a contract of sale has been concluded, although there has been no offer and acceptance by the parties. So much so that if on the following day corn has gone up half a pound in price per kile, the vendor is bound to deliver at one pound. If, on the other hand, the price of corn has gone down, the purchaser cannot refuse for this reason to accept delivery at the original price.

  (4). A purchaser asks a butcher to weigh him so much money's worth of meat from such and such a part. The butcher cuts the meat up and weighs it. A contract of sale has been concluded, and the purchaser cannot refuse to accept the meat.

- 176. If as a result of fresh bargaining after the conclusion of the contract, the price is changed, increased or decreased, the second contract is valid.

Example:- A contract is concluded for the purchase of an article for one hundred piastres. Later on fresh bargaining takes place and as a result the original hundred piastres is substituted for a gold piece of one hundred piastres, of for one hundred and ten piastres, or for one hundred and ten piastres or for ninety piastres. The second contract is valid.

SECTION II. AGREEMENT OF ACCEPTANCE WITH OFFER.

- 177. The acceptance of one of the two contracting parties must agree exactly with the offer of the other contracting party as regards the price or subject matter. Such party has no power to separate or divide either the price or the subject matter.

  Example:-
  (1) A vendor tells a purchaser that he has sold him certain cloth for one hundred piastres and the purchaser agrees thereto. He is then obliged to take the whole of such cloth for one hundred piastres. He cannot claim to take the cloth or a half thereof for fifty piastres.
  (2) A tells B that he has sold him two horses for three thousand piastres and B accepts. B must take the two for three thousand piastres. He cannot take one of them for one thousand five hundred piastres.

- 178. It is sufficient if the acceptance agrees with the offer by implication.

  Examples:-
  (1). A vendor informs a purchaser that he has sold him certain property for a thousand piastres. The purchaser tells the vendor that he accepts for one thousand five hundred piastres. The contract of sale is for one thousand piastres. If the vendor, however, agrees to the increase of price at the time it is mentioned, the purchaser is bound to pay the additional five hundred piastres.
  (2) A purchaser states that he has bought certain property for one thousand piastres. The vendor states that he has sold it for eight hundred piastres. A contract of sale has been concluded, and the two hundred piastres must be deducted.

- 179. If one of the two parties to a sale enumerates the prices of various articles, and proposes the sale of such articles en bloc and the other party accepts such offer, the latter may buy the whole lot for the whole price. If he does not do so, he may not divide up the lot and agree to buy any article he wishes at the fixed price.

  Example:-
  (1) A vendor states that he has sold two particular horses for three thousand piastres. The first one for one thousand piastres and the second for two thousand piastres; or each of them for one thousand five hundred piastres. The purchaser can take the two for three thousands piastres. He cannot, however, take the one he prefers of the two for the fixed price.

  (2) A vendor states that he has sold three pieces of cloth for one hundred piastres. The purchaser states that he has bought one piece for one hundred piastres, or two pieces for two hundred piastres. No sale is concluded.

- 180. If one of the two parties to a sale enumerates the price of the various articles, and offers them for sale separately and the other party accepts the article he desires, at the fixed price, a contract of sale is concluded.

Example:- A vendor enumerates the prices of various articles for sale and repeats that he has sold them, this one for a thousand piastres and that one for two thousand piastres. In that case, the purchaser may accept one of the two for the fixed price and buy the same.

SECTION III. THE PLACE WHERE THE SALE IS CONCLUDED.

- 181. The place where the sale is concluded is the place where the parties meet together with a view to the conclusion of the sale.

- 182. Both parties posses an option during the meeting at the place of sale, after the offer has been made, up to the termination of the meeting.

Example:- One of the two parties to the sale makes an offer at the meeting place of the parties to the sale by stating that he has sold such and such property for a certain sum of money, or that he has bought such property, and the other party fails to state immediately afterwards that he has bought or has sold and some time later accepts at the same meeting. The sale is concluded, no matter how long the meeting may have lasted or how long the period between offer and acceptance may have been.

- 183. If one of the parties gives any indication of dissent after the offer and prior to acceptance, either by word or by deed, the offer becomes void and there is no longer any reason for acceptance.

Example:- one of the two parties to the sale, after stating that he has bought or that he has sold, occupies himself with some other matter, or discusses some other question. The offer becomes void, and thereafter the sale cannot be concluded by acceptance.

- 184. If one of the two parties to the sale makes an offer, but revokes such offer before the other party has accepted, the offer becomes void, and thereafter the sale cannot be concluded by acceptance.

Example:- A vendor states that he has sold such and such goods for so much money, but revokes such offer before the purchaser has accepted, and the purchaser later states that he has accepted such offer. No sale is concluded.

- 185. A renewal of the offer before acceptance cancels the first offer and its place is taken by the second offer.

Example:- The vendor states that he has sold such and such property for one hundred piastres, but before the purchaser has accepted, revokes the offer, and states that he has sold for one hundred and twenty piastres, and the purchaser accepts such offer. The first offer is of no effect, and the sale is concluded on the basis of one hundred and twenty piastres.

SECTION IV. SALE SUBJECT TO A CONDITION.

- 186. If a contract of a sale is concluded with an essential condition attached, both sale and condition are valid.

EXAMPLE:- A vendor sells subject to a right of retaining the thing sold until he has received payment of the price. This condition is no way prejudices the sale, but on the contrary is an essential condition of the contract.

- 187. In the case of a sale concluded subject to a condition of the object of which is to assure the due performance of the contract, both sale and condition are valid.

  Example:- A certain thing is sold subject to the condition that some other thing shall be pledged or that a certain individual shall become a surety. Both sale and condition are valid. Moreover, should the purchaser fail to observe the condition, the vendor may cancel the sale. The reason for this is that these conditions assure the handing over of the price, which is an essential condition of the contract.

- 188. In the case of a sale concluded subject to a condition sanctioned by custom established and recognised is a particular locality, both sale and condition are valid.

  Example :- The sale of a fur subject to a condition that it shall be nailed to its place; or of a suit of clothes subject to the condition that they shall be repaired. In these cases the condition must be observed in carrying out the sale.

- 189. In the case of sale subject to a condition which is not to the benefit of either party, the sale is valid, but the condition is voidable.

  Example:- The sale of an animal subject to a condition that it shall not be sold to a third party, or that it shall be put out to graze. In such a case the sale is valid, but the condition is of no effect.

SECTION V RESCISSION OF THE SALE.

- 190. The two contracting parties may, by mutual agreement, rescind the sale after the conclusion of the contract.

- 191. As in the case of sale, rescission is carried out by means of offer and acceptance.

  Example:- One of the two contracting parties states that he has rescinded or cancelled a sale and the other states that he has agreed thereto; or one of the parties tells the other to rescind the sale and the latter states that he has done so. The rescission is valid and the sale cancelled.

- 192. A valid rescission may also be effected by conduct which takes the place of offer and acceptance.

- 193. As in the case of sale, a meeting of the parties must take place in the case of rescission. That is to say, acceptance must be made known at the place where the offer is made. If this is done, and one of the contracting parties states that he has rescinded the sale, and the other party leaves without expressing his concurrence, or if one of the parties does anything which indicates dissent, the subsequent acceptance by the other is of no effect.

- 194. It is an essential condition that the thing sold should be in the possession of the purchaser at the time of the rescission. Consequently, if the thing sold is destroyed, the rescission is invalid.

- 195. If a portion of the thing sold is destroyed, rescission is valid as regards the remainder.

  Example:- A vendor sells land he owns in absolute ownership, together with growing crops. After the crops have been reaped by the purchasers, the parties rescind the contract. The rescission is valid in so far as that part of the price concerning the land is concerned.

- 196. The loss of the price does not affect the validity of the rescission.

CHAPTER II. THE SUBJECT MATTER OF THE SALE.

SECTION I. Conditions affecting the subject matter of the sale and description.

- 197. The thing sold must be in existence.
- 198. The thing sold must be capable of delivery.
- 199. The thing sold must be property of some specific value.
- 200. The thing sold must be known to the purchaser.
- 201. The fact that the thing sold is known is ascertained by referring to its state and description which distinguish it from other things.

  Example:- A specific quantity of red corn, or a piece of land bounded by specific boundaries. If these are sold, the nature thereof is known and the sale is valid.

- 202. If the thing sold is present at the meeting place of the parties to the sale, it is sufficient if such thing is pointed out by signs.

  Example:- The vendor states that he has sold a particular animal. The purchaser sees that animal and accepts it. The sale is valid.

- 203. Since it is enough for the nature of the thing sold to be known to the purchaser, there is no need for any other sort of description or particularisation.

- 204. The thing sold must be the particular thing with reference to which the contract is concluded.

  Example:- A vendor, pointing to a particular watch, states that he has sold it. Upon the purchaser accepting, the vendor is bound to deliver that identical watch. He cannot put that particular watch on one side and deliver another of the same sort.

SECTION II. Things which may and may not be sold.

- 205. The sale of a thing not in existence is void. Example:- The sale of the fruit of a tree which has not yet appeared is void.
- 206. The sale of fruit which is completely visible while on a tree is valid, whether it is fit for consumption or not.
- 207. The sale at one and the same time of dependent part which are connected together is valid. For example, in the case of fruit, flowers, leaves and vegetables, which do not arrive at maturity simultaneously, a portion thereof only having come out, that portion which has not yet arrived at maturity may be sold together with the rest.
- 208. If the species of the thing sold has been stated, and the thing sold turns out to be of another species, the sale is void. Example:- The vendor sells a piece of glass stating that it is a diamond. The sale is void.
- 209. The sale of a thing which is not capable of delivery is void. Example:- The sale of a rowing-boat which has sunk in the sea and cannot be raised, or of a runaway animal which cannot be caught and delivered.

- 210. The sale of a thing which is not not generally recognised as property or the purchase of property therewith is void. Example:- The sale of a corpse or of a free man, or the purchase of property in exchange for them is void.

- 211. The sale of things which do not possess any specific value is void.

- 212. The purchase of property with property which does not possess any specific value is voidable.

- 213. The sale of a thing the nature of which is not known is voidable.

Example :- A vendor tells a purchaser that he has sold him the whole of the property he owns for a certain sum of money, and the purchaser states that he has bought the same. The nature of the things bought by the purchaser, however, is unknown. the sale is voidable.

- 214. The sale of an ascertained, jointly owned undivided share in a piece of real property owned in absolute ownership prior to division, such as a half, a third or a tenth, is valid.

- 215. A person may sell his undivided jointly owned share to some other person without obtaining the permission of his partner.

- 216. The sale of a right of way, and of a right of taking water and of a right of flow attached to land and of water attached to canals is valid.

SECTION III. PROCEDURE AT THE SALE.

- 217. The sale of things estimated by measure of capacity, or by weight, or by enumeration, or by length, may be sold individuality or en bloc. Example :- A vendor sells a heap of corn, or a barn full of straw,or a load of bricks, or a bale of merchandise en bloc. The sale is valid.

- 218. If grain is sold in a specified vessel or measured in a measure, or by weighing it according to a fixed weight, the sale is valid, although the capacity of the vessel or measure, or the heaviness of the weight may not known.

- 219. A thing which may be sold separately may validly be separated from the thing sold.

Example:- The vendor stipulates to retain a certain number of okes of the fruit of a tree that he has sold. The stipulation is valid.

- 220. The sale en bloc of things estimated by quantity on the basis of the price of each thing or part thereof is valid.

Example:- The sale of a heap of corn, a ship-load of wood, a flock of sheep, and a roll of cloth, on the basis of the price of each kile, or measure, or oke, or herd of sheep, or yard, is valid.

- 221. Real property may be sold by defining the boundaries thereof. In cases where the boundaries have already been defined, it may be sold by the yard or the donum.

- 222. The contract of sale is only valid in respect to the amount stipulated in the contract.

- 223. The sale of things estimated by measure of capacity, or by enumeration and which closely resemble each other and things estimated by weight, and which do not suffer damage by being separated from the whole, may be sold en bloc if the amount thereof is made known, whether the price is named in respect to the whole amount, or in respect to each individual unit. If on delivery the amount is found to be correct, the sale is irrevocable. If it is found to be shot, however, the purchaser has the option of cancelling the sale, or of purchasing the amount actually delivered for the proportionate part of the price. If more than the stipulated amount is delivered, the excess belongs to the vendor.

Examples:-

(1). A vendor sells a heap of corn said to be fifty kiles, at five hundred piastres, or, on the basis of fifty kiles, at ten piastres a kiles. If the amount delivered is correct, the sale is irrevocable. If forty-five kiles only are delivered, the purchaser has an option of cancelling the sale, or of taking forty-five kiles for four hundred and fifty piastres. If fifty-five kiles are delivered, the kiles in excess belong to the vendor.

(2). A basket of eggs said to contain one hundred is sold for fifty piastres, or at twenty paras for each egg. if it turns out on delivery that there are only ninety eggs, the purchaser has an option of cancelling the sale or of taking the ninety eggs for forty-five piastres. If one hundred and ten are delivered, the ten eggs remaining over belong to the vendor.

(3). A barrel of oil is sold as containing one hundred okes. The principle explained above applies.

- 224. In the case of the sale of a whole amount of things estimated by weight which suffer by being separated from the whole, the price of the whole amount only being named, the purchaser has the option of cancelling the sale on delivery, if the amount proves to be short, or of taking the portion delivered for the price fixed for the whole. If more than the amount is delivered, it belongs to the purchaser and the vendor has no option in the matter. Example:- a Diamond stated to be five carat is sold for twenty thousands piastres. It turns out to be four and a half carat. The purchaser has the option of rejecting the diamond, or of taking the stone for twenty thousand piastres. If it turns out to be five and a half carat, the purchaser can have it for twenty thousand piastres, the vendor having no option in the matter.

- 225. In the case of the sale of a whole amount of things estimated by weight which suffer damage by being separated from the whole, stating the amount thereof and the price fixed for parts or portions thereof, the purchaser has a option on delivery, if the amount delivered turns out to be less or more, of cancelling the sale, or of taking the amount delivered on the basis of the price fixed for the parts and portions thereof. Example:- A copper brazier said to weigh five okes is sold at the rate of forty piastres per oke. If it turns out to weigh either four and a half or five and a half okes, the purchaser has two options. He can either decline to accept the brazier, or, if it weighs four and a half okes he can purchase it for one hundred and eighty piastres, and if it weighs five and a half okes, he can purchase it for two hundred and twenty piastres.

- 226. In the case of the sale of a whole amount of things estimated by measure of length, whether land, goods, or similar things on the basis of the price for the whole amount, or of the price per yard, they are dealt with in both cases as in the case of things estimated by weight which suffer damage by being separated from the whole. Goods and articles such as linens and woollens which do not suffer damage by being cut and separated, are treated in the same manner as things estimated by measure of capacity.

Examples:-

(1). A piece of land said to measure one hundred yards is sold for one thousand piastres. It turns out to measure ninety-five yards only. The purchaser has an option of leaving it or of buying it for one thousand piastres. If it turns out to be larger, the purchaser can take the whole piece for one thousand piastres.

(2). A piece of cloth said to measure eight yards is sold for four hundred piastres with a view to being made up into a suit of clothes. It turns out to measure seven yards only. The purchaser has an option of leaving it or buying it for four hundred piastres. If it turns out to measure nine yards, the purchaser can take the whole piece for four hundred piastres.

(3). A piece of land said to measure one hundred yards is sold at the rate of ten piastres per yard. If it turns out to measure ninety-five or one hundred and five yards, the purchaser has an option of leaving it, or, if it turns out to be ninety-five yards, of buying it for nine hundred and fifty piastres, or if it turns out to be one hundred and five yards, of buying it for one thousand and fifty piastres.

(4). Some cloth said to measure eight yards is sold at the rate of fifty piastres per yard with a view to being made up into suit of clothes. If it turns out to measure seven or nine yards, the purchaser has an option of either rejecting it or, if it turns out to be seven yards, of buying it for three hundred and fifty piastres, and if it turns out to be nine yards of buying it for four hundred and fifty piastres.

(5). If a whole piece of cloth, however, said to measure one hundred and fifty yards is sold for seven thousand five hundred piastres, or at the rate of fifty piastres per yard, the purchaser has the option of cancelling the sale or of taking the hundred and forty yards for seven thousand piastres. If it turns out to be more, the balance belongs to the vendor.

- 227. In the event of the sale of things estimated by enumeration and which are dissimilar from each other, the price of the whole amount only named and the number of such things is found to be exact on delivery, the sale is valid and irrevocable. If the number is greater or smaller, however, the sale is voidable in both cases. Example:- A flock of sheep said to contain fifty head of sheep is sold for two thousand five hundred piastres. If on delivery the flock is found to consist of forty-five or fifty-five sheep, the sale is voidable.

- 228. In the event of the sale of a portion of a whole amount of things estimated by enumeration, and which are dissimilar from each other, stating the amount thereof, and a price calculated at so much per piece or per unit, and on delivery the number is found to be exact, the sale is irrevocable. If the number is found to be smaller, the purchaser has the option of leaving the things or of taking them for the proportionate share of the fixed price. If more than the stated number are delivered, the sale is voidable.

Example:- A flock of sheep said to consist of fifty is sold at the rate of fifty piastres per head. If it turns out to consist of forty-five head of sheep, the purchaser has the option of leaving them or of buying the forty-five head of sheep for two thousand two hundred and fifty piastres. If it turns out to be fifty-five head of sheep, the sale is voidable.

- 229. The purchaser, after having taken delivery of the thing sold, loses the option of cancelling the sale conferred upon him by the preceding Articles, if he knew that less than the stipulated amount had in fact been delivered.

SECTION IV. MATTERS INCLUDED BUT NOT EXPLICITLY MENTIONED IN THE SALE.

- 230. The sale includes everything which by local custom is included in the thing sold, even though not specifically mentioned. Example:- In the case of the sale of a house, the kitchen and the cellar are included; and in the event of the sale of an olive grove, the olive trees are included, even though not specifically mentioned. The reason for this is that the kitchen and cellar are appurtenances of the house, and the olive grove is so called because it is a piece of land containing olive trees. A mere piece of land, on the other hand, is not called an olive grove.

- 231. Things which are considered to be part of the thing sold, that is to say, things which cannot be separated from the thing sold, having regard to the object of the purchase, are included in the sale without being specifically mentioned.

Example:- In the case of the sale of a lock, the key is included; and in the case of the sale of a milch cow, the sucking calf of such cow is included in the sale without being specifically mentioned.

- 232. Fixtures attached to the thing sold are included in the sale, even though not specifically mentioned.

Example:- In the event of a sale of a large country house, things which have been fixed or constructed permanently, such as locks which have been nailed, and fixed cupboards and divans, are included in the sale. Similarly, the garden included in the boundaries of the house, together with the paths leading to the public road or to a blind alley are included in the sale, even though this was not specifically stated at the time the bargain was concluded.

- 233. Things which are neither appurtenances or permanent fixtures attached to the thing sold, and things which are not considered to be part of the thing sold, or things which are not by reason of custom included in the thing sold, are not included in the sale unless they are specifically mentioned at the time the sale was concluded. But things which by reason of local custom go with the thing sold, are included in the sale without being specifically mentioned. Example:- In the case of the sale of a house, things which are not fixtures, but have been placed so that they may be removed, such as cupboards, sofas and chairs, are not included in the sale unless specifically mentioned. And in the event of the sale of an orchard or a garden, flower pots, and pots for lemons and young plants which have been planted with a view to their removal elsewhere, are not included in the sale, unless specifically mentioned. Similarly when land is sold, the growing crops, and when trees are sold, the fruit thereof, are not included in the sale, unless some special stipulation to that effect was made at the time the bargain was concluded. But the bridle of the riding horse and the halter of a draught horse are included in the sale although not specifically mentioned, in places where such is the custom.

- 234. The thing included in the sale as being attached thereto is not a part of the price of such sale.

Example:- If the halters of draught horses are stolen before the delivery thereof, there is no necessity to deduct anything from the fixed price.

- 235. Things comprised in any general expressions added at the time of the sale are included in the sale.

Example:- The vendor states that he has sold a particular house " with all rights ". Any right of way, or right of taking water, or right of flow attaching to the house are included in the sale.

- 236. Any fruit or increase occurring after the conclusion of the contract and before the delivery of the thing sold belong to the purchaser.

Example:-
(1). In the case of the sale of a garden, any fruit or vegetables that are produced before delivery belong to the purchaser.
(2). Where a cow has been sold, a calf born before delivery of the cow becomes the property of the purchaser.

CHAPTER III. MATTERS RELATING TO PRICE.

SECTION I. NATURE OF AND CIRCUMSTANCES AFFECTING PRICE.

- 237. The price must be named at the time of the sale. Consequently, if the price of the thing sold is not mentioned, the sale is voidable.
- 238. The price must be ascertained.
- 239. The price is ascertained by being seen, if it is visible. If not, it is ascertained by stating the amount and description thereof.
- 240. If the price is stated to be so many gold coins in a locality in which different types of gold coins are in circulation, without stating the particular type of gold coin, the sale is voidable. The same rules applies to silver coins.
- 241. If the price is stated in piastres, the purchaser can give any type of coin he likes, provided that the circulation thereof is not forbidden.
- 242. When a contract is drawn up expressing the nature of the price, payment must be made in whatever kind of currency is mentioned.

  Example:- A contract is made for payment in Turkish, English, or French pounds, or in pieces of twenty medjidies each, or in dollars. Payment must be made in whatever currency is stipulated.

- 243. Anything produced at the time of the conclusion of the contract cannot be regarded as determining the nature of the price.

  Example:- A purchaser shows a gold piece of one hundred piastres which he has in his hand, and states that he has bought such and such a piece of property with that particular gold coin. The vendor agrees to sell. The purchaser is not obliged to give that particular gold coin itself, but may substitute for it another gold piece of one hundred piastres of the same type.

- 244. Fractions of coins may be given instead of a particular type of coinage. In this case, however, local custom must be followed.

  Example:- A bargain is concluded for payment by medjidies of twenty piastres. Payment may also be made with pieces of ten and five. But in view of custom now prevailing in constantinople, fraction of pieces of forty and two may be given instead of pieces of twenty.

SECTION II. SALE SUBJECT TO PAYMENT AT A FUTURE DATE.

- 245. A valid sale may be concluded in which payment of the price is deferred and is made by instalments.
- 246. In the event of deferment and payment of the price by instalments, the period thereof must be definitely ascertained and fixed.
- 247. if a bargain is concluded with a promise for payment at some definite future date which is

fixed by two contracting parties, such as in so many days, or months, or years time, or the 26th October next, the sale is valid.

- 248. If a bargain is concluded stipulating for payment at a time which is not clearly fixed, such as "when it rains " the sale is voidable.

- 249. If a bargain is concluded whereby credit is given for an undefined period, payment becomes due within one month.

- 250. The time agreed upon for deferred payment, or payment by instalments, begins to run from the time the thing sold is delivered. Example:- Goods are sold to be paid for in a year's time. The vendor after keeping them for a year, delivers them to the purchaser. The money must be paid after a period of one year from the date of delivery, that is, upon the expiration of precisely two years from the the time of the sale.

- 251. An unconditional sale is concluded with a view to payment forthwith. But in places where by custom an unconditional sale is concluded for payment by some definite date, or by instalments, payment becomes due on the date in question. Example:- A purchases a thing from the market without stipulating as to whether payment is to be made forthwith or whether purchased on credit. Payment must be made forthwith. But where by local custom the whole or a part of the price is payable at the end of a week or month, such custom must be observed.

CHAPTER IV. POWER TO DEAL WITH THE PRICE AND THE THING SOLD AFTER THE SALE.

SECTION I. RIGHT OF VENDOR TO DISPOSE OF THE PRICE AND OF THE PURCHASER TO DISPOSE OF THE THING SOLD AFTER THE CONCLUSION OF THE CONTRACT AND PRIOR TO DELIVERY.

- 252. The vendor has a right to dispose of the price of the thing sold before receiving the same.

  Example:- A person who has sold property, of his own can transfer the price thereof to meet a debt.

- 253. If the thing sold is real property, the purchaser can sell such real property to another person before taking delivery thereof. He may not, however, sell movable property.

SECTION II. INCREASE AND DECREASE IN THE PRICE AND IN THE THING SOLD AFTER THE CONCLUSION OF THE CONTRACT.

- 254. The vendor may increase the amount of the thing sold after the conclusion of the contact. If the purchaser agrees to such increase at the meeting place of the parties, he has a right to insist upon such increase and the vendor may not go back upon his offer. An Acceptance by the purchaser after the meeting, however, is invalid.

Example:- A bargain is concluded for the purchase of twenty melons at twenty piastres. The vendor states that he has given five more. If the purchaser accepts at the meeting, he has the right of taking twenty-five melons for twenty piastres. If he fails to accept at the meeting however, but seeks to accept subsequently, the vendor cannot be obliged to give the additional number.

- 255. The purchaser may increase the fixed price after the conclusion of the sale. If the vendor accepts such increase at the meeting where the offer is made, he has the right to insist upon such increase and the purchaser may not go back upon his offer. If the vendor accepts after the meeting, however, such acceptance is invalid.

Example:- A bargain is concluded for the sale of an animal for one thousand piastres. After the conclusion of the sale, the purchaser states that he has added an additional two hundred piastres. If the vendor accepts at the meeting where the offer is made, he must pay one thousand two hundred piastres for the animal. If the vendor fails to accept at the meeting, however, but signifies his acceptance later, the purchaser cannot be forced to pay the additional two hundred piastres which he has undertaken to give.

- 256. The vendor may validly deduct a portion of the fixed price after the conclusion of the contract.

Example:- A bargain is concluded for the sale of certain property for one hundred piastres. Later, the vendor states that he has deducted twenty piastres. He can only obtain eight piastres for the property in question.

- 257. Any increase made by the vendor in thing sold and by the purchaser in the fixed price, or any decrease on the part of the vendor of the fixed price after the conclusion of contract becomes a part of the original contract. That is to say, such increase or decrease is contemplated as having been part of the original contract at the time such contract was concluded.

- 258. If the vendor increases the thing sold after the conclusion of the contract, the increase becomes part of the fixed price. Example:-
(1). A vendor adds two water melons to the eight water melons which he has sold for ten piastres. The purchaser agrees and the ten water melons are sold for ten piastres. If the two water melons are destroyed before delivery, the price thereof is deducted from the total price and the vendor can only demand eight piastres for the eight water melons.
(2). A vendor sells a piece of land measuring one thousand yards for ten thousand piastres. After the sale he adds one hundred yards, to which the purchaser agrees. If a person claiming a right of pre-emption comes forward, he can take the whole amount represented by the ten thousand piastres, that is to say, one thousand on hundred yards.

- 259. If the purchaser increases the fixed price after the conclusion of the contract, the sum total of the fixed price together with the increase becomes the corresponding value of the thing sold in respect to the two contracting parties. Example :- A purchaser buys a piece of real property held in absolute ownership for ten thousand piastres. Before taking delivery he adds five hundred piastres, to which the vendor agrees. The price of the real property in question is ten thousand five hundred piastres. If a person who is entitled to such property comes forward, proves his case, obtains judgement, and takes possession of the real property in question, the purchaser is entitled to claim the sum of ten thousand five hundred piastres from the vendor. If a person claiming a right of pre-emption to such real property comes forward, such person can take the real property in question for ten thousand piastres, but the vendor cannot claim the five hundred piastres subsequently added from the person claiming the right of pre-emption, because such person's right is based upon the fixed price in the original contract, the subsequent increase to the original contract, the subsequent increase to the original contract affecting the contracting parties only and in no way invalidating such person's claim.

- 260. If the vendor reduces the price of the thing sold after the conclusion of the contract, the remainder of the fixed price is the corresponding value of the whole of the thing sold.

  Example:- A piece of real property held in absolute ownership is bought for ten thousand piastres. The vendor deducts one thousand piastres. The price of the real property is question is nine thousand piastres. Consequently, If a person claiming a right of pre-emption comes forward, he may take such property for nine thousand piastres.

- 261. The vendor may deduct the whole of the price of the thing sold before delivery, but this is not part of the original contract.

  Example:- The vendor sells a piece of real property held in absolute ownership for ten thousand piastres. Prior to delivery he forgoes the price thereof altogether. A person claiming to have a right of pre-emption may take such property for ten thousand piastres. He may not claim to take it for nothing.

CHAPTER V. GIVING AND TAKING DELIVERY.

SECTION I. PROCEDURE ON GIVING AND TAKING DELIVERY.

- 262. Taking delivery is not an essential condition of sale. After the conclusion of the contract, however, the purchaser must first deliver the price to the vendor, and the vendor is then bound to deliver the thing sold to the purchaser.
- 263. The thing sold must be delivered in such a way that the purchaser may take delivery thereof without hindrance. The vendor must give permission for such delivery.
- 264. As soon as the thing sold has been delivered, the purchaser is considered to have taken delivery thereof.
- 265. The method of delivery differs, according to the nature of the thing sold.
- 266. If the purchaser in on a piece of land, or in any field, or if the purchaser sees such land or fields from near by, any permission given by the vendor to take delivery thereof, is considered to be delivery.
- 267. If land is sold upon which crops are growing, the vendor must clear the land of such crops by reaping them or by pasturing animals thereon.
- 268. In the event of delivery of a tree bearing fruit, such fruit must first be gathered and the tree then handed over by the vendor.
- 269. If fruit is sold while upon a tree, and the vendor gives permission to the purchaser to pick such fruit, delivery thereof has been effected.

- 270 If the purchaser is within any real property, such as a house or an orchard, which can be closed by locking, and is informed by the vendor that the latter has delivered such real property to him, delivery thereof has been effected. If he is outside such property, and the purchaser is so near thereto that he could immediately lock the same, delivery thereof is effected by the vendor merely stating that he has made delivery. If he is not in such close proximity to such property, however, delivery is effected after the expiration of such time as is necessary for him to arrive and enter therein.

- 271. Delivery of real property which can be locked is effected by handing over the key.

- 272. Delivery of an animal is taken by seizing it by the head or by the ear or by the halter. Delivery of such animals may also be given by the vendor merely pointing to them and giving permission for them to be taken, if they are in such a place that the purchaser can take delivery thereof without inconvenience.

- 273. Delivery of things estimated by measure of capacity, or by weight, may be given by placing them in a cover or receptacle prepared by order of the purchaser.

- 274. Delivery of articles of merchandise is effected by placing them in the hands of the purchaser or by placing them beside him, or, if they are exposed to view, by pointing to them and giving him permission to take them.

- 275. Delivery of things sold en bloc and kept in a locked place, such as a store or box, is effected by giving the key to the purchaser and giving him permission to take them.

  Example:- A store full of corn or a box of books is sold en bloc. Delivery of things sold is effected by handing over the key.

- 276. If the purchaser takes delivery of the things sold and the vendor, seeing this, makes no objection, permission to take delivery is given.

- 277. If the purchaser takes delivery of the thing sold without paying the price and without the permission of the vendor, such taking delivery is invalid. But if the thing sold is taken by the purchaser without permission and is destroyed or damaged while in his possession, such taking delivery is invalid.

SECTION II. RIGHT OF RETENTION OVER THE THING SOLD.

- 278. In the case of a sale for immediate payment, the vendor has a right of retaining the thing sold until the price is fully paid by the purchaser.

- 279. If the vendor sells various articles en bloc, the whole of the things sold may be retained until the full price has been paid, even though a separate price has been stated for each article.

- 280. The fact that a pledge or a guarantor has been furnished by the purchaser does not invalidate the vendor's right of retention.

- 281. If the vendor gives delivery of the thing sold without receiving the price, he loses his right of retention. He cannot ask for the return of the thing sold in order to hold it until payment of the price is made.

- 282. If the vendor transfers the right of receiving the price of the thing sold from the purchaser to some other person, he loses his right of retention. In this case, the thing sold must be delivered to the purchaser forthwith.

- 283. In the case of a sale on credit, there is no right of retention on the part of the vendor. He must deliver the thing sold to the purchaser forthwith in order to receive payment on due date.
- 284. Should the vendor postpone payment of the price after having sold for immediate payment, he loses his right of retention. He must hand the thing sold to the purchaser forthwith in order to receive payment on due date.

SECTION III. THE PLACE OF DELIVERY.

- 285. In an unconditional contract the thing sold must be delivered at the place where it was when the sale was concluded.

  Example:- A sells wheat at Tekfur Dagh to B in Constantinople. A delivers the wheat in Tekfur Dagh. He cannot be forced to deliver the wheat in Constantinople.
- 286. If at the time of the sale the purchaser did not know where the thing sold was, but received information thereof after the conclusion of the contract, he has an option. He may either cancel the sale, or take delivery of the thing sold at the place where it was at the time the sale was concluded.
- 287. Property sold with a condition for delivery at a given place must be delivered at that place.

SECTION IV. EXPENSES CONNECTED WITH DELIVERY.

- 288. Expenses connected with the price fall upon the purchaser.

  Example:- Fees in connection with money-changing, such as counting and weighing the money, fall upon the purchaser.
- 289. Expenses connected with the delivery of the thing sold fall upon the vendor.

  Example:- Fees of measurers and weighers must be borne by the vendor.
- 290. Any charges connected with things sold en bloc must be borne by the purchaser. Examples:-
  (1). If grapes in an orchard are sold en bloc, the purchaser must gather them.
  (2). If a store full of corn is sold en bloc, the purchaser must take such corn away from the store.
- 291. In the case of things sold which are loaded upon animals, such as wood and charcoal, the question of transport to the house of the purchaser is decided in accordance with local custom.
- 292. The cost of drawing up contracts and written instruments falls upon the purchaser. The vendor, however, must declare the sale and attest the same in Court.

SECTION V. DESTRUCTION OF THE THING SOLD.

- 293. If the thing sold is destroyed while in the possession of the vendor prior to delivery, no liability attaches to the purchaser, and the loss must be borne by the vendor.
- 294. If the thing sold is destroyed after having taken delivery, no liability attaches to the vendor, and the loss must be borne by the purchaser.
- 295. If the purchaser dies bankrupt after having taken delivery of the thing sold, but without having paid the price, the vendor cannot demand the return of the thing sold, but becomes one of the creditors.

- 296. If the purchaser dies bankrupt before the delivery of the thing sold and payment of the price, the vendor has a right of retaining the thing sold until payment has been made from the estate of the purchaser. Thus, the thing sold is disposed of by the Court and if the sum realised is sufficient, the amount due to the vendor is paid in full, any surplus being paid to the other creditors. If less that the sum due to the vendor is realised, the full amount thereof is paid to the vendor, and the balance still remaining due is deducted from the estate of the purchaser.

- 297. If the vendor dies bankrupt after having received the price, but without having delivered the thing sold to the purchaser, such thing remains in the possession of the vendor on trust. Thus, the purchaser takes the thing sold, and the other creditors cannot intervene.

SECTION VI. SALE ON APPROVAL AND SUBJECT TO INSPECTION.

- 298. If property bought on approval as to price, that is to say, property the price of which has been fixed, is delivered to the purchaser and while in his possession is destroyed or lost, the price thereof must be paid to the vendor, if it is in the nature of a thing the like of which cannot be found in the market. If it is a thing the like of which can be found in the market, a similar article must be given to the vendor. If the price has not been fixed, however, it is considered to be in the possession of the purchaser on trust, and if it is destroyed or lost without any fault of the purchaser, there is no need to make good the loss.

  Example:- A vendor offers an animal for one thousand piastres, asking the purchaser to buy it if he is pleased with it. If the purchaser takes it with a view to buying it and the animal is destroyed while in his possession, the purchaser must pay the price to the vendor. But if the price is not stated and the vendor asks the purchaser to buy the animal if he is pleased with it, and the purchaser, being satisfied with it, later to enter into negotiations with a view to purchase, and the animal is destroyed without any fault of the purchaser, while in the latter's possession, the purchaser is not obliged to make good the loss.

- 299. If delivery is taken of the property on approval subject to inspection, that is today, to be examined or shown, and such property is destroyed or lost while in the possession of the prospective purchaser without any fault on his part, such purchaser is considered to have held the property on trust and there is no need to make good the loss, whether the price has been stated or not.

CHAPTER VI. OPTIONS.

SECTION I. CONTRACTUAL OPTIONS

- 300. The vendor, or the purchaser, or both, may insert a condition in the contract of sale giving them an option, within a fixed period, to cancel the sale or to ratify it by carrying out the term thereof.

- 301. The person is the enjoyment of an option conferred by the contract is empowered either to cancel or to ratify the contract within the period of the validity of the option.

- 302. Both cancellation and ratification of the contract may be by word of mouth or by conduct.

- 303. Words importing ratification are words implying satisfaction, such as, "I ratify", or " I am pleased". Words importing cancellation are words implying dissatisfaction such as," I have cancelled" or, "I have gone back".

- 304. Acts importing ratification are those acts implying satisfaction and acts importing cancellation are those acts implying dissatisfaction.

  Example:- A purchaser having a right to an option performs some act within the period during which the option is valid, indicative of a right of ownership is such property, such as putting it up for sale, or pledging it, or letting it on hire. Such act is an act of ratification by conduct. If the vendor has an option and deals with the property in the same way, it is an act of cancellation by conduct.

- 305. If the person possession the allows the period during which the option is valid to expire without either cancelling the sale or ratifying it, the sale becomes irrevocable.

- 306. An option conferred by contract is not transmissible by way of inheritance. Thus, if the person possessing the option is the vendor, the purchaser becomes the owner of the thing sold upon the death of the vendor. If the purchaser is the person having the option and dies, his heirs become owners of the thing sold without any option.

- 307. If both vendor and purchaser have an option, the sale can be cancelled by whichever party so desires. if one party only ratifies, that party loses his option, the other retaining his.

- 308. If the vendor alone has an option, he does not lose his title in the thing sold, which is still considered to be a part of his own property. if the thing sold is destroyed while in the possession of the purchaser after delivery thereof, the fixed price does not become due, but the purchaser must pay the value thereof on the day he took delivery.

- 309. If the purchaser alone has an option he acquires a title in the thing sold, which is considered to be a part of his own property. If the thing sold is destroyed while in the possession of the purchaser after delivery thereof, the fixed price must be paid.

SECTION II. OPTION FOR MISDESCRIPTION.

- 310. If the vendor sells property as possessing a certain desirable quality and such property proves to be devoid of such quality, the purchaser has the option of either cancelling the sale, or of accepting the thing sold for the whole of the fixed price. This is called option for MISDESCRIPTION. Examples:-
  (1). If a cow is sold described as giving milk and it proves that she has ceased to give milk, the purchaser acquires an option.
  (2). If a stone sold at night-time as a red ruby proves to be yellow ruby, the purchaser acquires an option.

- 311. The option for misdescription is transmissible by way of inheritance. That is to say, that if on the death of the purchaser who has an option for misdescription, it turns out that the thing sold does not conform to the description given, the heir also has the power of cancelling the sale.

- 312. If the purchaser having an option for misdescription deals with the thing sold in manner indicative of a right of ownership over such thing, he loses his option thereby.

SECTION III. OPTION AS TO PAYMENT.

- 313. Vendor and purchaser may validly conclude a bargain whereby payment of the price is to be made by a certain time and in the event of payment not being made, the sale is not to take place. This option is called an option as to payment.

- 314. If the purchaser does not pay the price within the stipulated period, a sale concluded subject to an option as to payment is voidable.

- 315. If a purchaser having an option as to payment dies within the prescribed period, the sale is void

SECTION IV. OPTION AS TO SELECTION.

- 316. A stipulation may validly be made in a sale whereby the purchaser may take whichever he likes of two or three things at different prices the like of which cannot be found in the market, or the vendor may give whichever one he pleases. This is called an option as to selection.

- 317. A period must be fixed during which the option as to selection is valid.

- 318. A person having an option as to selection is bound to choose the thing he has bought on the expiration of the prescribed period.

- 319. An option as to to selection is transmissible by way of inheritance.

Example:- If the vendor sells three pieces of cloth all being of one type and consisting of superior, medium and inferior quality, the purchaser to take the piece he prefers within a period of three or four days, and such purchaser agrees thereto, a valid sale is concluded, and on the expiration of the stipulated period, the purchaser must choose one and pay the fixed price thereof. If he dies before exercising his option, his heir must choose one in the same manner.

SECTION V. OPTION AS TO INSPECTION.

- 320. If a person buys a piece of property without seeing such property, he has an option upon inspection thereof of either cancelling the sale or of ratifying it. This is called option as to inspection

- 321. The option of inspection is not transmissible by way of inheritance. Consequently, if the purchaser dies without having seen the property which he has bought, his heir becomes owner of the property without having any option in the matter.

- 322. No option of inspection accrues to the vendor who sells property without seeing it .

Example:- A sells property which he has not seen and which has come to him by way of inheritance. The sale is concluded without any right of option.

- 323. The object of the option of inspection is to ascertain the nature of the thing sold and the whereabouts thereof. Example:- A person who examines the outside of a plain piece of cloth which is the same on both sides; or a piece of cloth marked with stripes or flowers; or the teat of a sheep bought for breeding; or the back of a sheep bought for killing; or who tries the taste of things for eating and drinking and who later makes a purchase, has no option of inspection.

- 324. It is sufficient to see a sample produced of things sold by sample.

- 325. If the thing sold proves to be inferior to the sample, the purchaser has an option of taking or rejecting it. Example:- If such things as corn or oil, and linen or wool manufactured so as to conform to a set standard of excellence are bought after inspecting a sample thereof, and are later found not to come up to sample, the purchaser has an option.

- 326. In the purchase of real property such as an inn or a house, every room must be inspected. If the rooms are all of one type, however, it is sufficient to inspect one of the rooms.

- 327. When things which are dissimilar to each other are purchased en bloc, each one must be inspected separately.

- 328. If the purchaser buys things which are dissimilar from each other en bloc and inspects some of them and fails to inspect the rest, and,upon inspection of the latter, is dissatisfied therewith, he has the option of accepting or rejecting the whole lot. He may not take those with which he is satisfied and reject the rest.

- 329. A blind person may validly buy and sell, but if he buys property the description of which is unknown to him, he has an option.

  Example:- If he buys a house the description of which is unknown to him, he has an option, upon learning the description thereof, of accepting or rejecting.

- 330. A blind person has no option if he purchases a thing which has been described to him beforehand.

- 331. If a blind person touches anything the nature of which can be ascertained by means of the sense of touch, and smells things the nature of which can be ascertained by means of the sense of smell, and tastes things the nature of which can be ascertained by means of the sense of taste, his right of option is destroyed. That is to say, if he touches or smells such things and afterwards purchases them, the sale is valid and irrevocable.

- 332.If a person who has inspected a piece of property with a view to purchase later buys such property knowing it is the property in question, such person has no option of inspection. Should any change have been made in such property, however such person has an option.

- 333. Inspection by an agent authorised to buy or receive the thing sold, is equivalent to inspection by the principal.

- 334. Inspection by a messenger, that is to say, a person sent, who merely has the power of collecting and dispatching the thing sold, does not destroy the purchaser's option of inspection.

- 335. If the purchaser deals with the thing sold in any way indicative of a right of ownership, his option of inspection is destroyed.

SECTION VI. OPTION FOR DEFECT.

- 336. In an unconditional sale, the thing sold must be free from any defect. that is to say, although property is sold without stipulating that it shall be free from faults, and without stating whether it is sound, or bad, or defective, or free from fault, such property nevertheless must be sound and free from defect.

- 337. If some defect of long standing is revealed upon the unconditional sale of any piece of property, the purchaser has the option of rejecting it or accepting it for the fixed price. He cannot keep the property and reduce the price on account of the defect. This is called the option of defect.

- 338. A defect consists of any faults which, in the opinion of persons competent to judge, cause a depreciation in the price of the property.

- 339. A defect of long standing is a fault which existed while the thing sold was in the possession of the vendor.

- 340. Any defect which occurs in the thing sold after sale and before delivery, while in the possession of the vendor, is considered a defect of long standing and justifies rejection.

- 341. If the vendor declares at the time of sale that there is a defect in the thing sold, and the purchaser accepts the thing sold with the defect, he has no option on account of such defect.

- 342. If the vendor sells property subject to the condition that he shall be free from any claim on account of any defect, the purchaser has no option on account of the defect found therein.

- 343. If a purchaser buys property, including all defects, he cannot make any claim on account of any defect found therein.

  Example:- If a purchaser buys an animal with all faults of any description whatsoever whether blind, lame, or worthless, he cannot return such animal asserting that it had a defect of long standing.

- 344. If the purchaser after becoming aware of a defect in the thing sold performs any act indicative of the exercise of a right of ownership, he loses his option of defect.

  Example:- The purchaser, after becoming aware of the existence of a defect of long standing in the thing sold, offers such thing for sale. He is taken to have acquiesced therein and cannot reject the thing sold.

- 345. If a defect appears in the thing sold while in the possession of the purchaser, and it proves to be a defect of long standing, the purchaser has no right to return the thing sold to the vendor, but has a right to claim a reduction in the price.

  Example:- If the purchaser discovers a defect of long standing in the thing he has purchased, such as a piece of cloth which after being cut up and measured is found to rotten and frayed, he cannot return the same, because by cutting it he caused a fresh defect. He can, however, claim a reduction in the price on account of the defect.

- 346. The amount of the reduction in the price is ascertained by a report drawn up by impartial experts. With this object in view, the value of the thing sold when sound and also when defective is ascertained, and a reduction is made from the fixed price on the basis of the difference between the two prices.

  Example:- A purchaser after buying a roll of cloth for sixty piastres and cutting it up and measuring it becomes aware of a defect of long standing. Experts estimate the value of such property at sixty piastres when sound and with the defect of long standing at forty-five piastres. The reduction to be made in the price is fifteen piastres, and the purchaser has a right to make a claim for that amount. If the expert report that the VAlue of such property when sound was eighty piastres and with the defect sixty piastres, the difference of twenty piastres between the two prices, that is to say a fourth of eighty piastres or a quarter of the fixed price may be claimed by the purchaser. If the value of the cloth when sound is reported to be fifty piastres and with the defect forty piastres, the difference of ten piastres between the two, that is to say, one fifth of the fixed price, is considered to be amount to be deducted from the price .

- 347. If a defect of recent origin disappears, a defect of long standing still justifies rejection.

    Example:- Horse is purchased and falls sick while in the possession of the purchaser. Thereupon a defect of long standing is revealed. The purchaser is unable to return the horse, but can obtain a reduction in the price. If the animal recovers from the illness, the purchaser can return the horse to the vendor on account of the defect of long standing.

- 348. If the vendor agrees to take back the thing sold after the occurrence of a defect while in the possession of the purchaser which reveals a defect of a long standing, and should there be nothing to prevent its return, the purchaser cannot claim a reduction in price, but must either return the thing sold or keep it and pay the full price. Should the purchaser sell the property to some third person after becoming aware of the existence of the defect of long standing, he is in no way entitled to claim a reduction of price.

    Example:- A purchaser buys a roll of linen and cuts it up to make shirts. He then finds it to be defective and sells it. He cannot claim any reduction of the price from the vendor. The reason for this is that while the vendor may state that he would take back the stuff with the defect of recent origin, that is to say, cut up, the sale thereof by the purchaser is tantamount to an adoption of the defect.

- 349. Any increase, that is to say, any addition of property belonging to the purchaser to the thing sold makes any return thereof impossible.

    Example:- A purchaser adds certain sewing or dyeing with his own thread or colour to a piece of cloth; or the purchaser of a piece of land plants trees therein. such acts prevent the return of the thing sold.

- 350. If there is anything to prevent the return of the thing sold, the vendor cannot receive back the defective thing sold, even though he is willing to do so, but must make a reduction in price. If the purchaser becomes aware of the existence of a defect of long standing in the property in question and sells the same, he can demand a reduction in price from the vendor.

    Example:- A purchaser buys a roll of linen to make into shirts. After measuring them and sewing them, he finds that the linen is defective. He cannot ask for the linen to be taken back, even though the vendor is prepared to so. The vendor is obliged to make a reduction in the price. If the purchaser sells the shirts, he can recover the reduction in the price from the vendor. The reason for this is that the thread belonging to the purchaser has been added to the thing sold and prevents its return. The vendor cannot say that he will take the thing back after it has been cut up and sewn, and the purchaser is not considered to have kept back the thing sold from the vendor.

- 351. Before taking delivery, the purchaser may reject the whole of of a number of things bought en bloc, if some of them prove to be defective, or he may elect to take them for the fixed price. He cannot reject the things which are defective and keep the rest. If the defect becomes apparent after delivery, and no loss is incurred by separation, he can return that portion in which the defect has appeared, against a proportionate share of the fixed price when sound sound. He cannot return the whole unless the vendor agrees thereto. If any loss is caused by the separation, however, he may return or keep the whole amount at the fixed price.

    Example:- If one of the two fezzes bought for forty piastres proves to be defective before delivery, both can be rejected together. If one of them proves to be defective after delivery, he can return that fez, deducting the value of such fez when sound from the forty piastres. If he has bought a pair of shoes, however, and after delivery, on of them turns out to be defective, he can return them both and can demand the return of the whole of his money.

- 352. If a person who has bought and taken delivery of a definite number of things estimated by measure of capacity or weight and which are of one type, finds a portion thereof to be defective, he has the option of accepting or rejecting the whole number.

- 353. If cereals such as wheat prove to be earthy, though to an extent considered by custom to be negligible, the sale is valid and irrevocable. If, however, such cereals are considered by local opinion to be positively defective, the purchaser has an option.

- 354. If such things as eggs and nuts prove to be bad and defective but not to a greater extent than that sanctioned by custom, such as three per cent, the sale is valid. If the defect is considerable, however, such as ten per cent, the sale is invalid and the purchaser can return the whole amount to the vendor and recover the entire price.

- 355. If the thing sold appears to be in such a state that no benefit can ever be derived therefrom, the sale is void and the purchaser can recover the whole of the price.

Example:- If eggs which have been bought prove to be so bad that they are useless, the purchaser can recover the whole of his money.

SECTION VII. MISREPRESENTATION AND DECEIT.

- 356. The existence of flagrant misrepresentation in a sale, but without actual deceit, does not enable the person who has been the victim of such misrepresentation to cancel the sale. But if the sale of the property of orphans is tainted by flagrant misrepresentation, although there is no actual deceit, such sale is invalid. Property belonging to a pious foundation and to the treasury is treated on the same basis as the property of orphans.

- 357. If one of the two parties to the sale deceives the other, and flagrant misrepresentation is also proved to be present in the sale, the person so deceived can cancel the sale.

- 358. If the person who is the victim of flagrant misrepresentation dies, no right to an action for deceit is transmitted to his heirs.

- 359. If the purchaser who is the victim of deceit becomes aware that the sale is tainted by flagrant misrepresentation and deals with the thing sold in any manner indicative of a right of ownership, he has no right whatsoever to cancel such sale.

- 360. If a thing sold which has been bought as a result of deceit or flagrant misrepresentation is destroyed, or perishes, or becomes defective, or if something new is added, such as a building to apiece of land, the victim of such misrepresentation has no right to cancel the sale.

CHAPTER VII. VARIOUS CATEGORIES OF THINGS SOLD AND THE EFFECT THEREOF.

SECTION I. TYPES OF SALE.

- 361. It is a condition precedent to the conclusion of the sale that the parties thereto should be sound be sound mind and perfect understanding and that the sale should be made with reference to some thing which may properly be subject of sale.

- 362. A sale which is defective in any essential condition, such as sale by lunatic, is void.

- 363. In order that any object may properly be the subject of sale, such object must be in existence, must be capable of delivery, and must be of some specific value. Consequently, the sale of thing which is not in existence, or is incapable of delivery, or is not of any specific value, is void.

- 364. If a sale is concluded validly, but is not legal as regards certain subsidiary matters, such as the thing sold being unknown, or defective as regards the price, the sale is voidable.

- 365. For a sale to be executory, the vendor must be the owner of the thing sold, or the agent of the owner, or his tutor or guardian, and no other person must be entitled thereto.

- 366. Avoidable sale becomes executory on taking delivery. That is to say, the purchaser may deal with the thing sold.

- 367. If one of the options attaches to the sale, such sale is not irrevocable.

- 368. A sale dependent upon the right of some third person may validly be concluded if the permission of such person is obtained, as in the case of a sale by an unauthorised person, to the sale of property given as a pledge.

SECTION II. EFFECT OF VARIOUS KINDS OF SALE.

- 369. The effect of the conclusion of a sale is ownership, that is to say, the purchaser becomes the owner of the thing sold and the vendor becomes the owner of the price.

- 370. A sale which is void is of no effect whatsoever. Consequently, if in the case of a sale which is void, the purchaser has taken delivery of the thing sold with the permission of the vendor, and such thing is destroyed without the fault of the purchaser while in his possession, there is no necessity for the purchaser to make good the loss, the thing sold being in the nature of a thing deposited on trust.

- 371. A voidable sale, on delivery, is effective, that is to say, if the purchaser takes possession of the thing sold with the permission of the vendor, he becomes the owner thereof. Consequently, if a thing bought as the result of a voidable sale is destroyed while in the possession of the purchaser, the purchaser must make good the loss. If the thing sold is one the like of which can be found in the market, a like thing must be given by the purchaser to the vendor, or if it is a thing the like of which cannot be found in the market, the value thereof on the day of delivery must be paid.

- 372. In the case of a voidable sale, each of the contracting parties has the right of cancelling the sale. But if the thing sold is destroyed while in the possession of the purchaser, or if the purchaser disposes of it in any way, such as consuming it, or selling it validly to some other person, or bestowing it upon upon someone by way of gift, or if the thing sold being a house, the purchaser adds to it in any way, such as repairing it, or, if it is a piece of land, planting trees on it, or, if it is corn, changes it by grinding it into flour, so that its name is changed there is no right of cancellation.

- 373. In the case of cancellation of a voidable sale, if the price has been received, the purchaser has the right of retaining the thing sold until the vendor has returned the price.

- 374. An executory sale becomes effective forthwith .
- 375. An executory sale is irrevocable, and neither of the two parties to the sale may go back thereon.
- 376. In the case of a revocable sale, a person possessing an option can cancel such sale.
- 377. A conditional sale becomes effective when the necessary permission is given.
- 378. In the event of a sale by an unauthorised person, such sale is executory if the owner of the property, or his agent, or his tutor, or his guardian give their permission. Otherwise it is of no effect. For the permission to be effective, however, it is necessary for the vendor, the purchaser, the person giving permission and the thing sold to be in existence. If any of these is absent permission is invalid.
- 379. In the case of sale by barter, the conditions applicable to a thing sold also apply, since the value of the two things exchanged is considered to constitute a thing sold. If a dispute arises as to delivery, however, the two parties to the sale must respectively give and take delivery simultaneously.

SECTION III. SALE BY IMMEDIATE PAYMENT AGAINST FUTURE DELIVERY.

- 380. A contract of sale by immediate payment against future delivery is concluded by offer and acceptance, as in the case of sale.

Example :- A purchaser tells a vendor that he has paid a thousand piastres immediately against future delivery of one hundred kiles of c corn. The vendor agrees. A contract of sale by immediate payment against future delivery has been concluded.

- 381. A sale by immediate payment against future delivery can only be concluded validly with reference to things the quantity and quality of which can be determined; for example, the highest and lowest.
- 382. The amount of things estimated by measure of capacity or by weight or by length is fixed by the kile, the weight, or the yard.
- 383. The amount of things estimated by enumeration and which closely resemble each other may be measured by counting, and also by the kile and by weight.
- 384. In the case of things estimated by enumeration, such as burnt bricks and sun-dried bricks, the mould thereof must be made known.
- 385. The length, breadth and thickness of things measured by length, such as linen and woollens, the material they are made from, and the place in which they were made, must be stated.
- 386. It is essential to the validity of a sale by immediate payment against future delivery that the type of thing sold should be stated; for instance, corn, rice or dates: and the particular variety; for example, whether produced by rain or by irrigation: and the quality ; for example, the highest or the lowest: the amount of the price of the thing sold, and the time and place of delivery thereof must be stated.
- 387. It is essential to the validity of the sale by immediate payment against future delivery that the

price should be paid at the meeting where the contract is concluded. If the two contracting parties separate before the price is handed over, the contract is cancelled.

SECTION IV. CONTRACT OF MANUFACTURE AND SALE.

- 388. If a person requests a
  (1). A purchaser displays his foot to boot-maker and asks him to make a pair of boots from such and such leather for so many piastres and the latter agrees to so so; or a bargain is struck with a ship's carpenter for the building of a rowing boat or ship, after describing the length and breadth and essential qualities thereof. A contract for manufacture and sale has been concluded.
  (2). A bargain is concluded with a manufacturer for the production of a certain number of needle guns at so much per gun, after describing the length and the size thereof, and other requirements. A contract for manufacture and sale has been concluded.

- 389. A contract for manufacture and sale is generally valid if it is customer to conclude such a contract. If a period is prescribed, however, in respect to things to which no such custom applies, the conditions applicable in the case of immediate payment against future delivery are in force. If no period is prescribed, however, the contract is in the nature of a contract for manufacture and sale.

- 390. In the case of contract for manufacture and sale, an identification and description of the article must be given as required.

- 391. It is not essential to a contract for manufacture and sale, that the money should be paid immediately.

- 392. After the conclusion of a contract for manufacture and sale, neither party can go back on the bargain they have struck. If, however, the object manufactured is not in accordance with the specification, the person who has given the order may exercise an option.

SECTION V. SALE BY A PERSON SUFFERING FROM A MORTAL SICKNESS.

- 393. If a person suffering from a mortal sickness sells a thing to one of his heirs, such sale is dependent upon the permission of the other heirs. If such heirs give their permission after death of the person suffering from the mortal sickness, such sale becomes executory. If they do not so give their permission, it is not executory.

- 394. If a person suffering from mortal sickness sells a things to a person who is not one his heirs at the time of his death for a price equal to the value of such thing, such sale is valid. If he gives favourable terms, that is to say, such thing for less than its value and gives delivery thereof, anyone third of his property allows thereof, and thereafter dies, the sale is valid. If a third of his property is insufficient to allow of such favourable terms, the purchaser must make good such deficiency. If he does not do so, the heir can cancel the sale.

Examples:-
(1). A person suffering from a mortal sickness, and who owns nothing but a house worth one thousand five hundred piastres, sell and delivers such house to a person who is not one of his heirs for one thousand piastres. Such sale is valid, since the five hundred piastres which he has made a

subject of his generosity do not exceed a third of his property, and the heir cannot cancel the sale. (2). If a person suffering from a mortal sickness sells a nd delivers the house fro five hundred piastres, the purchaser is obliged to increase the price to two thirds, upon being requested to do so by the heirs, since the thousand piastres which he has made the subject of hiss generosity is twice as much as one third of his property. If he does so, the heir cannot cancel the sale. If he fails to do so, the heirs can cancel the sale and demand the return of the house.

- 395. If a person whose estate is overwhelmed by debts and who is suffering from a mortal sickness sells his property for a price less than the true value and then dies, the creditors can oblige the purchaser to make good the balance of the price. If he does not do so, the creditors can cancel the sale.

SECTION VI. SALE SUBJECT TO A RIGHT OF REDEMPTION.

- 396. In sale subject to a right of redemption the vendor may return the price and claim back the thing sold. The purchaser likewise can return the thing sold and claim back the price.
- 397. A thing sold subject to a right of redemption may not be sold to any other person by either the vendor or the purchaser.
- 398. A condition may validly be made that a portion of the profits of the thing sold shall be for the purchaser.

  Example:- If it is mutually agreed to make a contract that the grapes of a vineyard sold subject to a right of redemption shall be equally divided between vendor and purchaser, the contract must be carried out.
- 399. If property sold subject to a right of redemption is equal to the amount of the debt and perishes while in the possession of the purchaser, the debt which it secures is cancelled.
- 400. If the value of the property sold subject to a right of redemption is less than the debt and perishes while in the possession of the purchaser, a sum equivalent to the amount of the debt is deducted, and the purchaser can claim the return of the balance from the vendor.
- 401. If the value of the property sold subject to a right of redemption is greater than the amount of the debt and perishes while in the possession of the purchaser, a sum equivalent to the amount of the debt is deducted. If the purchaser has been guilty of some wrongful act, he must make good the balance. If he has not been guilty of any wrongful act, and the property has been destroyed, the purchaser is not obliged to make good the balance.
- 402. If one of the two parties to a sale subject to a right of redemption dies, the right of cancellation is transmitted to his heirs by way of inheritance.
- 403. No other creditors of the vendor have the right of interfering with property sold subject to a right of redemption, until the purchaser thereof has recovered payment of what is due to him.

PROMULGATED BY ROYAL IRADAH, 26 SHAABAN, 1293.

AL-MAJALLA AL AHKAM AL ADALIYYAH
(The Ottoman Courts Manual (Hanafi))

BOOK II. HIRE.

INTRODUCTION

TERMS OF ISLAMIC JURISPRUDENCE RELATING TO HIRE.

- 404. Rent is hire. that is to say, the price paid for use of a thing ; letting is giving on hire, and hiring is taking on hire.

- 405. (has no meaning for the English reader)

- 406. An irrevocable contract of hire is any valid contract of hire which is not burdened by a contractual option, or by an option for defect or by an option for inspection, and which neither of the parties may cancel without some lawful excuse.

- 407. An immediate contract of hire is a contract of hire which comes into force immediately upon the conclusion of the contract.

- 408. A future contract of hire is a contract of hire which comes into force as from some definite future date. Example :- A house is given on hire as from the beginning of some future month for a certain period and for a certain sum of money. A future contract of hire has been concluded.

- 409. The lessor is the person who gives on hire.

- 410. The lessee is the person who takes on hire.

- 411. The thing hired is the thing which is given on hire.

- 412. Property given to work upon is property handed to a person employed by the employer, so that the person employed may do the work which has been entrusted to him, such as stuff given to a tailor to make into clothes, or a load given to a porter to carry.

- 413. The employee is the person giving his services on hire.

- 414. Estimated rent is the rent fixed by disinterested experts.

- 415. Fixed rent is the rent mentioned and fixed at the time of the conclusion of the contract .

- 416. Indemnification consists of giving a similar thing if it is a thing the like of which can be found in the market, or the value thereof, if it is a thing the like of which cannot be found.

- 417. Prepared for hire is said of any thing designed and prepared to be let on hire. It relates to real property such as inns, houses, baths, and shops originally built or bought in order to be let on hire. If a thing is continuously on hire for a period of three years, it is a proof that it is prepared for hire. If a person has a thing made for himself and tells people that it is prepared for hire, such thing is deemed to be prepared for hire.

- 418. A hirer of a wet nurse is a person who hires a nurse to give milk to a baby.

- 419. Partition of usufruct consists of a division of benefit.

Example:- Two persons who are joint owners of a house agree to take the benefit arising therefrom separately in alternate years.

CHAPTER I. GENERAL.

- 420. In a contract of hire, the subject matter of the contract consists of some advantage to be derived from such contract.

- 421. Hire is relation to the subject matter of the contract is of two categories. The first is a contract for hire made with reference to an interest in specific things. The thing which is the subject of hire is called both the object given on hire and the object taken on hire.
The first category is divided into three classes.
(1). The first class relates to the lease of real property, such as the hire of houses and lands.
(2). The second class relates to the hire of merchandise such as the hire of clothes and utensils.
(3). The third class relates to the hire of animals.
The second category is a contract of hire with regard to labour. In this category, the person hired is called the employee, as in the case of workmen and servants employed for a wage. Hiring the services of craftsmen and artisans is also included in this category.

Example:- A contract for manufacture and sale is concluded when clothes are ordered to be made by a tailor who supplies the cloth. If the cloth is given to the tailor in order that he should make the clothes, such person's labour has been hired.

- 422. Employees are of two classes.
The first class comprises private employees, that is, persons whose services are retained by one employer only, as in the case of a servant paid a monthly wage.
The second class comprises public employees, that is persons who are not bound by an undertaking not to work for more than one employer. Example:- Porters, brokers, tailors, clock-makers, jewellers, harbour boatmen, cab- drivers, and village shepherds are all public employees; that is, persons who are not employed specially by one particular individual, but work for anyone. But if any one of such persons undertakes to give his services on hire to one employer only for a specific period, he becomes during that period a private employee. Again, a porter, or a cab-driver, or a boatman who gives his services on hire to one employer alone to take such employer to a certain place, and who works for no other person is, until he arrives at his destination, a private employee.

- 423. The person employing a private employee may be one single individual or several persons contemplated as one individual only. Consequently, when the inhabitants of a village hire the services of a shepherd for themselves alone by means of a single contract, such shepherd becomes a private employee. But should those persons permit the shepherd to tend some other person's animals, such shepherd becomes a public employee.

- 424. The wages of a public employee are due when the work is done.

- 425. The wages of a private employee are due if he is ready to work during the period for which he services were hired. It is not essential that he should actually have performed the work. He cannot, however, decline to do the work. If he does so, he is not entitled to his wages.

- 426. A person who is entitled to a definite advantage arising out of a contract of hire may obtain enjoyment of such advantage or the equivalent thereof, or of some lesser advantage. He cannot, However, obtain any greater advantage. Example:-
(1). A blacksmith hires a shop in order to carry on his trade there. He can carry on any other trade there which causes no greater injury to the lessor, or a trade causing a lesser degree of injury.
(2). If a person does not live a house which he has hired for purposes of habitation, he may store goods therein. But he may not carry on trade as a blacksmith in a shop which he has hired as a grocer's shop.

- 427. Anything which becomes altered by any change in the person using it may validly be made the subject of a restriction. Example:- A person hires a horse to ride himself. No other person may ride it.

- 428. Any restriction imposed in connection with any thing which does not become altered by any change in the person using it is inoperative. Example:- A hires a house to dwell in. B can also dwell in it.

- 429. The owner of a share of undivided jointly owned property may let such share to his co-owner whether such share is capable of division or not. He may not let it to any other person. He may, however, after a partition of the usufruct has been made, let his share to some other person.

- 430. The existence of undivided shares of jointly owned property after the conclusion of a contract of hire does not invalidate such contract.
Example:- A lets his house and after doing so a half share is seized by a person entitled thereto. The lease relating to the other undivided share remains in force.

- 431. Two joint owners may simultaneously let property jointly owned to some other person.

- 432. One particular thing may be let to two particular persons. Each one must pay the amount of the rent which falls to his own share. The share of one may not be obtained from the other unless they are guarantors of one another.

CHAPTER II. QUESTIONS RELATING TO THE CONTRACT OF HIRE.

SECTION I. THE FUNDAMENTAL BASIS OF THE CONTRACT OF HIRE.

- 433. As in the case of sale, the contract of hire is concluded by offer and acceptance.

- 434. In a contact of hire, statements made indicative of offer and acceptance are such expression as " i have given on hire", "I have let", " I have taken on hire" and " I have accepted".

- 435. As in the case of sale, the contract of hire is concluded by the use of the past tense. It cannot be concluded by the use of the future tense. Example :- A says " I will give on hire" and B says " i have taken on hire"; or A says"hire" and B says " I have hired". In both cases no contract of hire has been concluded.

- 436. A contract of hire may be concluded by word of mouth, or by writing, or by the use of generally recognised signs by dumb persons.

- 437. A contract of hire may also be concluded by conduct. Thus, if a traveller boards a steam boat or a harbour rowing boat or rides a hired pony, the rate of hire of which is well known, without concluded any oral contract, the amount of hire involved must be paid. If such rate is not known, an estimated rate must be paid.

- 438. In a contract of hire, silence is considered to indicate assent and acceptance. Examples :-
(1). A leases a shop at a monthly rent of fifty piastres. After staying there for a few months, the lessor informs him that if he agrees to pay sixty piastres on the first of the month he can remain, but if not, he must leave. A refuses to pay sixty piastres and remains in the shop. He is only obliged to pay fifty piastres as hitherto. If, however, he remains silent and continues to reside in the shop without interruption, he must pay a monthly rent of sixty piastres.
(2). An owner of a shop proposes a rent of one hundred piastres and the lessee a rent of eighty piastres. The owner leaves the lessee, who remains in the shop. The rent is eighty piastres. If the two parties persist in their contention, and the lessee remains in possession an estimated rent must be paid.

- 439. If fresh negotiations are commenced after the conclusion of the contract with regard to any change, increase or decrease of the rent, the second contract takes the place of the first.

- 440. A contract of hire may validly be concluded to take effect at some future date. It is irrevocable, although it may not yet have come into force. Consequently, neither of the contracting parties may cancel such contract merely on the ground that it has not yet come into force.

- 441. If after the conclusion of a valid contract of hire, some other person offers a higher rent, the contract of hire may not be cancelled by the lessor by reason of that fact alone. If a guardian or trustee of a pious foundation, however, lets the real property of an orphan or of a pious foundation for a rent which is less that the estimated rent, the contract of hire is voidable and the rent must be increased to the estimated rent.

- 442. If the person taking the property on hire becomes owner of the hired property in any manner, such as by way of inheritance or gift, such property loses its quality of hired property.

- 443. If any event happens whereby the reason for conclusion for the contract disappears, so that the contract cannot be carried out, such contract is cancelled. Examples:-
(1). A cook is hired for a wedding feast. One of the spouses dies. The contract of hire is cancelled.
(2). A person suffering from toothache makes a contract with dentist to extract his tooth for a certain fee. The pain ceases. The contract of hire is cancelled.
(3) A person seeking a wet-nurse dies. The contract of hire is not cancelled. But upon the death of the child or the wet-nurse, such contract is cancelled.

SECTION II. CONDITION RELATING TO THE CONCLUSION AND EXECUTION OF THE CONTRACT OF HIRE.

- 444. To conclude a contract of hire, the two contracting parties must possess the requisite capacity, that is to say, they must be of sound mind and perfect understanding.

- 445. In a contract of hire offer and acceptance must agree and the parties must met together at the same time and place, as in the case of sale.

- 446. The person letting a thing on hire must be owner of the thing he lets on hire, or the agent of the owner, or his tutor or guardian.

- 447. If any unauthorised person lets anything on hire, such letting is dependent upon the ratification of the owner, and if the owner is minor or is mad, and a contract of letting on hire has been concluded for an estimated rent, such contract is dependent upon the ratification of the tutor or guardian. There are four essentials to the validity of such permission which remain constant: the two contacting parties; the property; the subject matter of the contract; and the rent, should it be payable from merchandise. If one of these essentials is lacking, the permission is valid.

SECTION III. ESSENTIALS TO THE VALIDITY OF A CONTACT OF HIRE.

- 448. The consent of the two contracting parties is essential to the validity of the contract of hire.

- 449. The subject matter of the contract of hire must be specified. Consequently, if one of two shops is let on hire, without the particular shop is question being specified, and the lessee being given an option as to which one he will take, such contract is invalid.

- 450. The rent must be clearly ascertained.

- 451 . In a contract of hire, the advantage to be derived from the subject matter of the contract must be specified in such a manner as to void any possibility of dispute.

- 452. In the case of the of such things as houses, shops and wet- nurse, the advantage to be derived therefrom is defined by stating the period of hire.

- 453. In the case of hire or a horse, it must be stated whether such horse is to be used as a draught horse, or a riding horse, and if so, who is to ride it: or it may be stated in general terms that whosoever wishes may ride such horse, and the period for which the contract is concluded, or the distance, must also be stated.

- 454. In the case of hire of land, the period of hire must be stated; the purpose for which such land is to be used; and, if it is to be used for cultivation, the nature of the things to be planted; or, if the person taking such land on hire so desires, a statement is general terms must be made to the effect that he may plant whatever he likes.

- 455. In the case of hire of the services of skilled workmen, the advantage to be derived from the services of such workmen may be specified by stating the nature of the work, that is to say, what work is to be done and how it is to be performed. Example:- When clothes are to be dyed, they must be shown to the dyer, the texture thereof must be specified, and the colour stated.

- 456. In the case of transport of goods, the advantage to be derived therefrom is specified by indicating them, and by stating the place to which they are to be transported. Example:- A instructs B to carry a certain load to a certain place. The advantage to be derived therefrom is specified by such load being inspected and the distance being made known.

- 457. The advantage to be derived from the thing hires must be capable of enjoyment. Consequently, a contract of hire in respect to a runaway animal is invalid.

SECTION IV. NULLITY OR VOIDABILITY OF THE CONTRACT OF HIRE.

- 458. If one of the conditions essential to the conclusion of a contract of hire is absent, such contract is void. Example:- A contract of letting or taking on hire entered into by madman or by a minor of imperfect understanding is void. But if the person giving or letting on hire becomes mad after the conclusion of the contract, such contract is not cancelled.

- 459. If a contract of hire which is void is carried out the amount of the hire need not be paid. But if the property is dedicated to pious purposes, or belongs to orphans, an estimated rent must be paid. A madman is treated on the same basis as an orphan.

- 460. If the conditions requisite for the conclusion of a contract of hire are present, but one of the conditions essential to the validity of the contract is absent, the contract of hire is voidable.

- 461. A voidable contract of hire is executory. But in a voidable contract of hire, the person giving on hire is not entitled to the fixed rent, but to the estimated rent only

- 462. The voidability of a contract of hire sometimes arises from the amount of the hire not being known and sometimes owing to the absence of other conditions essential to the validity of the contract. In the first case, the estimated rent must be paid, whatever the amount thereof may be . In the second case, the estimated rent is payable, provided that it does not exceed the fixed rent.

CHAPTER III. QUESTION AFFECTING THE AMOUNT OF THE HIRE.

SECTION I. RENT.

- 463. A thing which is valid as the price in a contract of sale, may be the rent in a contract of hire. On the other hand, a thing which is not valid as the price in a contract of sale may nevertheless be valid as the rent in a contract of hire. Example:- A garden may be taken on hire in exchange for an animal, or in exchange for the right of dwelling in a house.

- 464. If the rent is cash, the amount thereof must be clearly ascertained, as in the case of the price of a thing sold.

- 465. If the rent consists of merchandise, or things estimated by measure of capacity, or by measure of weight, or things estimated by enumeration and which closely resemble each other, such rent must be made known by stating both the amount and description thereof.
In the case of things which require loading and entail expense on account of transport such things must be delivered at the place agreed upon for delivery. If no place has been designated for delivery and the thing hired consists of real property, delivery of such real property must be given at the place where such real property is situated, and if it consists of labour, delivery thereof must be given at the place where the person hired performs his work; if it consists of loading, delivery thereof must be given in the place where the hire becomes payable.
In the case of things which do not require loading and do not entail expense on account of transport, however, delivery thereof must be given at any place that may be required.

SECTION II. NECESSITY FOR RENT: RIGHT OF THE PERSON GIVING ON HIRE TO TAKE RENT.

- 446. Rent does not become payable irrevocably by the conclusion of an unconditional contract: that is to say, there is no necessity to hand over the rent immediately, owing to the mere conclusion of a contract of hire.

- 467. Rent which is payable immediately is irrevocable: that is to say, if the person taking the thing on hire pays the rent in advance, the person letting the thing on hire becomes the owner thereof, and the person taking the thing on hire cannot demand the return thereof.

- 468. Rent with a condition for immediate payment is irrevocable; that is to say, if it is stipulated that rent must be paid in advance, the person taking the thing on hire is bound in any case and first of all to hand over the rent, whether the contract of hire is for the use of some specific thing, or for the performance of any piece of work.
  In the first case, the person letting the thing on hire may refuse to hand over the thing hired until the rent has been paid. In the second case, the person giving his services on hire may refuse to perform the work until his wages have been paid.
  In both cases, if the person letting the thing on hire demands payment of the rent in advance and the person taking the thing on hire refuses, the contract of hire may be cancelled.

- 469. Rent becomes payable when the thing is put to the use for which it is hired.

  Example:- A the owner of a horse, lets such horse on hire to B is order that he may ride it to a certain place. Upon arrival at that place, A is entitled to the amount of the hire.

- 470. In a valid contract of hire, the rent is also payable when there is ability to put the thing to the use for which it was hired. Example:- A takes possession of a house which he has taken on hire by means of a valid contract of hire. A is obliged to pay the rent, even though he does not inhabit such house.

- 471. In a voidable contract of hire, mere ability to put the thing to the use for which it was hired is not enough. The rent is not payable unless the thing is actually put to the use for which it was hired.

- 472. If a person uses the property of another person without the conclusion of a contract and without such person's permission, and if it is property prepared for hire, an estimated rent must be paid, but not otherwise. But if the owner of the property has previously demanded payment of rent, and such person uses such property, rent is payable, even though no benefit can be derived from such property. The reason for this is that by using the property, such person is deemed to have agreed to pay the rent.

- 473. Effect is given to any condition agreed upon by the two contracting parties regarding immediate or deferred payment of the rent.

- 474. If a stipulation is made for a deferred payment of the price of the hire, the person giving the thing on hire must first of all deliver such thing; and a person giving his services on hire, must perform his work. The price of the contract of hire is not payable until after the expiration of the period agreed upon.

- 475. If an unconditional contract of hire is concluded for the use of some specific object, or for the performance of any piece of work, and no stipulation is made as to immediate of deferred payment, the person giving the thing on hire must in any case first of all give delivery of the thing hired, and the person giving his services on hire must perform the work.

- 476. If the rent is payable by some specified period, such as monthly or yearly, such rent must be paid at expiration of that period.

  Example:- Rent payable monthly must be paid at the end of the month. Rent payable yearly must be paid at the end of the year.

- 477. When the rent falls due, delivery must be given of the thing hired; that is to say, rent falls due as from the time of delivery. Thus, the person giving the thing on hire is not entitled to rent in respect to the period expiring prior to delivery. If the period of hire terminates prior to delivery, no part of the rent is payable.

- 478. If the benefit to be obtained from the thing hired is entirely lost, no rent is payable. Example:-
(1). A bath is in need of repairs. If it cannot be used during that period, the portion of the rent corresponding to such period is deducted.
(2). The water of a mill is cut off and the mill remains idle. No rent is payable from the time at which the water was cut off. But if the person hiring the mill uses it for any purpose other than that of grinding corn, such person is bound to pay a portion of the rent corresponding thereto.

- 479. If a person takes a shop on hire and is given delivery thereof and alleges that on account of slackness of business his trade has stopped and his shop has been shut, such person cannot refuse to pay rent for that period.

- 480. If a boat is taken on hire for a certain period, and the period expires while on the journey, the period of hire is extended until the shore is reached. The person taking the boat on hire must pay as estimated rent in respect to such excess period.

- 481. If one person gives his house to another person in order that the latter may repair it and live in it rent free, and such person does in fact effect such repairs himself and dwells in such house for a certain period, the expenses occasioned by such repairs fall upon such person, since the giving of the house is in the nature of a loan for use. The owner of the house cannot claim anything from him by way of rent in respect to such period.

SECTION III. RIGHT OF LIEN OF A PERSON TO WHOM A THING HAS BEEN ENTRUSTED TO WORK UPON.

- 482. A person hired to do work, and whose work causes a change in the thing given to him to work upon, such as a tailor, a dyer, or a cleaner, and who has made no contract whereby his work is to be done on a credit basis, has a right of retention over the thing entrusted to him to work upon, for payment of his wage. If he exercises such right of retention and the property is destroyed while in his possession, he cannot be called upon to make good the loss. He cannot, however, claim his wages in addition.

- 483. A person hired to do work, and whose work causes no change in the thing upon which he works, such as a porter or a sailor, has no right of retention over the thing upon which he working, for payment of his wage. Thus if exercises a right of retention and the property is destroyed while in his possession, he is liable to make good the value thereof.
The owner of the property has an option either of claiming compensation on the basis of the value of the thing destroyed, plus cost of transport and of paying the wages, or of merely claiming the value of the thing destroyed, without paying the wages.

CHAPTER IV. THE PERIOD OF HIRE.

- 484. A person may give his property on hire, whatever the form of ownership, for a fixed period, whether of short duration, such as a day, or whether of long duration, such as a period of years.

- 485. The commencement of the period of hire is deemed to be the time named when the contract was concluded.

- 486. If no time is mentioned as the commencement of the period of hire when the contract is concluded, such time is deemed to be the time when the contract was concluded.

- 487. Real property may validly be let on hire for a period of a year, either at a rent of so much per month, or of so much of the year, without stating the rent per month.

- 488. If a contract of hire is made at the beginning of the month for a period of one month, or for any period in excess thereof, such contract is a monthly contract. In such a case, if the month is less than thirty days, a full month's rent must be paid.

- 489. If a contract is made, for a period of one month and a portion thereof has expired, the period of one month is considered to consist of thirty days.

- 490. If a portion of the month has expired and a contract has been concluded for a period of months, and the first month is not complete, such month is completed by the payment of rent at so much per day, from days taken from the last month, so as to make thirty days. The intervening months are calculated as from the first day of each lunar month.

- 491. If a portion of the month has expired and the number of months is not expressed, and a certain sum is agreed upon as being payable as rent for each month, the first incomplete month is considered to consist of thirty days in the same manner as the other months.

- 492. If a contract of hire is concluded for a period of one year at the beginning of the month, the year is considered to consist of twelve months.

- 493. If a portion of the month has expired and a contract of hire has been concluded for a period of one year, the first month is calculated according to days, and the other eleven months as from the first of the lunar month.

- 494. If real property is hired at a rent of so much per month and the number of months is not mentioned, a valid contract has been concluded. Upon the completion of the first month, however, both the person giving and the person taking such real property on hire may cancel the contact of hire on the first night and day, however, have expired, such contract cannot be cancelled. If one of the two contracting parties alleges that he has cancelled the contract during the course of the month, such contract is cancelled as from the end of the month. If during the course of the month one of the parties states that he has cancelled the contract as from the beginning of following month, such contract cancelled as from the beginning of the following month. If payment is made in advance for two or more months, neither party may cancel the contract of hire in respect to those months.

- 495. If a person hires another to work for a day from sunrise to the time of evening prayer or till sunset, the conditions prescribed by local custom must be observed as regards the performance of the work.

- 496. If a person is hired to work for a period of days, as for example, a carpenter for a period of ten days, the contract is presumed to be concluded with reference to the days following. If he is hired to do ten days work during the summer, the contract of employment is invalid unless the month is stated and the day from which the work is to commence.

CHAPTER V. OPTIONS.

SECTION I. CONTRACTUAL OPTIONS.

- 497. A contractual option exists in the case of hire, as in the case of sale. Either or both of the parties may give or take on hire, subject to an option of a certain number of days.

- 498. The person having the option may cancel the contract of hire during the period of the option or may ratify such contract.

- 499. Both cancellation and ratification may be by word of mouth, or in writing, or by conduct, as is set forth in Article 302,303 and 304. Consequently, if person giving on hire possesses an option and performs any act with regard to the thing hired indicative of the exercise of a right of ownership, the contact of hire is cancelled by conduct. If the person taking on hire possesses an option and performs any act with regard to the thing hired indicative of the exercise of a right of ownership, the contract of hire is cancelled by conduct. If the person taking on hire possesses an option and performs any act with regard to the thing hired indicative of the exercise of the right of a lessee, the contract of hire is ratified by conduct.

- 500. If the person possessing an option allows the period of the option to expire without cancelling or carrying out the contract, the option is lost and the contract of hire becomes irrevocable.

- 501. The period of option is presumed to run from the time of the conclusion of the contract.

- 502. The commencement of the contract of hire is presumed to run from the time when the option was lost.

- 503. If a piece of land taken on hire and said to consist of so many yards or donums proves to be of greater or smaller extent, the contract of hire is valid and the fixed rent becomes payable. Should it prove to be smaller, however, the person taking the land on hire has the option of cancelling the contract of hire.

- 504. If a piece of land is taken on hire at so much per donum the rent is payable at so much per donum.

- 505. If a wage is fixed as payment for work to be performed by a given period, the contract of hire is valid and the condition effective.
Examples:-
(1). A gives cloth to a tailor to be cut up and made into a shirt to be ready on the same day.
(2). A hires a camel from B to carry him to Mecca in so many days.
In both cases the contract of hire is executory, and if the person giving the thing on hire fulfils the condition, he can claim the fixed wage. If he fails to do so, however, he is entitled to an estimated wage, provided such wage does not exceed the wage.

- 506. The wages my validly be fixed alternatively in two or three ways as regards the work, the workman, the load, the distance, the place and the time, and the wages must be paid according to whichever way the work is carried out. Examples:-
(1). A contract is made for back-stitching a thing for so much, and for over- stitching it for so much. The wages must be paid according to the way in which it is sewn.

(2). A contract is concluded for so much in respect to a shop to be used as a perfumery and for so much as a forge. The person taking the thing on hire must pay the fixed rent according to the way in which he uses the shop.

(3). A contract is concluded to load corn on a draught animal for so much and iron for so much. The hire agreed upon must be paid according to the load used.

(4). A muleteer states that he has let a particular animal on hire to go to CHORLU for one hundred piastres and to ADRIANOPLE for two hundred piastres and to PHILIPOLIS for three hundred piastres. The person taking the animal on hire must pay a sum corresponding to the place to which he goes.

(5). A states that he has let one particular house on hire for one hundred piastres and another house for two hundred piastres. The person taking the house on hire agrees. Such person must then pay the fixed rent according to whichever house he lives in.

(6). A hands a cloak to a tailor stating that he will pay fifty piastres if it stitched on the same day, and thirty piastres if it is stitched on the following day. The contract is executory and the condition is valid.

SECTION II. OPTION OF INSPECTION.

- 507. The person taking the thing on hire has an option of inspection.

- 508. An inspection of the thing hired is equivalent to an inspection of the advantage to be derived therefrom.

- 509. If a person takes a piece of real property on hire without seeing it, he may exercise an option as soon as he sees it.

- 510. If a person takes on hire a house which he has seen previously, he has no option of inspection in respect to such house. However, if the place is dilapidated and unfit for habitation to such an extent that its original form is changed, such person may exercise an option.

- 511. A person hired to do a piece of work which changes in accordance with any change in the subject-matter of such work, has an option of inspection. Example:- An agreement is concluded with a tailor to stitch a cloak. Upon seeing the cloth or the cloak, the tailor may exercise an option.

- 512. There is no option of inspection attaching to a thing which is not changed in accordance with any change in the subject-matter of such work. Example:- A contract is made to clean a certain amount of cotton seed for a certain sum of money . Although the person so employed has a not seen the cotton seed, he has no option of inspection.

SECTION III. OPTION FOR DEFECT.

- 513. There is an option for defect in the case of a contract of hire, as in a contract of sale.

- 514. In a contract of hire, the circumstance which creates an option on account of defect is something which causes the complete loss of or interference with the benefits sought to be obtained. Example:- A house is entirely destroyed ; the utility of a mill is negatived by the water being cut off; the frame of the roof of a house sinks; a place is knocked down so as to be unsuitable for habitation; the back of a horse which is hired is injured by galling. In all these cases there is an option for defect if they are taken on hire, on account of the benefits sought to be obtained being destroyed. But defects which do not interfere with the benefits sought to be obtained give no right to an option for defect in the case of a contract of hire, as where the plaster of a house falls off, but not to such an extent that rain and cold can enter; or where the mane or tail of a horse is cut.

- 515. If a defect occurs in the thing hired before such thing has been put to the use for which it was hired, such defect is considered to have existed at the time the contract was concluded.

- 516. If a defect occurs in the thing hired, the person taking on hire may exercise an option. He may either put the thing hired to the use for which it was hired in spite of the defect, in which case he must pay the whole of the rent, or he may cancel the contract of hire.

- 517. If the person giving a thing on hire removes a defect of recent origin before the cancellation of the contract of hire by the person taking such thing on hire, the latter has no right of cancellation. And if the person taking the thing on hire wishes to take possession thereof for the remainder of the period, the person giving such thing on hire cannot prevent him from doing so.

- 518. If the person taking a thing on hire wishes to cancel the contract of hire prior to the removal of a defeat of recent origin which prevents the thing hired being put to the use for which it was hired, such person may cancel the contract in the presence of the person giving the thing on hire. He may not do so in his absence. If he cancels the contract in the presence of the person giving the thing on hire, that is to say, without giving him notice thereof, such cancellation is of no effect, and the rent continues to be payable as heretofore.
If the benefits sought to be obtained are entirely lost, however, the contract may be cancelled in the absence of the person giving the thing on hire.
whether the contract is cancelled or not the rent is not due, as is set forth in Article 478. Example:- A place collapses and destroy the use to which a house taken on hire can be put. The person taking the house on hire may cancel the contract of hire .The cancellation, however, must take place in the presence of the person letting the house on hire. If he fails to give notice and leaves the house, he is bound to pay rent as though he had not left the house. If the house is entirely destroyed, however, the person taking the house on hire may cancel the contract without the necessity of doing so in the presence of the person giving the house on hire. In any case the rent is not due.

- 519. If a room or a wall of a house collapses and the person taking the house on hire does not cancel the contract of hire, but dwells in the rest of the house, no portion of the rent is remitted.

- 520. If a person takes two houses on hire together for a certain some of money and one of them collapses, he may leave both of them together.

- 521. If a house taken on hire as containing so many rooms proves to contain fewer rooms that the stipulated number, the person taking the house on hire has the option of cancelling the contract of hire or of agreeing to the contract of hire and of paying the fixed rent. If he carries out the terms of the contract of hire, however, he is not entitled to any reduction in the rent.

CHAPTER VI. TYPE OF THING HIRED AND MATTERS RELATING THERETO.

SECTION I. MATTERS RELATING TO THE HIRE OF REAL PROPERTY.

- 522. A person may validly take a house or shop on hire without stating who is to live therein.

- 523. If a person lets his house or shop on hire containing his goods or effects, the contract of hire is valid, but the person letting such house or shop on hire is bound to deliver the house or shop after taking out the goods or effects.

- 524. If a person takes a piece of land on hire without stating what he will sow therein or without making a stipulation of a general nature to the effect that he may sow whatever he likes, the contract of hire is voidable. But if such matter is defined before cancellation, and the person giving the land or hire agrees thereto, such contract becomes a valid contract of hire.

- 525. If a person takes a piece of land of hire with a right of sowing what he likes, he may cultivate such land more than once in a year with a view to winter and summer crops.

- 526. If the period of the contract of hire expires before the crops are ripe, such crops may remain on the land until they are ripe, the person taking such land on hire paying an estimated rent.

- 527. A person may validly conclude a contract of hire for a shop or house without stating the use to which it is to be put, which matter is settled according to custom.

- 528. Person who takes a house on hire without stating the use to which it is to be put, may dwell in it himself or let some other person dwell therein, and may place his effects therein.
  He may perform any kind of work therein, provided it is not of such a nature as to weaken or damage the building. He may not perform any work of such a nature as to damage the building unless he receives the permission of the owner. Local custom is followed as regards the tethering of animals. The same stipulations are in force as regards shops.

- 529. The person giving the thing on hire must put right anything likely to interfere with the benefits sought to be obtained from the thing hired. Examples:-
  (1). The owner must clean the water channel of a mill.
  (2). Repairs and improvements to the house and water courses and pipes, the repair of things detrimental to habitation and other; matters relating to the building must all be performed by the owner. If the owner refuses to do these, The person taking the house on hire may leave the same. If, however, such person was aware that the house was in that state when he took it on hire, he is considered to have agreed to the defect. He cannot later make this a pretext for leaving the house. If the person taking the house on hire does these things himself, such act is in the nature of a gift and he cannot claim the expenses incurred thereby from the person giving the house on hire.

- 530. If the person taking property on hire does repairs with the consent of the person giving such property on hire, and such repairs are for the improvement of the property, such as changing the tiles of the roof, or preventing any harm being done thereto, the person taking the property on hire may call upon the person giving the property on hire to make good the expenses incurred by such repairs, even though no stipulation has been made to that effect. However, if such repairs are purely in the interest of the person taking the property on hire, such as repairing the oven of the house, the person taking the house on hire cannot claim the expenses from the person giving the house on hire, unless a stipulation has been made to that effect.

- 531. If the person taking real property on hire erects buildings or plants trees thereon, the person giving such real property on hire has the option, on the expiration of the period of hire, either of having such building pulled down, or of having such trees uprooted, or of keeping them upon payment of value thereof, whatever that may be.

- 532. Dust, earth and sweepings which have accumulated during the period of the contract of hire must be cleaned and removed by the person taking the thing on hire.

- 533. In the event of the person taking the thing on hire damaging such thing, the person giving such thing on hire, may, if he is unable to prevent such damage, apply to the Court for an order cancelling the contract of hire.

SECTION II. HIRE OF MERCHANDISE.

- 534. A valid contract of hire may be concluded for a definite period and for a definite rent with regard to movable property such as clothing, weapons and tents.

- 535. If a person takes clothing on hire to go to any particular place, and fails to go to such place and wears them in his house, or does not wear them at all, he must nevertheless pay the hire thereof.

- 536. A person who takes clothes on hire to wear himself may not give such clothing to another person to wear.

- 537. Jewellery is treated on the same basis as clothing.

SECTION III. HIRE OF ANIMALS.

- 538. A contract may validly be made to take a specific animal on hire and a valid contract may also be made with an owner of animals to be carried to a specific.

- 539. If a specific animal is taken on hire to proceed to a certain place, and such animal becomes fatigued and stops on the way, the person taking such animal on hire has the option either of waiting till the animal gets better or of avoiding the contract of hire, in which case he is obliged to pay a portion of the fixed hire proportionate to the distance he has been carried.

- 540. If a bargain has been struck to carry a certain place and the animal becomes fatigued and stops on the way, the owner of the animal is bound to charge such load on to another animal and carry it to the place in question.

- 541. A contract to take an unspecified animal on hire is of no effect. if such animal is specified after the conclusion of the contract, however, and the person taking such animal on hire agrees thereto, such contract is valid. But it it is customary to take an animal of no particular type on hire, such hire is valid, and is governed by such custom. Example:- A horse is hired from a horse-owner to take a person as far as a particular place in accordance with custom. The owner is obliged to transport that person to such place by horse in accordance with the particular custom.

- 542. In a contract of hire it is not enough to designate the end of a journey be mentioning the name of a particular territory, such as a SANJAK or vilayet. On the other hand, this may validly be done if by custom the name of such territory is applied to a town. Example:- A valid contract of hire cannot be concluded to take an animal on hire to go to Bosnia or Arabia. The name of the town, township or village to which such person is going must be mentioned. The word Sham, however, the name of a certain territory, is by custom applied to the town of Damascus, and therefore a valid contract may be concluded to hire an animal to go as far as Sham.

- 543. If an animal is taken on hire to proceed to a certain place, and it so happens that there are two places of that name, an estimated sum by way of hire must be paid in respect to whichever place the person taking the animal on hire goes.
  Example:- An animal is taken on hire to proceed from Constantinople to Chekmeje, and it is not specified as to whether the animal is to go to Greater or Lesser Chekmeje. An estimated sum by way of hire must be paid according to the distance to the place in question.

- 544. If an animal is taken on hire to proceed to a certain town, the person taking such animal on hire must be taken to his house in such town.

- 545. A person who takes an animal on hire to proceed to a specified place may not go beyond that place without the permission of the owner. If he does in fact go beyond such place, the person taking such animal on hire is responsible for handling over the animal safe and sound, and if such animal is destroyed either on the outward or return journey, he must make good the loss.

- 546. If an animal is taken on hire to go to a specified place, the person taking such animal on hire cannot go with him to another place. If he does so and the animal is destroyed, he must make good the loss. Example:- If an animal is taken on hire to go to Tekfur Dagh. But instead goes to Islimiyeh and the animal is destroyed, the loss must be made good.

- 547.If an animal is taken on hire to go to a specified place, and there are several roads leading thereto, the person taking such animal on hire may proceed by whichever road he prefers which is commonly used by the public. If the owner of the animal prescribes the road which is to be taken, and the person taking such animal on hire proceeds by another road and the animal is destroyed, the loss must be made good if the road taken is more winding or difficult than that prescribed by the owner of the animal. But if it is of equal length or easier, the loss need not be made good.

- 548. The person taking the animal on hire for a specified period may not use it for longer than that period. If he does so, and the animal is destroyed while in his possession, he must make good the loss.

- 549. A valid contract may be made to take an animal on hire to be ridden be a specified person. A valid contract may also be made in general terms to take an animal on hire to be ridden by anyone.

- 550. An animal which is taken on hire for riding may not be used as a draught animal. If it is so used and the animal is destroyed, the loss must be made good. In this case, however, no hire need be paid. (See Article 86.)

- 551. If an animal is hired to be by a certain person, no other person may ride such animal. If he does so, and the animal is destroyed, the loss must be made good.

552. A person who has taken an animal on hire in order that it may be ridden by any person he likes, may either ride such animal himself, or allow some other person to do so. Bur whether; he rides it himself or allows some other person to ride it, once the particular person to ride such animal is known, no other person may ride it.

- 553. If an animal is taken on hire for riding and it is not stated who is to ride it, nor laid down in general terms that any particular person who wishes may ride it, the contract of hire is voidable.

But if this is made clear before the contract is cancelled,such contract becomes valid. In this case also, one a particular person has been named no other person may be allowed to ride the animal.

- 554. If an animal is taken on hire as a draught animal, local custom is binding as regards the saddle, rope and sack.

- 555. If the amount of the load is not stated or made clear by signs, the amount of such load is determined by custom when an animal is taken on hire.

- 556. The person taking an animal on hire may not beat such animal without the owner's permission. If he does so, and the animal is destroyed as a result thereof, he must make good the loss.

- 557. If the owner gives his permission for an animal taken on hire to be beaten, the person taking the animal the animal on hire may only beat such animal on a place where it is usual to do so. If he beats him on any other place, as for example, on the head, instead of the quarter, and the animal is destroyed as a result thereof, such loss must be made good.

- 558. An animal hired to carry loads may also be used for riding purposes.

- 559. When an animal is taken on hire and the nature and quantity of the load is stated, a load of another; nature equal to or lesser than such load may also be placed upon such animal. But no greater load may be placed thereon. Examples:-

  (1). A takes a horse on hire to carry five kiles of wheat. A may load five kiles of his own wheat, or of anybody else's wheat of whatsoever sort upon such horse. He may also load five kiles of barley. But he may not load five kiles of wheat on an animal hired to carry five kiles of barley.

  (2). A hundred okes of iron may not be loaded upon an animal hired to carry a hundred okes of cotton.

- 560. The owner of the animal taken on hire must unload such animal.

- 561. The person giving the animal on hire is responsible for feeding such animal. Example:- The feeding and watering of an animal taken on hire fall upon the owner. If the person taking the animal on hire, however, feeds it without the permission of the owner, such feeding, is an involuntary gift and the value thereof cannot later be claimed from the owner.

SECTION IV. HIRE OF PERSONAL SERVICES.

- 562. A contract may validly be made for the hire of personal services or the performance of skilled labour for a specified period or in some other way, as by specifying the nature of the work, as is set forth in Section III of Chapter II.

- 563. If a person works for some other person at the latter's request without entering into any contract in regard to the wage to be paid, he is entitled to receive an estimated wage if he is of the class of persons who work for a wage. If he is not of such class, however, he is not entitled to receive anything.

- 564. If a person requests some other person to do a certain piece of work for him and promises him something in return without mentioning the amount thereof, and such person does that work, he is entitled to an estimated wage.

- 565. If a person employs workmen without fixing the amount of the wage to be paid, and if the daily sage of such workmen is known, they are entitled to receive the daily wage. If it is not known, they are entitled to an estimated wage. The work performed by skilled workmen is also of this type.

- 556. If a contract of hire is entered into with an employee whereby payment is to be made by giving a thing the like of which cannot be found in the market, and the nature of which has not been defined, an estimated wage must be paid.

Example:- A calls B and asks B to work for him for a certain number of days in return for which A promises to give B a pair of oxen. There is no need to give the pair of oxen, but an estimated wage must be paid. It is customary, however, when a wet nurse is taken on hire for clothes to be made for her. If the nature of the clothes has not been defined beforehand, they are to be of medium quality.

- 567. Tips given to servants from outside cannot be included in wages.

- 568. If a teacher is employed to teach any science or art and the period is defined, the contract of employment is concluded in respect to that particular period. Such person is entitled to his fee if he is ready and willing to teach, whether the pupil studies or not. If the period is not defined, the contract of hire voidable. If the pupil studies under these circumstances, the teacher is entitled to his fee. If not, he is not entitled to his fee.

- 569. If a person sends his son to a master to learn a trade and no agreement is made between the two as to the fee to be paid, and they both claim a fee after the boy has learnt the trade, the question is decided in accordance with local custom.

- 570. If the inhabitants of a village hire the services of a khoja or an imam or a muezzin, and such persons perform their duties, they are entitled to receive their wages from the inhabitants of that village.

- 571. When a person has been employed to do work personally, he may not employ anyone to do the work in his place.

Example:- A contracts with B for B to sew a cloak with his own hand for so many piastres. The tailor may not have it sewn by any other person. It must be sewn by B himself. If B has it sewn by any other person and it is destroyed, he must make good the loss.

- 572. If an unconditional contract has been made, the employee may employ another person in his place.

- 573. If the employer gives a definite order to the employee to do a certain piece of work, such order is unconditional.

Example:- A instructs a tailor to sew a cloak for so much money without binding him to do the work personally. After the conclusion of the contract, the tailor has the cloak sewn by his assistant or by another tailor. The tailor is entitled to the fixed price. If the cloak is destroyed without his fault, he may not be called upon to make good the loss.

- 574. Matters connected with the work done are settled in accordance with local custom when there is no specific condition binding the person employed. Thus, custom has it that the thread shall be the tailor's thread.

- 575. A porter must carry the load inside the house, but he is not bound to put it in position.

Example:- It is not the duty of the porter to take the load up to the top floor; nor to put grain into a barn.

- 576. The employer is not bound to feed the employee unless local custom is to that effect.

- 577. If a broker hawks property round but cannot sell it, and the owner sells it at some later date, the broker is not entitled to a fee. If another broker sells such property, such second broker takes the whole of the fee, and the first broker is not entitled to anything.

- 578. If a person gives his property to a broker, instructing him to sell it for so many piastres, and such broker sells it for more than the stipulated sum, the owner of the property is entitled to the whole of such sum in excess, and the broker is not entitled to anything more than the brokerage fee.

- 579. In the case of a sale, where the broker has received his fee, and some person appears who is entitled to the thing sold and takes possession of the same, or if the thing sold is returned on account of some defect, the return of the brokerage fee cannot be claimed.

- 580. If a person employs reapers to reap crops in his field for a certain sum of money, and after such reapers have reaped a portion thereof, the rest is destroyed by a fall of hail or by some other accident, the reapers are entitled to a share of the fixed wage proportionate to the quantity reaped, but not to the balance.

- 581. If a wet nurse falls sick she is entitled to cancel the contract of employment. The employer may cancel the contract of employment if she becomes sick or pregnant, or if the child refuses to take her breasts, or if it brings up the milk.

CHAPTER VII. RIGHTS AND OBLIGATIONS OF THE PERSON GIVING AND THE PERSON TAKING ON HIRE AFTER THE CONCLUSION OF THE CONTRACT.

SECTION I. DELIVERY OF THE THING HIRED.

- 582. Delivery of the thing hired consists of permission being given by the person giving the thing on hire to the person taking the thing on hire to enjoy such thing without let or hindrance. <1815>

- 583. Upon the conclusion of a valid contract of hire for a particular time or for a particular journey, the thing hire must be delivered to the person taking the thing on hire to be continuously in his possession until the expiration of such period, or the end of such journey.

Example:- A takes a cart on hire for a certain period, or in order to go to a certain place. A can use the cart during such period or until he has arrived at his destination. The owner may not use it for his own purposes during that period.

- 584. If a person who owns real property in absolute ownership containing other property of his own, gives such real property on hire, no rent is payable until it is delivered free from all such encumbrances, unless they have been sold to the person taking the property on hire.

- 585. When the lessor of the house hands the house over minus a room in which he has stored his goods, the proportion of the rent represented by such room must be deducted. As regards the rest of the house the lessee may exercise an option. If the lessor evacuates the house entirely and hands it over before cancellation of the contract, such contract is irrevocable; that is to say, the right of the lessee to cancel the contract is lost.

SECTION II. RIGHT OF THE CONTRACTING PARTIES TO DEAL WITH THE THING HIRED AFTER THE CONCLUSION OF THE CONTRACT.

- 586. If the thing hired consists of real property, the person taking such real property on hire may give it on hire to some third person before taking delivery thereof. He may not do so, however,however, if it is movable property.

- 587. The person taking the thing on hire may let such thing on hire to some third person if it is not changed by use or enjoyment.

- 588. In the case of a voidable contract of hire the person taking the thing on hire may validly give it on hire to some third person after taking delivery thereof.

- 589. If a person who has given his property on hire to some other person for a definite period in accordance with the terms of an irrevocable contract of hire, again gives such property on hire to some third person, the second contract of hire ineffective.

- 590. If the person giving the thing on hire sells the thing hired without the permission of the person taking the thing on hire, the sale is not executory as regards the latter, but is executory as regards the vendor and the purchaser, and on the expiration of the period of hire, the sale is irrevocable as regards the purchaser and he may not refuse to take delivery thereof. However, if before the expiration of the period of hire the purchaser asks the vendor to hand over the thing sold, and it is impossible to do so, the Court shall cancel the contract of sale. If the person taking the property on hire ratifies the sale, the sale becomes executory in respect to each party. If the person taking the thing on hire, however, has made payment in advance, the thing hired cannot be taken from him until he has received payment of the amount of the rent paid by him in respect to the unexpired portion of the lease. If the person taking the thing on hire hands it over without receiving payment, he loses his right of retention.

SECTION III. RETURN OF THE THING HIRED.

- 591. On the termination of the contract of hire, the person taking the thing on hire must give up the thing hired.

- 592. The person taking the thing on hire may not use the thing hired after the termination of the contract of hire.

- 593. If the person giving the thing on hire asks for the return of his property upon the termination of the contract of hire, the person taking the thing on hire is bound to return it to him.

- 594. The person taking the thing on hire is not bound to return the thing hired, but the person giving the thing on hire is bound to take over the thing hired on the expiration of the contract of hire.

Examples:- (1). Upon the termination of the lease of a house the owner must come and take delivery thereof. (2). An animal is taken on hire is in that place, he must take over his animal. If he arrives and does not take it over, and it is destroyed while in the possession of the person hiring the animal without such person's fault, or neglect, such person may not be called upon to make good the loss. If, however, the animal is hired to leave and return to a definite place, it must be brought to that place. If it is not brought to such place, but is brought to the house of the person taking the animal on hire and is destroyed while there, the loss must be made good by such person.

- 595. If the return of the thing hired involves expenditure for transport, such expenses fall upon the person giving the thing on hire.

CHAPTER VIII. COMPENSATION

SECTION I. COMPENSATION IS RESPECT TO USE.

- 596. If a person uses any property without the permission of the owner thereof, this amounts to wrongful appropriation, and he is not obliged to pay for the use thereof. If. however, the property has been dedicated to pious purposes, or is the property of a minor, an estimated rent must be paid in any case. If it is property owned in absolute ownership, nor as a result of contract, payment for use must be made; that is, an estimated rent must be paid.

Example:-

(1). A lives in B's house for a certain period without concluding a contract of hire. He is not obliged to pay rent. But if the house has been dedicated to pious purposes or is the property of the minor, an estimated rent must be paid in respect to the period during which it has been inhabited, whether it is claimed to be property held in absolute ownership, or as a result of contract.

(2). In the case of a house for hire, an estimated rent must be paid if it not claimed to be property held in absolute ownership nor a a result of contract.

(3). A takes B's horse, which B lets out on hire, and uses it for a certain period without the permission of B. An estimated sum by way of hire must be paid.

- 597. If property is used which is claimed to be property owned in absolute ownership, even though it is prepared for hire, nothing need be paid in respect to such use.

Example:- One of the joint owners of a piece of jointly owned property uses such property for a certain period independently and without the consent of the other joint owner, asserting that it is his own property owned in absolute ownership. The other joint owner cannot claim rent in respect to his share, even though it is property prepared for hire.

- 598. If use is made of property which is claimed to be owned as a result of contract, even though it is prepared for hire, nothing need be paid in respect to such use.

Examples:-

(1). A is joint owner of a shop and sells such shop to B without the permission of the other joint-owner. B holds such shop for a certain period. The other joint-owner does not give his assent to the sale and seizes his share. He cannot claim rent in respect to his share, however, much the shop may have been prepared for giving on hire, because the purchaser, having asserted that he has used it as an owner, his ownership being claimed to be used upon a contract, that is to say, upon a contract of sale, is not obliged to pay for the benefit received.

(2). A sells and delivers his mill to B which he asserts is his own property held in absolute ownership. After having held it for a certain period, another person appears claiming the mill and after proving his case and obtaining judgement, takes it from the purchaser. Such person cannot claim anything from B in the way of rent in respect to that period, since this is claimed to be based on a contract.

- 599. If any person employs a minor without the consent of his tutor, such minor is entitled to receive an estimated wage for his services upon his reaching the age of puberty. If the minor dies, his heirs may claim an estimated wage from the employer is respect to the period of the employment.

SECTION II. COMPENSATION BY PERSON TAKING THE THING ON HIRE.

- 600. Whether the contract of hire is valid or not, the thing taken on hire is on trust while in the possession of the person taking such thing on hire.
- 601. If the thing taken on hire is destroyed while in the possession of the person taking such thing on hire, the latter may not be called upon to make good the loss, unless he has committed some wrongful act, or negligence, or performed any act which he is not authorised to do.
- 602. If the thing hired is destroyed by reason of the wrongful act of the person taking the thing on hire, or the value thereof is diminished, such person must make good the loss.

Example:- The person taking an animal or hire beats it and it dies,or is destroyed by reason of his brutal and violent driving. Such person must make good the loss.

- 603. If the person taking the thing on hire acts in a way contrary to what is customary, such act is wrongful and he must make good any damage or loss resulting therefrom.

Examples:-

(1). Clothes which are taken on hire are used in a way contrary to what is customary and become tattered. The loss must be made good.

(2). A fire breaks out in a house which has been hired by reason of a fire being lighted which is larger than what is customary and house is burnt. The loss must be made good.

- 604. If the thing is destroyed owing to the failure of the person taking the thing on hire to take proper care, or the value thereof is decreased, the loss must be made good.

Example:- A person takes an animal on hire and drives it is not a deserted place so that it is lost. He must make good the loss.

- 605. If the person taking the thing on hire goes beyond what he has agreed to do, acting in contravention of what he has been authorised to do, he must make good any loss caused thereby. But if his act in contravention results in something equivalent to or less than what he has agreed to do, he incurs no liability.

Example:- A takes an animal on hire to load so many okes of oil and instead loads the same number of okes of iron upon it and the animal is destroyed. A must make good the loss. But if a load equal to or lighter than oil is loaded and the animal is destroyed, there is no liability to make good the loss.

- 606. On the expiration of the contract of hire, the thing hired remains on trust in the possession of the person taking the thing on hire for safe keeping. Consequently, if the person taking the thing on hire uses such thing on the expiration of the period of hire and such thing is destroyed, he must make good the loss. Again, if the person giving the thing on hire asks for his property to be returned on the termination of the contract of hire, and the person taking the thing on hire fails to do so, he must make good the loss if such property is destroyed.

SECTION III. LOSS CAUSED BY EMPLOYEES.

- 607. If the thing entrusted to an employee to work upon is destroyed by the wrongful act or negligence of such person, the latter must make good the loss.
- 608. A wrongful act of an employee consists of any act or conduct contrary to the express or implied order of his employer.

Examples:-

1. A instructs his shepherd who is his private employee to pasture his flock in a certain place and no other. The shepherd takes the flock to another place. He has committed a wrongful act, and if the animals are destroyed in that place, the shepherd must make good the loss.

(2). A hands cloth to a tailor instructing him to cut it and make him a long coat therefrom, if the cloth is sufficient. The tailor tells him that it is sufficient. If it turns out after the cloth is cut up that it is not sufficient for the purpose, A can claim to have the loss made good by the tailor.

- 609. Negligence of the employee consists of any fault of his of which he is guilty without excuse in the preservation of the thing entrusted to him on account of his employment.

Example:- An animal strays from the flock and is lost purely on account of the neglect of the shepherd to come and catch such animal. The shepherd must make good the loss. He is not liable, however, if his failure to go after the animal arose out of the probability that is so doing he would lose the other animals.

- 610. A private employee is a trustee. Consequently, he is under no obligation to make good any loss arising out or the destruction of property in his possession not caused by any act of his. Similarly, if property is destroyed by his own act without his fault he is not liable to make good the loss.
- 611. A public employee is liable to make good any damage or loss incurred by his own act, whether resulting from any wrongful act or negligence of his or not.

PROMULGATED BY ROYAL IRADAH 6TH. ZIL QADA, 1286.

AL-MAJALLA AL AHKAM AL ADALIYYAH

(The Ottoman Courts Manual (Hanafi))

BOOK III. GUARANTEE.

INTRODUCTION

TERMS OF ISLAMIC JURISPRUDENCE RELATING TO GUARANTEE.

- 612. A guarantee consists of the addition of an obligation to an obligation in respect to a demand for a particular thing. This is to say, it consists of one person joining himself to another person, and binding himself also to meet the obligation which accrues to that other person.

- 613. A personal guarantee is constituted by a person becoming a guarantor for another man personally.

- 614. A guarantee of property is constituted by a person becoming guarantor for the payment of something.

- 615. A guarantee for delivery is constituted by a person becoming guarantor for the delivery of something.

- 616. A contingent guarantee is constituted by a person becoming guarantor for the payment of the price of the property sold, in the event of its being appropriated by a person having a right thereto, or for the vendor personally.

- 617. An unconditional guarantee is a guarantee constituted independently of any condition or of any future time.

- 618. A guarantor is a person who adds an obligation of his own to that of some other person. In other words, a person who undertakes to do a thing which some other person has undertaken to do. The latter person is called the principal, or the person guaranteed.

- 619. The person is whose favour the guarantee is made is the person demanding the guarantee and who is the creditor.

- 620. The subject matter of the guarantee is the thing which the guarantor undertakes to hand over or pay. In the case of a personal guarantee the person guaranteed and the subject matter of the guarantee are one and the same thing.

CHAPTER I. THE CONTRACT OF GUARANTEE.

SECTION I. FUNDAMENTAL BASIS OF A CONTRACT OF GUARANTEE.

- 621. A guarantee may be concluded and become executory by the mere offer of the guarantor. The person in whose favour the guarantee is made decline to accept such guarantee. Until such time as he does so, however, the guarantee is valid. Thus, if in the absence of the person in whose favour the guarantee is made, a person stands security for the latter recovering any amount due to him, and the creditor dies without receiving information that such person has stood security, the guarantor is bound thereby.

- 622. The offer of the guarantor, that is, words used importing guarantee, are any words which by custom are evidence of an undertaking to be bound.

  Example:- A states that he has stood security, or that he is a guarantor, or that he is ready to indemnify someone. A valid contract of guarantee is thereby concluded.

- 623. A contract of guarantee may also be concluded by means of a promise dependent on a condition. (see Article 84).

  Example:- A tells B that he will stand security for the payment of any sum due to B in the event of B not receiving payment thereof. A valid contract of guarantee is thereby concluded, and if the person in whose favour the guarantee is made claims the sum due to him, and the debtor fails to pay, such person may demand payment from the guarantor.

- 624. Should a person undertake to be a guarantor for any limited period of time, a contract of guarantee of limited duration is thereby concluded independently of any condition or of any future time.

- 625. In addition to the conclusion of an unconditional contract of guarantee, a contract of guarantee subject to a condition for immediate or future performance may also be concluded. That is to say, a guarantee may be concluded for payment forthwith or at some future date.

- 626. A person may validly be a guarantor of a guarantor.

- 627. There may also be more than one guarantor.

SECTION II. CONDITION ATTACHING TO A CONTRACT OF GUARANTEE.

- 628. In order to be able to make a contract of guarantee, a surety must be of sound mind and must have arrived at the age of puberty. Consequently, a madman, an imbecile and a minor cannot make a valid contract of guarantee. If a minor becomes a guarantor while a minor and after arriving at the age of puberty ratifies the contract of guarantee, he cannot be made to abide thereby.

- 629. It is not essential for the person guaranteed to be of sound mind, nor to have arrived at the age of puberty. Consequently, a valid contract of guarantee may be entered into in respect of the debt of a madman or a minor.

- 630. If the subject matter of the guarantee is a person, the identity of such person must be clearly established. If it is property, however, there is no need for such property to be identified. Consequently, if a person becomes guarantor for the debt of another owing to some third person, the amount of such debt being unknown, a valid contract of guarantee is concluded.

- 631. In the case of a guarantee of property, the obligation must fall upon the principal debtor, that is to say, the performance of such obligation must be binding on the principal debtor. Consequently, a valid contract of a thing sold, rent and other proved debts. Similarly, a valid contract of guarantee may be concluded with regard to property which has been wrongfully appropriated, and on demand, the guarantor is bound to make good the same in kind or in cash. Again, a valid contract of guarantee may be concluded with regard to property bought on approval as to price, provided the price has been fixed. But a valid contract of guarantee cannot be made with regard to any actual property sold before the receipt thereof, because if the property sold perishes while in possession of the vendor, there is no obligation upon him to deliver the actual property sold,since the sale is cancelled, he being merely obliged to return the price thereof if he has received the same. Likewise, a valid contract of guarantee cannot be concluded with regard to property pledged or lent for use, or let on hire or in other cases where property has been entrusted to some third party, the responsibility for which does not fall upon the principal. But a person may validly undertake to be guarantor for the person guaranteed if such things are wasted or destroyed. A valid contract of guarantee may also be concluded in respect to both the property sold and the delivery thereof. Upon demand, the guarantor is bound to deliver such goods, provided there is no right of retention. If they are destroyed, however, the guarantor is in no way liable, just as the death of the person with regard to whom a contract of guarantee has been concluded frees the guarantor from liability.

- 632. No substitution is permissible in criminal punishment. Consequently, no valid contract of guarantee can be concluded in respect to capital punishment and other criminal matters and punishments of a personal nature. But a valid contract of guarantee may be concluded with reference to indemnities for personal injury payable by persons who may have inflicted bodily injury, including blood money payable by a murderer.

- 633. It is not a condition that the person guaranteed should be solvent, since a valid contract of guaranteed should be solvent, since a valid contract of guarantee may be concluded with regard to a bankrupt also.

CHAPTER II. THE CONTRACT OF GUARANTEE.

SECTION I. UNCONDITIONAL, CONDITIONAL AND FUTURE CONTRACTS OF GUARANTEE.

- 634. The effect of a contract of guarantee is a claim. That is to say, it consists of the right of the person in whose favour the guarantee is made to claim the subject matter of the guarantee from the guarantor.

- 635. In an unconditional contract of guarantee, the sum guaranteed may be claimed forthwith if the debt is payable immediately by the principal debtor, and at the expiration of the period prescribed for payment, if payable at some future date.

  Example:- A states that he guarantees the debt of B. If the debt is payable forthwith, payment may be demanded by the creditor at once from the guarantor, and if it is payable at some future date, then upon the expiration of the prescribed period.

- 636. Where a contract of guarantee is concluded subject to a condition, or is to take effect at some future date, the guarantor may not be called upon to make payment until the condition has been fulfilled, and the time has arrived.

Examples:-

(1). A tells B that if C does not pay his debt to B, he will stand security for the debt. A conditional contract of guarantee has been concluded, and if C does not pay his debt when it falls due, payment may be demanded from the guarantor. But no claim may be made against the guarantor until the principal debtor has been asked to pay.

(2). A tells B that if C steals his property he will make good the loss. A valid contract of guarantee has been concluded, and if B is robbed by C, payment may be demanded from the guarantor.

(3). A becomes guarantor on condition that when the person in whose favour the guarantee is made makes a claim for payment he shall be given so many days grace. The person in whose favour the guarantee is made entitled to ask for payment at any time whatsoever after the expiration of the period of grace as from the time at which the demand for payment was made. The guarantor has no right of asking for the same period of grace a second time.

(4). A tells B that he is guarantor for any sum that may be due to him, or for any sum that may be lent by him, or in respect to anything that may be wrongfully appropriated from him, or in respect to the price of anything that he may sell. The guarantor is only liable in the circumstances contemplated, that is to say, when the debt falls due, or when the money is lent, or wrongful appropriated is proved, or when the property is sold and delivery thereof is given.

(5). A stands security for the appearance of B upon a certain day. No claim may be made upon the guarantor to produce the person guaranteed before the day in question.

- 637. Upon the fulfilment of a condition, all matters in amplification or restriction thereof must also be fulfilled.

Example:- A undertakes to be guarantor of B for the payment of any sum which may be given in judgement against him. B admits that he is in debt for a certain sum of money. The guarantor is not liable to pay the sum of money is question, until judgement has been given by the Court.

- 638. In the case of a contingent guarantee, the guarantor may not be called upon for payment should any person prove that he is entitled to the thing sold, until the Court has given judgement for the return of the price be the vendor.

- 639. In cases of guarantee of limited duration, no demand may be made from the guarantor except during the period of the guarantee.

Example:- A states that he is guarantor for B for a period of one month as from today. A is only liable during that period, and thereafter is discharged from the guarantee.

- 640. After the conclusion of a contract of guarantee, the guarantor cannot withdraw from the guarantee. In the case of a conditional or future contract of guarantee, however, the guarantor can withdraw from the guarantee before the debtor has become liable in respect to any debt.

Example:- A becomes guarantor absolutely for B, either personally or in respect to a debt. A cannot withdraw from the contract. Nor can he withdraw if he states that he will make good any sum which may be owing to C from D, because the debt came into existence before the conclusion of the contract of guarantee, notwithstanding the fact that it was proved after the conclusion of the contract. But if A undertakes to be guarantor for anything which B may sell to C, or for the price of any goods which he may sell, A is responsible to the person in whose favour the guarantee is made for anything sold to C. He may, however, withdraw from the contract of guarantee prior to the sale. And if A states that he has withdrawn from the contract and requests B not to sell to *c and B nevertheless does sell to C, A is not bound as guarantor for the price.

- 641. A person who is guarantor for the return and delivery of property wrongfully appropriated or lent for use and who delivers such property to the owner, may claim indemnification for the cost of transport from the person wrongfully appropriating or borrowing such property for use.

SECTION II. GUARANTEE FOR THE PRODUCTION OF A PARTICULAR PERSON.

- 642. A personal guarantee consists of producing the person guaranteed. Thus, the guarantor must produce the person guaranteed at any time stipulated, in the event of his being called upon to do so. If he produces such person, he is discharged from his obligation. If he fails, he shall be compelled to produce him.

SECTION III. GUARANTEE OF PROPERTY.

- 643. A guarantor is obliged to make good the loss suffered.
- 644. The person claiming under the guarantee has the option of claiming either against the guarantor or against the principal debtor. The exercise of his right against the one in no way destroys his right of claiming from the other. He may claim first from the one and then from the other or from both simultaneously.
- 645. If a person who is guarantor of property has been guaranteed by some third person for any sum for which he may become liable by reason of his guarantee, the creditor may have recourse against whichever one of them he wishes.
- 646. If persons who are jointly indebted on one particular account guarantee each other, action may be taken against any one of them for the whole amount.
- 647. If there are several guarantors of one debt who have become guarantor for such debt separately, action may be taken against any one of them for the whole amount of the debt.

If they become guarantors at one and the same time, action shall be taken against each one for his share of the debt. But if they have also each guaranteed the amount to be paid by the others, each of them is liable for the whole amount of the debt.

Example:- A is guarantor for a debt of one thousand piastres contracted by B. C also becomes a guarantor for the thousand piastres. The creditor can demand payment of his sum from whichever of the two guarantors he wishes. But if the two guarantors jointly guarantee the debt, they are each liable for the half of the sum only. If they each guarantee the amount for which the other is liable, however, they can both be called upon to pay the whole amount of one thousand piastres.

- 648. If there is a condition in the contract of guarantee whereby the principal debtor becomes freed from his liability, the contract is changed into a transfer of debt.

- 649. A transfer of debt subject to a condition that the debtor shall not be freed from the liability is a contract of guarantee. Consequently, if a creditor instructs his debtor to transfer the sum he is owing to some other person on condition that the debtor is to guarantee payment, and he does so, such person may demand payment from whichever of the two he wishes.

- 650. A person who holds property belonging to some other person on trust may validly become the guarantor of that person for the payment of a debt owing by him, on condition that payment shall be made out of such property and the guarantor is then obliged to make payment from such property. If the property is destroyed, the guarantor is not obliged to pay anything. If he returns the property to the owner thereof after becoming guarantor, he is then personally liable.

- 651. If any person guarantees to produce another at a given time and in the event of his failing to do so, guarantees to pay the debt of such person, the guarantor is obliged to pay such debt. In the event of the death of the guarantor, the heirs must produce the person whose appearance is guaranteed at the time agreed upon, or if such person surrenders himself in accordance with the contract of guarantee, the guarantor's property is freed from all liability. If they fail to produce the person guaranteed, or if such person fails to surrender himself, the estate of the guarantor becomes liable for payment of debt. In the event of the death of the person in whose favour the guarantee is given, his heirs may claim the sum in question.

  If the guarantor produces the person guaranteed at the time agreed upon and the person in whose favour the guarantee has been given cannot be found, the guarantor may make application to the Court for the appointment of a representative of such person for the appointment of a representative of such person and for the person guaranteed to be handed over to him.

- 652. In the case of an absolute contract of guarantee, if the debt is payable forthwith by the principal debtor, payment thereof may also be demanded forthwith from the guarantor. If the principal debtor is to make payment at some future definite date, however, payment may only be demanded from the guarantor on that date.

- 653. In the case of a restricted contract of guarantee, payment may be demanded from the guarantor in accordance with the nature of the guarantee, that is to say, whether for immediate payment, or for payment at some future definite date.

- 654. A contract of guarantee may validly be concluded in respect to a debt payable at some future definite date for a period to coincide with such date, and also for a period beyond that date.

- 655. If the creditor postpones his claim in respect to the principal debtor, he is considered to have postponed his claim both in respect to the guarantor and any person guaranteeing him. Any postponement in respect to a first guarantor acts as a postponement of the second guarantor. A postponement in respect to the guarantor, however, does not act as a postponement in respect to the principal debtor.

- 656. If a person who has contracted debts repayable at some future definite date wishes to leave for some other country before such debts fall due for payment, such person must find a guarantor upon creditor applying to the Court to that effect.

- 657. If a person requests another to guarantee a debt which he owes to some third person and such person agrees, and pays the debt, and wishes to exercise his right of recourse against the debtor, he may do so, in respect to what he has guaranteed and not what he has paid. But if he has paid a portion of the debt as a result of a settlement with the creditor, he has a right of recourse in respect to that amount only, and not to the whole debt.

Examples:-

(1). A is a guarantor for sound coin. He pays with base coin. He is entitled to receive sound coin from the principal debtor. On the other hand, if he is guarantor in respect to base coin and pays in sound coin, he is only entitled to receive base coin from the principal debtor.

(2).A is a guarantor for so may piastres and as the result of a settlement pays with goods. A recovers from the principal debtor in cash the amount that he has guaranteed. But if A is guarantor in respect to one thousand piastres and as a result of a settlement pays five hundred piastres, A can only recover five hundred piastres from the principal debtor.

- 658. If any party to a contract based upon consideration deceives another party thereto, such party must make good any loss caused to the other.

Examples:-

(1).A buys a piece of land and erects a building thereon. Thereupon, a person appears who proves to be entitled to such land and takes possession thereof. A is entitled to recover the value of the land from the vendor and in addition the value of the building at the time of handing it over.

(2). A requests certain merchants to sell certain goods to his son, who is a minor, stating that he has given him permission to engage in trade. It is later proved that the boy is the son of some other person. The merchants are entitled to recover the value of the good which they have sold to the boys from A.

CHAPTER III. RELEASE FROM THE CONTRACT OF GUARANTEE.

SECTION I. GENERAL.

- 659. When the subject matter of the guarantee is made over to the person in whose favour the guarantee was made, whether by the principal debtor or the guarantor the guarantor is released from the contract of guarantee.
- 660. If the person in whose favour the guarantee is made informs the guarantor that he has released him from the contract of guarantee, or that he has renounced any rights he may have against him, the guarantor is freed from all liability.
- 661. The release of the guarantor does not bring about the release of the principal debtor.
- 662. The release of the principal debtor from the liability brings about the release of the guarantor.

SECTION II. RELEASE FROM A CONTRACT OF GUARANTEE TO PRODUCE A PARTICULAR PERSON.

- 663. Upon the guarantor producing the person whose appearance was guaranteed to the person in whose favour the guarantee was given in a place where it is possible to take legal proceedings, such as a town or township, he is released from the contract of guarantee, whether such person agrees or not. If it has been stipulated that he shall deliver him in some specified town, however, and delivers him elsewhere, he is not released from the contract of guarantee. If he has agreed to produce him in Court, but hands him over in the street, he is not freed from the contract of guarantee. If he hands him over in presence of a police officer, however, he is released from the guarantee.

- 664. The guarantor is released from the contract of guarantee by simply handing over the person guaranteed when requested to do so. But if he hands over the person guaranteed without being requested to do so, he is not released from the contract unless he states that he is handing him over in pursuance of the contract of guarantee.

- 665. If a person who has guaranteed to produce a certain person on a certain day produces such person before that day, he is released from the contract of guarantee, even though the person in whose favour the contract is given does not agree thereto.

- 666. If the person whose appearance is guaranteed dies, the guarantor is released from the contract of guarantee, and if there is any person guaranteeing the guarantor, he also is released. Again, if the guarantor dies, he is released from the contract of guarantee and any person guaranteeing him is also released from the contract. Should the person in whose favour the guarantee is given die, however, the guarantor is not released from the contract of guarantee, and a claim may be made by such person's heirs.

SECTION III. RELEASE FROM A CONTRACT OF GUARANTEE OF PROPERTY.

- 667. In the event of the death of the creditor, the guarantor is released from the contract of guarantee, should the debtor be the sole heir of the creditor. Should there be some other heir of the debtor, however, the guarantor is only released from the share of the debtor, and not from the share of the other heir.

- 668. In the event of the guarantor or of the principal debtor coming to a settlement with the creditor in respect to a portion of the debt, both of them are released from the contract of guarantee, if a stipulation has been inserted to the effect that both of them or the principal debtor are to released, or if no condition has been inserted at all. If a condition has been inserted stipulating for the release of the guarantor only, the guarantor alone is freed, and the creditor has the option of claiming the whole of the debt from the principal debtor or of claiming the amount covered by the settlement from the guarantor and the balance from the principal debtor.

- 669. If the guarantor transfers liability in respect to the person in whose favour he has concluded the contract of guarantee to some other person, and both such persons agree thereto, the guarantor and the principal debtor are released from the liability.

- 670. In the event of the death of the guarantor of property, the property guaranteed may be claimed from the guarantor's estate.

- 671. If a person becomes the guarantor for the price of a thing sold and the contract of sale is cancelled or the thing sold is claimed by some person who is entitled thereto or is returned on account of some defect, the guarantor is released from the contract of guarantee.

- 672. If property is taken on hire for a fixed period and some person becomes guarantor fro the rent to be paid in respect thereto, the contract of guarantee terminates at the end of such period. Should a fresh contract of hire be concluded in respect to that property, such contract does not include the contract of guarantee.

PROMULGATED BY ROYAL IRADAH, 18TH MUHARRAM, 1287.

AL-MAJALLA AL AHKAM AL ADALIYYAH
(The Ottoman Courts Manual (Hanafi))
BOOK IV. TRANSFER OF DEBT.

INTRODUCTION.

TERMS OF ISLAMIC JURISPRUDENCE RELATING TO TRANSFER OF DEBT.

- 673. By transfer of debt is meant transferring a debt from the account of one person to that of another.
- 674. The transferor is the debtor who makes the transfer.
- 675. The person in whose favour the debt is transferred is the creditor.
- 676. The transferee is the person who agrees the transfer of the debt to himself.
- 677. The subject matter of the transfer is the property transferred.
- 678. A restricted transfer of debt is a transfer of debt whereby the transferor limits the payment by the transferee to property of his owing by the transferee or in his possession.
- 679. An absolute transfer of debt is a transfer of debt whereby the transferor does not limit the payment to property of his in the possession of the transferee.

CHAPTER I. THE CONTRACT OF TRANSFER OF DEBT.

SECTION I. THE FUNDAMENTAL BASIS OF A TRANSFER OF DEBT.

- 680. A contract for the transfer of a debt is concluded by the transferor informing his creditor that he has transferred his debt to some other person, and by the agreement thereto of the creditor and such other person.
- 681. A contract for the transfer of a debt may be concluded between the person in whose favour the transfer is made and the transferee alone.Example:- A informs B that he has transferred to him a certain sum of money owing to him by C, and B agrees thereto; or A tells B to transfer to him a sum of money owing to him by C and B agrees thereto. In both cases a valid contract for the transfer of the debt has been concluded and the transferee may not thereafter go back on the transaction.
- 682. A contract for the transfer of a debt may validly be concluded between the transferor and the

person in whose favour the transfer is made alone, provided the transferee, on being informed thereof,agrees thereto.

Example:- A transfers a debt which he owes B, to C, who is resident in some other country. B agrees thereto. If the transferee, on being informed thereof, agrees thereto, a valid contract for the transfer of the debt is concluded.

- 683. A contract for the transfer of a debt may be concluded between the transferor and the transferee only, subject to the agreement of the person in whose favour the transfer is made.

Example:- A transfers a debt owing to him by B to C. C agrees. The contract for the transfer of a debt has been concluded, subject to the consent of the person in whose favour the transfer has been made, and if the latter agrees thereto, such transfer becomes executory.

SECTION II. CONDITIONS RELATING TO TRANSFER OF DEBT.

- 684. To conclude a contract for the transfer of a debt, the transferor and the person in whose favour the transfer is made must be of sound mind, and the transferee must be of sound mind and have reached the age of puberty. Consequently, any transfer or acceptance of the transfer of a debt by a minor of imperfect understanding is void, and any acceptance of the of the transfer of a debt by a minor whether of perfect or imperfect understanding, or whether permitted by his tutor to undertake business, or whether interdicted, is void.

- 685. for the contract of transfer of debt to be executory, the transferor and the person in whose favour the transfer is made must have reached the age of puberty. Consequently, The transfer or acceptance of the transfer of a debt by a minor of perfect understanding is dependent upon ratification by the tutor. If the tutor ratifies, the contract becomes executory. Moreover, if the minor accepts the transfer of a debt and the tutor gives his permission, the transferee must be wealthier than the transferor.

- 686. It is not essential to the validity of a contract for the transfer of a debt that the transferee should be indebted to the transferor, nor that the transferor should be entitled to receive something from him.

- 687. A contract for the transfer of a debt in respect to which a valid contract of guarantee cannot be concluded, is invalid.

- 688. Any contract for the transfer of debt in respect to which a valid contract of guarantee can be concluded, is valid. The subject matter of the contract must, however, be clearly ascertained. Consequently, any contract for the transfer of a adept which is unknown is invalid.

Example:- A agrees to accept the transfer by B of some debt which may be proved in the future to be due to him. The contract is invalid.

- 689. A contract for the transfer of a debt incurred by reason of a guarantee or arising out of a contract for the transfer of a debt may be validly concluded, in the same way as a contract for the transfer of debts which have been incurred directly.

CHAPTER II. EFFECT OF A CONTRACT FOR THE TRANSFER OF DEBT.

- 690. The effect of a contract for the transfer of a debt is that the transferor, and his guarantor, if any, are liberated from all responsibility for the debt. The person in whose favour the contract is made then has the right of demanding payment thereof from the transferee. A pledgee who transfers his right to claim the debt from the pledge or to some third person loses all right of retention over the pledge.

- 691. If any person who makes an absolute transfer of a debt has no claim against the transferee, the latter may have recourse against the former, after he has paid his debt. If such person has a claim against the transferee, the amount of the claim is set off against the debt after payment has been made.

- 692. In the case of a restricted contract for the transfer of a debt, the transferor loses his right to claim on account of the subject matter of the transfer. The transferee is under no obligation whatsoever to give the subject matter of the transfer to the transferor. If he does so, he is liable to make good any loss resulting therefrom. Upon making good, such loss, he has a right of recourse against the transferor. If the tranferor dies before making payment, his debts being greater than the value of his estate, the other creditors have no right to touch the subject matter of the transfer.

- 693. If a restricted contract for the transfer of a debt is concluded whereby payment is to be made from the sum to be received in respect to the price of a thing sold due to the vendor from the purchaser, and the thing sold is destroyed before the delivery, the price in consequence being no longer due, or if the thing sold is returned by virtue of a contractual option, or by reason of an option of inspection or an option for defect, or if the sale is rescinded, such transfer is not void and the transferee has a right of recourse against the tranferor after payment. That is to say, he may obtain what he has given from the transferor. But if any person appears who is entitled to the thing sold and takes possession of the same whereby it is proved that the transferee is free from the debt, the contract of transfer is void.

- 694. If a restricted contract for the transfer of a debt is concluded whereby payment is to be made from a sum of money deposited on trust by the transferor with the transferee, and some person appears who is entitled to such money and takes possession of the same, the contract of transfer is void, and the debt reverts to the transferor.

- 695. If a restricted contract for the transfer of a debt in concluded whereby payment is to be made from a sum of money belonging to the transferor in the possession of the transferee, and such sum of money is not subject to compensation, the contact is void and the debt reverts to the transferor. If it is subject to compensation, however, the contact continues in force.

  Example:- A transfers to C a debt which is due to B, to be paid from money which he has deposited with C on trust, and such money is lost without any fault being attributable, before payment is made. The transfer is void and the sum due to the creditor reverts to the transferor. If such money has been wrongfully appropriated, or if, being deposited on trust, it has been lost by the act of C and must be repaid by him, the contract is not void.

- 696. If any person transfers a debt to some other person and provides that payment is to be made from the price realised on the sale of some specific property of his, and such person agrees to the transfer on that condition, the contract is valid, and the transferee is bound to sell the property and pay the debt from the price realised.

- 697. In the case of a vague transfer of debt, that is to say, in the case of a transfer of debt where it is not stipulated whether the subject matter of the transfer is payable forthwith, if the debt is likewise payable forthwith by the transferor. If the debt is payable at some future definite date, the transfer is of the same nature, and payment must be made when the debt falls due.

- 698. There is no right of recourse against the transferor until the transferee has paid the debt; and when recourse is made, the subject matter of the transfer may be claimed. That is to say, the transferee takes from the transferor exactly the same type of money that was the subject of the transfer. He cannot, however, claim the identical money which has been paid.

Examples:-

(1). Silver money is transferred. Payment is made in gold. Silver money may be claimed from the transferor and not gold.

(2). Payment is made with goods and effects. The money which was the subject of the transfer may be claimed.

- 699. If the subject matter of the transfer is paid, or it is transferred to some other person, or the person in whose favour the transfer is made liberates the transferee from the debt, or the person in whose favour the transfer is made makes a gift of the subject matter of the transfer or disposes of it as alms and the transferee accepts, he is liberated from the debt.

- 700. In the event of the death of the person in whose favour the transfer is made, and of the transferee becoming his heir, the transfer becomes devoid of effect.

PROMULGATED BY ROYAL IRADAH, 25 SEFER, 1288

AL-MAJALLA AL AHKAM AL ADALIYYAH
(The Ottoman Courts Manual (Hanafi))

BOOK V. PLEDGES.

INTRODUCTION.

TERMS OF ISLAMIC JURISPRUDENCE RELATING TO PLEDGES.

- 701. A pledge consists of setting aside property from which it is possible to obtain payment or satisfaction of some claim. Such property is then said to be pledged, or given in pledge.
- 702. The act of accepting property as a pledge is called taking on pledge.
- 703. The person who gives his property as security is called the pledgor.
- 704. The person who accepts property as security is called the pledgee.
- 705. The person with whom the pledgor and the pledgee deposit the pledge on trust is called the bailee.

CHAPTER I. MATTERS RELATING TO THE CONTRACT OF PLEDGE.

SECTION I. FUNDAMENTAL BASIS OF THE CONTRACT OF PLEDGE.

- 706. A contract of pledge is concluded by the offer and acceptance of the pledgor and the pledgee. If the pledge is not transferred to the effective possession of the pledgee, however, such contract is incomplete and revocable. The pledgor may, therefore, denounce such contract before delivery of the pledge.
- 707. In a contract of pledge, offer and acceptance is made by words purporting to imply agreement, as where the pledgor states that he has given such and such property as for his debt to the pledgee, or similar words to that effect, and here the pledgee states that he has accepted such pledge or has assented thereto, or words indicating consent. It is not an essential condition that the word pledge should be mentioned.yvT A Example. A person having purchased an article for so much, hands the vendor certain of his property, telling him to keep it until the price is paid. Such property is then validly given in pledge.

SECTION II. CONDITIONS INCIDENTAL TO A CONTRACT OF PLEDGE.

- 708. The pledgor and pledgee must be of sound mind. They need not have reached the age of puberty. Consequently, a minor of perfect understanding may be either pledgor or pledgee.
- 709. The subject matter of the pledge must be something which may be validly sold. Consequently, it must be in existence at the time of the contract, must have some specific value, and also be capable of delivery.
- 710. The property is respect of which the pledge is given must be capable of sustaining a claim in respect to such pledge. Consequently, a pledge may be taken in respect to property wrongfully appropriated. But a pledge taken is respect to property held on trust is invalid.

SECTION III. MATTERS ATTACHED TO THE PLEDGE: CHANGE AND INCREASE.

- 711. Things which are implicitly included in sale are also included in pledge. Thus, when a piece of land is pledged, all trees growing thereon, together with the fruits thereof and all plants and growing crops are included therein even though not explicitly mentioned.
- 712. A pledge may be exchanged for another pledge.

  Example:- A person who has pledged his watch for so many piastres may ask pledgee to take a sword instead of the watch and if the pledgee returns the watch and accepts the sword, such sword thereupon becomes the pledge for the debt in question.
- 713. The subject matter of the pledge may be increased by the pledgor after the conclusion of the contract. That is to say, a second piece of property may be added to the first after the contract relating thereto has been concluded, the first pledge remaining intact. The additional pledge is added to the pledge of the original contract, as though the original contract had been concluded with reference to the two pledges, both becoming one pledge for the debt as it stood at the time the pledge was increased.
- 714. The debt secured by the pledge may be validly increased in respect to the same pledge.yvT Example:- A person pledges a watch worth two thousand piastres to secure a debt of one thousand piastres. If such person contracts a further loan from the creditor of five hundred piastres, the watch becomes a pledge for one thousand five hundred piastres.
- 715. Any increase arising out of the pledge is part of the original pledge.

CHAPTER II. PLEDGOR AND PLEDGEE.

- 716. The pledgee may of his own accord cancel the contract of pledge.
- 717. The pledgor may not cancel the contract of pledge without the consent of the pledgee.
- 718. The pledgor and pledgee may cancel the contract of pledge by agreement. The pledgee, however, may retain the pledge after the cancellation of the contract, until the sum secured by such pledge has been paid.

- 719. A principal debtor may validly give a pledge to his guarantor.
- 720. A pledge may be validly taken from a debtor by two creditors, whether such creditors are partners or not, such pledge securing both debts.
- 721. A creditor may validly take a pledge in respect to sums due from two persons, such pledge securing both debts.

CHAPTER III. THE PLEDGE.

SECTION I. PRESERVATION OF THE PLEDGE AND EXPENSES CONNECTED THEREWITH.

- 722. The pledgee may keep the pledge himself or may have it kept by some person in whom he has confidence, such as members of his family, or a partner, or a servant.
- 723. The pledgee is responsible for expenses incurred in connection with the preservation of the pledge, such as rent of the premises and wages of the watchman.
- 724. If the pledge consists of an animal. the cost of forage and the wages of the keeper must be paid by the pledgor. If the pledge consists of movable property, all expenses incurred in connection with the improvement and maintenance thereof, such as repairs, irrigation, grafting, weeding, and the cleansing of watercourses must be borne by the pledgor.
- 725. Should either the pledgor or the pledgee of their own accord defray expenses which should rightly be met by the other, such payment is in the nature of a gift, with regard to which no subsequent claim may be made.

SECTION II. PLEDGE OF BORROWED ARTICLES.

- 726. A person may make a valid pledge of property borrowed from some third person, provided he has received the permission of that person. This is known as a pledge of a borrowed article.
- 727. Should the owner of property give permission unconditionally, the borrower may pledge such property in any way whatsoever.
- 728. Should the owner of such property have given permission subject to a condition as to the amount of money, or the nature of the property to be secured, or that the pledge is to be made to a certain person, or in a certain town, the borrower must strictly observe such condition.

CHAPTER IV. FUNDAMENTAL RULES RELATING TO A PLEDGE.

SECTION I. GENERAL.

- 729. It is a fundamental rule that the pledgee has the right of retaining possession of the pledge until the redemption thereof. In the event of the death of the pledgor, the pledgee has a prior right over other creditors and may obtain payment of the debt from the pledge.

- 730. The pledge does not extinguish the right to claim the debt. The pledgee after taking possession of the pledge preserves intact his right to demand payment from the pledgor.

- 731. Upon part payment of the debt there is no necessity to return a portion of the pledge equivalent to such part payment, the pledgee having a right to retain the entire pledge until the whole debt is repaid. When two things have been pledged, however, each one in respect to a specified portion of the debt, and the sum relating to one such specified portion has been repaid, the pledgor may claim the return of such thing only.

- 732. The owner of borrowed property which has been pledged may call upon the pledgor to redeem the pledge and return it to him. Should the borrower of such property be unable to repay his debt by reason of lack of funds, the person lending such property may himself pay the debt and thus redeem the property pledged.

- 733. In the event of the death of either the pledgor or the pledgee, the pledge remains intact.

- 734. Upon the death of the pledgor, his heirs of age stand in his stead. They must redeem the pledge by payment of the debt from the estate of the deceased person. If the heirs are minors, however, or if, being of age, they are absent, that is to say, they are elsewhere in the course of a long journey, the guardian of such heirs may sell the pledge subject to the permission of the pledgee, and repay the debt from the sum realised.

- 735. The lender of property which has been given as security for a debt may not claim such property from the pledgee until the debt in respect to which it has been given as security has been repaid, and this whether the pledgor or the borrowed property be alive or has died before the redemption of the pledge.

- 736. In the event of the death in a state of bankruptcy of a person who has pledged borrowed property, such borrowed property continues as a pledge in the possession of the pledgee and cannot be sold without the consent of the lender. Should the lender of the pledge seek to repay the debt by means of the sale of the pledge, such pledge shall be sold independently of the consent of the pledgee, provided the value thereof is sufficient to meet the debt, however, such pledge may not be sold without the consent of the pledgee.

- 737. In the event of the death of the lender of a pledge and of his debts being greater than his estate, the pledgor shall be called upon personally to pay his debt and to redeem the pledge which he has borrowed. Should he be unable to do so, however, by reason of lack of means, the borrowed property continues as a pledge in the possession of the pledgee. The heirs of the lender of the pledge may redeem such pledge by repaying the debt. In the event of the creditors of the lender of the pledge claiming the sale of such pledge, the pledge, if the value thereof is sufficient to repay the debt, shall be sold regardless of the consent of the pledgee. If it is insufficient to repay the debt, such pledge may be sold with the consent of the pledgee.

- 738. Upon the death of the pledgee, the pledge devolves upon his heirs.

- 739. Should a pledgor give a pledge in respect to debts due to two persons, and repay the debt of one of them, such pledgor may not demand the return of half of the pledge, having no right to redeem the pledge until he has repaid in full the debt due to both creditors.

- 740. A person taking a pledge from two debtors may retain such pledge until the debt of both has been paid in full.

- 741. In the event of a pledgor destroying or damaging the pledge, he must make good such destruction or damage. Should a pledgee destroy or damage the pledge, a sum corresponding to the amount of such destruction or damage shall be deducted from the debt.

- 742. In the event of a third person destroying the pledge, such person shall make good the value thereof as on the day it was destroyed. The sum in question shall be held as a pledge by the pledgee.

SECTION II. RIGHTS OF PLEDGOR AND PLEDGEE OVER THE PLEDGE.

- 743. A pledge by either pledgor or pledgee of the original pledge to some third person is null and void, unless the permission of either the pledgor or pledgee has been obtained.
- 744. In the event of a pledge of the original pledge being made by the pledgor to some third person with the permission of the pledgee, the second pledge stands in the place of the first pledge, which becomes null and void.
- 745. In the event of a pledge of the original pledge being made by the pledgee, with the permission of the pledgor, the first pledge becomes null and void, and the second pledge is valid, being in the nature of a pledge made of a borrowed object.
- 746. In the event of the pledgee selling the pledge without the permission of the pledgor, the pledgor may either adopt or cancel such sale.
- 747. In the event of the pledgor selling the pledge without the permission of the pledgee, such sale is invalid and the pledgee may retain possession of the pledge. If the debt is repaid, however, such sale is valid. Moreover, if the pledgee adopts such sale it is valid, the sale acting as a release of the pledge, the debt being unaffected. The price realised by the sale becomes the pledge of the thing sold. Should the pledgee not agree, however, the purchaser may either wait until the pledge has been redeemed, or apply to the Court for an order cancelling the sale.
- 748. Provided permission is mutually given, both the pledgor and the pledgee may lend the pledge to a third person. Either of them may afterwards restore it to a state of pledge.
- 749. The pledgee may lend the pledge to the pledgor. If he does so and the pledgor dies, the pledgee has a right of preference over other creditors of the pledgor in respect to the pledge.
- 750. The pledgee may not make use of the pledge without the permission of the pledgor. The pledgee, however, may use the pledge with the permission of the pledgor and may take the produce thereof, such as fruit and milk. In such case there is no reduction of the debt is consideration thereof.
- 751. The pledgee, upon removing to another place may take the pledge with him, provided the road is safe.

SECTION III. DEPOSIT OF THE PLEDGE WITH A BAILEE.

- 752. Possession by a bailee is equivalent to possession by the pledgee. That is to say, should the pledgor and pledgee agree to deposit the pledge with some person in whom they have confidence, and such person agrees to take possession thereof, the pledge becomes irrevocable. The bailee then stands in the place of the pledgee.
- 753. In cases where at the time of the conclusion of the contract it has been agreed that the pledgee shall take possession of the pledge, the pledgor and the pledgee may buy mutual consent deposit

the pledge with a bailee.

- 754. The bailee may not give the pledge to either the pledgor or the pledgee during the continuance of the debt without the consent of the other. Should he do so, the return thereof may be demanded. Should the pledge be destroyed before it is returned, the bailee must make good the value thereof.

- 755. In the event of the death of the bailee, the pledge may, subject to the consent of the two contracting parties, be deposited with some other bailee, and in the event of their failing to agree, the pledge shall be deposited with a bailee appointed by the Court.

SECTION IV. SALE OF THE PLEDGE.

- 756. Neither the pledgor nor the pledgee may sell the pledge without the consent of the other.

- 757. Should the pledgor refuse to make payment when the debt falls due, he shall be directed by the Court to sell the pledge and pay the debt. Should he still persist in his refusal, the pledge shall be sold by the Court and the debt repaid.

- 758. Should the pledgor be absent and should it be uncertain whether he is alive or dead, the pledgee may apply to the Court for an order for the sale of the pledge and the satisfaction of the debt from the proceeds.

- 759. If there is good ground for believing that the pledge is likely to deteriorate, the pledgee may apply to the Court for an order directing him to sell the pledge and he thereupon holds the proceeds of the sale as the pledge. Should the pledgee sell the pledge without having obtained an order from the Court, he becomes responsible therefor. Thus, if there is good ground for believing that the ripe fruit and vegetables of an orchard and garden which may have been pledged are likely to perish, they may be sold by order of the Court. Should the pledgee, however, sell them on his own initiative, he is liable to make good any loss which may be incurred thereby.

- 760. The pledgor may validly appoint the pledgee or the bailee, or some third person his agent for the sale of the pledge when the debt falls due for payment. Thereafter revoke the power of such agent, nor can he be removed in the event of the death of either the pledgor or the pledgee.

- 761. An agent for all sale of a pledge shall, when the debt falls due for payment, sell such such pledge and hand the proceeds to the pledgee. Should he refuse to do so, the pledgor shall be forced to sell the pledge himself. In the event of the pledgor likewise refusing to sell, such pledge shall be sold by the Court. Should either the pledgor or his heirs be absent, the agent shall be obliged to sell the pledge. Should he refuse to do so, such pledge shall be sold by the Court.

PROMULGATED BY ROYAL IRADAH, 25, SEFER, 1288.

AL-MAJALLA AL AHKAM AL ADALIYYAH
(The Ottoman Courts Manual (Hanafi))

BOOK VI. TRUST AND TRUSTEESHIP.

INTRODUCTION

TERMS OF ISLAMIC JURISPRUDENCE RELATING TO TRUSTS AND TRUSTEESHIP.

- 762. The subject matter of the trust is the thing entrusted to the person who is responsible for the safe keeping thereof, whether placed on trust for safe keeping in pursuance of an express contract, such as a contract of deposit for safe keeping, or by implication, as in the case of a thing taken on hire or borrowed, or intention, as where wind blows into the house of a certain person the property of such person's neighbour. Such property does not become property deposited for safe keeping with the owner of the house, since there is no contract to that effect, but is held by him on trust.

- 763. By deposit for safe keeping is meant handing property to any particular person in order that it may be kept safely.

- 764. By delivery for safe keeping is meant handing over one's own property to some other person for safe keeping. The person handing over such property is called the person delivering and the person accepting such property is called the custodian or keeper.

- 765. By loan for use is meant conferring upon somebody the usufruct of a thing gratuitously, that is to say, without payment.

- 766. By loaning for use is meant giving on loan in order what the usufruct of the loan may be enjoyed.

- 767. By taking a loan for use is meant accepting a loan in order that the usufruct of the thing borrowed may be enjoyed.

CHAPTER I. GENERAL.

- 768. A trust is not subject to compensation. That is to say, if the trustee is not guilty of any wrongful act or negligence and the subject of the trust is destroyed or lost, the trustee is not obliged to make the loss.

- 769. If any person finds anything in the highway or in any other place and keeps such thing as his own, he is considered to be a person wrongfully appropriating property. Consequently, if such property is destroyed or lost, even without such person's wrongful act or negligence, he is obliged to make good the loss. But if he takes it with the intention of restoring it to owner thereof, and it is known who such person is, such property is held in trust while in his possession and must be restored to its rightful owner. If the owner thereof is unknown, such property is lost property and is held in trust by the finder.

- 770. The finder of lost property must make known the fact that he has found such property, and must keep it in his possession on trust until such time as the owner appears and proves that such property is his, the property in question must be handed over to him.

- 771. In the event of property belonging to one being destroyed accidentally while in the possession of another, and such person has taken such property without the permission of the owner, the loss must be in any case be made good by the former. If such property is taken with the permission of the owner thereof, the person so taking the property is under no such obligation to make good the loss, since he held such property on trust. But in the case of property purchased on approval as to price, the price of which has been fixed, the loss must be made good.yvT E Examples: -
(1) A takes a cup from a china shop of his own accord. The cup falls from his hand and is broken. A must make good the loss. If he takes it with the permission of the owner, and it is accidentally destroyed by falling from A's hand while in the act of inspecting the cup, A is not obliged to make the loss. But if such cup falls upon a number of other cups and the latter are also broken, the loss thereof must be made good. AS regards the first cup, however, there is no need to make good the loss, since it was held in trust. If A enquires the price of the cup, however, and the shopkeeper informs him of the price thereof, and tell him to take it, and A does in fact take it in his hand and it falls to the ground and is broken, A must make good the loss.
(2). A is drinking sherbet and while doing so drops the glass belonging to the sherbet vendor, and it is broken. A is not obliged to make good the loss, since the glass is in his possession on trust as a loan for use. But if the glass was dropped as a result of some improper use, A is obliged to make good the loss.

- 772. Permission given by implication is the same as permission given explicitly. But in the presence of an express prohibition, any permission given by implication is of no effect.yvT ¦
Example:- A enters B's house with the latter's permission. A is permitted by implication to drink water by means of a glass which he finds in the house. If the glass falls from A's hand while he is drinking the water and is broken, a need not make good the loss. But if the owner of the house tells A not to touch the glass and A does so in spite of the prohibition, and the glass falls and is broken, A must make good the loss.

CHAPTER II. DEPOSIT FOR SAFE KEEPING.

SECTION I. CONCLUSION OF THE CONTRACT OF DEPOSIT FOR SAFE KEEPING AND CONDITIONS RELATING THERETO.

- 773. A contract of deposit for safe keeping may be concluded by offer and acceptance either expressly or by implication. Examples:-

(1). A informs B that he has deposited with him for safe keeping certain property of which he is the owner, or that he has placed such property with him on trust, and the person with whom such property is deposited agrees thereto. An express contract for the deposit of a thing for safe keeping has been concluded.

(2). A enters an inn and asks the inn-keeper where he should tie up his animal. The latter shows him a certain place and A ties his animal up there. A contract for deposit for safe keeping has been concluded by implication.

(3). A leaves certain property with a shopkeeper. The shopkeeper is aware thereof, and keeps silence. The property in question is deposited for safe keeping with the shop keeper, however, declines to keep the property, no contract for safe keeping is concluded.

(4). A leaves property of his with certain persons for safe keeping. The property in question is deposited for safe keeping with all of such persons. BUt if such persons leave the place in question one by one, such property is deposited for safe keeping with the last remaining person, who is responsible for its preservation.

- 774. The person making the deposit for safe keeping and the person so receiving it may either of them cancel the contract of deposit for safe keeping at any time they wish.

- 775. The thing deposited for safe keeping must be capable of possession and delivery. Consequently, a deposit for safe keeping of a bird in the air is invalid.

- 776. The person making the deposit for safe keeping and the person so receiving it must be of sound mind and perfect understanding, though they need not have arrived at the age of puberty. Consequently, a madman or a minor of imperfect understanding cannot validly make or receive a deposit for safe keeping. A deposit for safe keeping or the receipt thereof by a minor of perfect understanding, however, who has been duly authorised thereunto, is valid.

SECTION II. EFFECT OF MAKING A DEPOSIT FOR SAFE KEEPING AND OF MAKING GOOD ANY LOSS ARISING THEREFROM.

- 777. The thing deposited for safe keeping is a trust in the possession of the person receiving such thing. Consequently, if it is destroyed or lost without the fault or negligence of the person keeping such thing, there is no necessity to make good the loss. But if such thing has been deposited for safe keeping in consideration of payment of a fee, and the thing has been destroyed or lost owing to some cause which might have been avoided, the loss must be made good.yvT , Examples:-

(1). A watch is entrusted to A for safe keeping, and A accidentally drops and breaks it. A cannot be called upon to make good the loss. But if A threads on the watch or drops something on it and it is broken, A must make good the loss.

(2). A entrust certain property to B for safe keeping and pays him a fee for doing so. Later, the property is stolen. The person receiving such property must make good the loss, since it arose from a cause which could have been avoided.

- 778. If the servant of the person receiving property for safe keeping drops something on to such property and it is destroyed, the servant must make good the loss.

- 779. The person receiving the property for safe keeping may not perform any act with regard to such property which he is not authorised to do by the owner thereof.

- 780. The person receiving property for safe keeping must keep such property personally and as though it were his own property, or cause it to be kept by some person in whom he has confidence. If such property is destroyed or lost while in the negligence on his part, neither he not the person receiving the property for safe keeping may be called upon to make good the loss.

- 781. The person receiving property for safe keeping may keep such property in the place where he keeps his own property.

- 782. The property entrusted for safe keeping must be kept in the same way as articles similar thereto are kept. Consequently, placing property such as cash and jewels in such places as stables and barns amounts to negligence, and if they are destroyed or lost while there, the loss must be made good.

- 783. If the persons receiving property for safe keeping are several, and the property deposited for safe keeping is not capable of division, one of them may keep such property with the permission of the others, or they keep it in turn. If the property entrusted for safe keeping in these circumstances is destroyed without any fault or negligence, none of them may be called upon to make good the loss. If the property de[posited for safe keeping, however, is capable of division, the persons receiving such property may divide it among themselves equally, each person keeping his own share. No one of them may give his share to any other person for safekeeping unless he obtains the permission of the person who has deposited his property with him. If he does so, and it is destroyed or lost without fault or negligence while in such other person's possession, the latter is not liable to make good the loss, but the former may be called upon to do so in respect to his share.

- 784. If any condition contained in the contract of deposit for safe keeping is capable of execution and beneficial, such condition is valid, if not it is null and void.yvT Examples:-

(1). A contract of deposit for the safe keeping of certain property is drawn up subject to the condition that such property is to be kept in the house of the person receiving such property. A fire breaks out, and the property has to be transferred to another place. The becomes invalid; and if the property after having been transferred to such other place is destroyed or lost without any fault or negligence, there is no obligation to make good the loss.

(2). A person entrusts property to another for safe keeping, instructing the latter to keep such property, and forbids him to entrust it to his wife or his son, or to a servant, or to a person to whom he has entrusted his own property, and such person is forced to disobey his instruction. The prohibition becomes invalid. If the property entrusted to such person in these circumstances is destroyed or lost, without any fault or negligence, there is no need to make good the loss. If he was under no necessity to do so, however, the loss must be made good.

(3). A contract of deposit for safe keeping is concluded subject to the condition that the property shall be kept in a particular room of the house. The person receiving such property stores it in another room. If such rooms are identical the one with the other, as regards safety, the condition is invalid; and if the property entrusted for safe keeping is destroyed in these circumstances, there is no need to make good the loss. But if one room differs from the other, as where one is made of stone and the other of wood, the condition is invalid and the person to whom the property is entrusted is bound to store the property in a room which is inferior to the room agreed upon as regards safety, and the property is destroyed, the loss must be made good.

- 785. If the owner of the property deposited for safe keeping is absent, and it is known whether he is alive or dead, the person receiving such thing must keep it until such time as it is proved that he is dead. If the property is of such nature, however, that it would spoil by being kept, it may be sold by the order of the Court, and such person may then keep the proceeds on trust. If the property is not sold and is ruined, there is no need to make good the loss.

- 786. The owner of a thing deposited for safe keeping which requires maintenance, such as a horse or a cow, is responsible for the maintenance thereof, In the event of the absence of the owner, the person receiving such thing for safe keeping may apply to the Court, which will decide upon the most suitable and useful manner for the owner in which to deal with the matter. Thus if the property can be let on hire, the person receiving the property can be let it on hire, subject to the approval of the Court, and may provide for its maintenance out of the proceeds, or may sell it for an estimated price. If it is not capable of being let on hire, he may, subject to the price forthwith, or after having provided for the maintenance thereof from his own property for a period of three days, the expenses incurred in connection with the three days upkeep being charged to the owner. If he incurs such expenditure without the sanction of the Court, however, he cannot recover it from the person depositing property for safe keeping.

- 787. If the property deposited for safe keeping is destroyed or the value thereof diminished by the fault or negligence of the person entrusted therewith, such person must make good the loss.yvT s Examples :-

(1). The person to whom money is entrusted for safe keeping uses such money for his own purposes. He must make good for the loss. If he spends a purse of money in this manner which has been left with him on trust, and afterwards replaces it with money of his own, and it is later lost without any fault or negligence on his part, he is nevertheless liable to make good the loss.

(2).A person to whom an animal has been entrusted for safe keeping rides the animal without the permission of the owner, and such animal is destroyed either by riding it in some manner, or for some other reason, or for no reason at all, or such animal is stolen while on the road. Such person must make good the loss.

(3). A person to whom property has been entrusted for safe keeping fails to transport the property entrusted to him to some other place upon the outbreak of a fire, although able to do so, and such property is destroyed by the fire. Such person must make good the loss.

- 788. If the person to whom property has been entrusted for safe keeping mixes such property without the permission of the owner with other property in such a manner that it cannot be distinguished therefrom, such person is guilty of negligence. Consequently, If the person to whom a quantity of gold pounds have been entrusted for safe keeping,mixes them without permission with gold pounds of his own, or with gold pounds delivered to him for safe keeping by some other person, and they are lost or stolen, he must make good the loss. Again, if any other than the person to whom they have been entrusted for safe keeping so mixes them, such person must make good the loss.

- 789. If the person to whom property has been entrusted for safe keeping mixes such property with the permission of the owner thereof with other property as is stated in the preceding Article, or if, without any fault on his part two pieces of property are mixed together in such a way that they cannot be distinguished the one from the other, as for example, where a purse of money which is delivered for safe keeping is put in a box and the purse is torn and the gold coins therein are mixed with other gold coins, the person to whom they have been entrusted for safe keeping and the owner become joint owners of the total amount of such coins in proportion to their shares. In these circumstances, if the coins are destroyed or lost without fault or negligence, there is no need to make good the loss.

- 790. The person to whom property has been entrusted for safe keeping may not transfer such property for safe keeping to any other person without permission. If he does so, and the property is destroyed, he must make good the loss. If the property is destroyed owing to the fault or negligence of the second person, the owner of the property may at his option claim to have the loss made good from either the second or the first. If he recovers from the first person, the latter has a right of recourse against the second.

- 791. If the person to whom property has been entrusted for the safe keeping deposits such property with some other person, and the owner of the property adopts the transaction, the first person is replaced by the second.

- 792. The person to whom property has been entrusted for safe keeping may, with the permission of the owner thereof, use such property or let it on hire, or lend it,or give it on pledge. If he does so without the permission of the owner, however, and such property is destroyed or lost while in the possession of the person taking it on hire, or the borrower, or the pledgee, or the value thereof is decreased, the person to whom the property has been entrusted for safe keeping must make good the loss.

- 793. If the person to whom money has been delivered on trust lends and delivers such money to some other person without permission, and the owner thereof does not adopt such transaction, the person to whom the money has been entrusted must make good any loss incurred. Again, if he repays a debt owing to some other person who has entrusted money to him out of such money, and the owner does not agree, he must make good the loss.

- 794. Upon the owner of the property entrusted for safe keeping asking for the return thereof, such property must be restored to him. Any charges and expenses occasioned thereby must be borne by the owner of the property. If the owner asks for the return of his property and the person to whom it has been entrusted fails to restore it to him, and the property is destroyed or lost, such person must make good the loss. But if the property is not restored by reason of some lawful excuse, as for example where the property is in some remote place when its return is asked for and it is destroyed or lost, there is then no liability to make good the loss.

- 795. The person to whom property has been entrusted for safe keeping may restore such property himself or by means of some person on whom he relies. If he returns the property through the latter, and before delivery to the owner, such property is destroyed or lost without any fault or negligence, there is no liability to make good the loss.

- 796. If two persons who are joint owners of various pieces of property deposit such property with any person for safekeeping, and one of the joint owners, in the absence of the other, requests delivery of his share from such person, the latter may restore to such joint owner his share of the property, providing they are things the like of which can be found in the market, but not otherwise.

- 797. The property delivered for safe keeping must be returned at the place where it was handed over for safe keeping.yvT A Example:- Goods handed over for safe keeping at Constantinople must be returned in Constantinople. The person to whom they have been entrusted cannot be obliged to hand them over to adrianople.

- 798. Any usufruct of the property deposited for safe keeping belongs to the owner.yvT u Example:- The, or the milk or the wool of an animal handed over for safe keeping belongs to the owner of such animal.

- 799. If a person who has deposited money for safe keeping is absent, any person dependent upon such person for support may apply to the Court for an order that a certain sum may be set aside therefrom for him; and if the person with whom such money has been so deposited pays such to him by way of maintenance, he is in no way liable. He is liable, however, if he does so without the order of the Court.

- 800. If the person to whom property is entrusted for safe keeping goes mad, and there is little hope of his recovery, and if the thing deposited for safe keeping prior to such person's madness is itself no longer in existence, the owner of such property may, upon producing a reliable guarantor, have the loss made good from the mad person's property. Should he recover from his madness, however, and allege that the property deposited has been returned to the owner thereof, or that such property has been destroyed or lost without any fault or negligence on his part, and should such statement be confirmed on oath, the money which has been taken must be returned.

- 801. If upon the death of the person to whom a thing has been entrusted for safe keeping such thing is found among the estate of the deceased, it is held on trust by the heir, and must be returned to the owner. If it cannot be found in the estate of the deceased person, however, and the heirs are able to prove that such person during his lifetime had stated that he had returned such thing to the owner thereof, or that it had been lost without any wrongful act on his part, there is no need to make good the loss.

Again if the heirs state that they know the thing that was handed over for safe keeping, and describe it, and allege that it was lost after the death of the person to whom it had been entrusted, without any fault or negligence on their part, and such statement is confirmed on oath, there is no need to make good for the loss. If the person to whom the thing has been entrusted dies without making any statement as to the condition of the property entrusted to him, the value thereof must be paid out of the estate, in the same manner as other debts.

Similarly, if the heirs fail to describe the thing which has been entrusted for safe keeping and merely state that they know of such thing and that it was lost, such statement, unless proved, is of no effect, and the value of such thing must be paid from the estate.

- 802. Upon the death of the person who has entrusted a thing for safe keeping, such thing must be handed to the heirs. If the estate is overwhelmed with debts, however, the matter must be referred to the Court. If the matter is not so referred, and the person to whom such thing has been entrusted hands it over to the heirs, who consume the same, the person to whom it has been entrusted for safe keeping must make good the loss.

- 803. Should it be necessary to make good the loss of the thing entrusted for safe keeping, and such thing is one the like of which can be found in the market, a similar thing must be given. If it is a thing the like of which cannot be found in the market, the value of such thing at the time it was lost must be made good.

CHAPTER III. PROPERTY LENT FOR USE.

SECTION I. THE CONTRACT OF LOAN FOR USE AND CONDITIONS RELATING THERETO.

- 804. A contract of loan for use is concluded by offer and acceptance and by conduct.yvT W

Example:- A tells B that he has lent him certain property for use or that he has made him a loan for use and B accepts, or without making any statement takes such thing. A contract has been concluded for a loan for use. Again, A asks B to lend him certain property to use and B lends him such property. A contract of loan for use is concluded.

- 805. The silence of the person giving the loan is not considered to be acceptance. Consequently, if one person asks another to lend him a thing for use, and the owner of such thing keeps silence, and the other takes it, such person becomes a person wrongfully appropriating property.

- 806. The person lending the thing for use may at any time withdraw from the contract.

- 807. A contract of loan for use is cancelled upon the death of either the person giving or the person taking the thing on loan for use.

- 808. The thing given of loan for use must be capable of enjoyment. Consequently, the giving or taking of a runaway animal on loan for use is invalid.

- 809. The person giving and the person taking a thing on loan for use must be of sound mind and perfect understanding. They need not have arrived at the age of puberty. Consequently, a madman or a minor of imperfect understanding cannot conclude a valid contract for giving or taking a thing on loan for use. A minor who has received permission from his tutor, however, may do so.

- 810. Taking delivery is essential to the validity of a contract of loan for use. The contract is devoid of effect before delivery.

- 811. The thing given on loan for use must be clearly defined.yvT

Example:- A contract is concluded for a loan for the use of one of two horses without stating which one or without giving an option for selection. The contract is invalid. The person making the loan must state which one he gives on loan. But if he gives the person taking the horse on loan the option of selecting whichever one he likes, the contract is valid.

SECTION II. EFFECT OF A CONTRACT OF LOAN FOR USE AND COMPENSATION FOR LOSS SUSTAINED IN CONNECTION THEREWITH.

- 812. The person to whom a thing has been lent for use becomes owner of the usufruct thereof without giving anything in return. Consequently, the person giving the thing on loan cannot demand any payment from the person taking such thing on loan after he has used it.

- 813. The thing lent for use is on trust while in the possession of the person to whom it has been lent. If it is destroyed without any fault or negligence, or if the value thereof is decreased, there is no need to make good the loss. Examples:-

(1). A person to whom a mirror has been lent for use accidentally drops it or slips and knocks it with his foot and it is broken. There is no need to make good the loss.

(2). A carpet lent for use is accidentally stained by something dropping on it so that its value is decreased. There is no need to make good the loss.

- 814. If the thing lent for use is destroyed or the value thereof decreased owing to any fault or negligence, or for any reason whatsoever on the part of the person receiving such thing, the loss must be made good. yvT -

Examples:-

(1). An animal is lent to A to go to a certain place with the proviso that he shall take two days to reach that place. He arrives there in one day and the animal is destroyed or is rendered so weak that its value is diminished. A must make good the loss.

(2). A borrows an animal to go to a certain place. On arrival there he continues his journey on the animal and it dies a natural death. A must make good for the loss.

(3). A borrows a necklace and puts it round the neck of a child. A leaves the child without anyone to look after it and the necklace is stolen. If the child is able to look after the thing which it is wearing, there is no need to make good the loss, but if the child is incapable of doing so, the loss must be made good.

- 815. Expenses occasioned by the upkeep of the thing lent must be borne by the person to whom it is lent. Consequently, if the person who borrows an animal fails to provide fodder for such animal and it dies4s, such person must make good the loss.

- 816.In the case of an absolute contract of loan for use, that is to say, when the person granting the loan makes no stipulation as to time or place or the use to which the thing lent is to be put, the person borrowing the thing may use such thing at any time or in any place he wishes, subject, however, to custom. Examples:-

(1). A lends B his horse absolutely as stated above. B can ride the horse whenever he likes, and to whichever place he likes. He may not ride it to a place in one hour, however, which by custom takes two hours to reach.

(2). A lends B the room of an inn absolutely. B may, if he wishes, live in it or store goods in it. But he may not, contrary to custom, carry on the trade of a blacksmith therein.

- 817. If the loan for use is restricted as to time and place, the restriction is valid and the person to whom the loan is made not act contravention thereof.yvT £ Example:- An animal borrowed for riding for a period of three hours, may not be ridden for four; and an animal borrowed to go to a specific place may not be taken to some other place.

- 818. If the loan for use is restricted as to the use to which it may be put, the person to whom it is lent may not put it to any more exacting use. But if it is out to a similar or less exacting use, the breach of the restriction is valid.yvT b Examples :-

(1). An animal is borrowed to carry a load of corn iron or stone may not be loaded on him. A load equal to or lighter than the weight of corn may, however, be loaded on him.

(2). A load may not be placed upon an animal which has been borrowed for riding. An animal which has been borrowed to carry loads, however, may be used for riding.

- 819. If the person making the loan makes it absolutely, without specifying the person to whom it is lent may use it as he likes. That is to say, he may use it himself or he may lend it to another person to use, and this, whether the thing lent is one which is not changed by the person using it, such a room, or one that is so changed such as a horse for riding.yvT + Examples:-

(1). A tells B that he has lent him his room. The person to whom the room is lent may either live in the room himself or let some other person live therein.

(2). A tells B that he has lent him a certain horse. B may either live in the room himself or let some other person ride him.

- 820. The person who is to enjoy may validly be specified in the case of things which change with the change of persons using such things. This is not the case with things which do not so change. If the person making the loan, however, states that it is not to be given to any other person, the person to whom such thing is loaned may not under any circumstances cause it to be used by another.yvT ^ Example:- A tells B that he has lent him a certain horse to ride. The person to whom it is lent may not give it to his servant to ride. But if A tells B that he has lent him a room in which to live, B can live in it himself or let some other person live in it. He may not do so, however, if A has told him not to allow any other person to live there.

- 821. If an animal is borrowed to go to a certain place, and there are several roads leading thereto, the borrower can proceed along whichever of the roads he likes in accordance with custom. But if he proceeds along a road which it is not customary to use, and the animal is destroyed, he must make good the loss. Again, if the borrower uses a road other than that prescribed by the lender and the animal is destroyed, the borrower must make good the loss if the road used by him is longer or less than that prescribed by the lender, or not customarily used.

- 822. If a person asks a woman to make him a loan for use of a thing which is the property of her husband, and she gives such thing on loan without her husband's permission, and it is lost, there is no need for either the woman or the borrower to make good the loss,if it is one of those things which are found in the wombs@s quarter of the house, and which by custom is in the possession of the wife. If the thing borrowed is not one of such things, however, but is a thing which is not in the p[possession of woman, such as horse, the husband ma, at his option, have the loss made good by the wife or the borrower.

- 823. The borrower may not give the thing borrowed on hire, nor pledge it without the permission of the lender, nor may the borrower pledge a piece of property which has been lent to secure a loan in one town as security for a loan in another town. If he does so, and the thing lent for use is destroyed or lost, the loss must be made good.

- 824. The borrower may deposit the thing borrowed for safe keeping with some other person. If it is destroyed without any fault or negligence while in the possession of the latter, there is no need to make good for the loss.yvT

Example :- A borrows a horse from B for the purpose of going to and returning from a certain place. Upon arrival at that place, the horse is found to be tired and unable to proceed, and B entrusts the horse to C to mind. Later the horse dies a natural death. A need not make good for the loss.

- 825. Upon the lender asking the borrower to return the thing lent, the latter must do so forthwith. If he keeps it delays returning it without any valid excuse and it is destroyed or lost, or there is a decrease in the value thereof, the borrower make good the loss.

- 828. A thing which has been lent for use for a definite period of time, whether express or implied, must be reduced to the lender in the expiration of such period. But any delay which is sanctioned by custom is excused.

Examples :-
(1). Ornaments are borrowed to be used on a certain day until the afternoon. When that time

arrives they must be returned.

(2). Ornaments are borrowed to be used at a certain person's wedding. When the wedding is over the ornaments must be returned. But the time ordinarily necessary for the return of the ornaments is allowed.

- 827. If a thing is borrowed for use in connection with any particular piece of work, such thing, on the completion of such work is regarded as property entrusted for safe keeping to the borrower. He may not use it in any way whatsoever and may not retain it for any period longer than is allowed by custom. If he does so and such property is destroyed, he must make good the loss.

- 828. The borrower must return the thing borrowed to the lender either personally or through some reliable person. If he returns such thing through a person who's is not reliable, and it is destroyed or lost, he must make good the loss.

- 829. Things borrowed for use which are of great value, such as jewels, must be returned to the lender personally. In other cases, however, it is sufficient to return them at the place where it is customary to do so, or to deliver them to the servant of the lender. Example:- Return of an animal borrowed for use may be effected by delivering it at the stable of the lender or by handing it over to him groom.

- 830. Upon the return of a thing borrowed for use which is in the possession of the borrower, all expenses occasioned thereby, including cost of transport, must be borne by the borrower.

- 831. A piece of land may validly be lent for use for the purpose of erecting buildings or planting trees. The lender, however, may at any time go back on the loan and oblige the borrower to pull down the building goes or uproot the trees. However, if the loan is for a definite period, the lender must make good the difference between the value of the buildings and trees they were pulled down or uprooted and what would have been the value thereof at the end of the period, had they remained standing.yvT c Example:- Should the pulled down and uprooted value of buildings and trees which are pulled down and uprooted forthwith be twelve gold pounds, and the value thereof if left standing up to the end of the period be twenty gold pounds, and should the lender cause them to be pulled down or uprooted forthwith, he is obliged to pay a sum of eight gold pounds.

- 832.If land is lent for cultivation, whether for a fixed period or not, the lender cannot withdraw from the contract and demand the return of the land from borrower before the harvest.

PROMULGATED BY ROYAL IRADAH, 24, ZIL HIJJA, 1288.

AL-MAJALLA AL AHKAM AL ADALIYYAH
(The Ottoman Courts Manual (Hanafi))

BOOK VII. GIFT.

INTRODUCTION.

TERMS OF ISLAMIC JURISPRUDENCE RELATING TO GIFT.

- 833. A gift consists of bestowing the ownership of property upon some other person without receiving anything in return. The person giving is called the property bestowed by way of gift; and the person who receives such property is called the recipient.

- 834. A present is property brought or sent to someone by way of gratification.

- 835. Alms consists of property given for some charitable object.

- 836. Allowing another person to eat and drink without receiving anything in exchange is called gratuitous feeding.

CHAPTER I. MATTERS RELATING TO THE CONTRACT OF GIFT.

SECTION I. FUNDAMENTAL BASIS AND RECEIPT OF A GIFT.

- 837. A contract of gift is concluded by offer and acceptance. Upon taking delivery the contract becomes complete.

- 838. Offer, as regards donation, consists of the employment of words importing the gratuitous transfer of ownership in property, such as " I have given for nothing": "I have given by way of gift": "I have given as a present". An offer of a gift is also made by the use of expressions importing the intention of transferring ownership in property gratuitously, as where a husband hands a pair of earrings or some other jewel to his wife, telling her to take such thing and wear it.

- 839. A contract of gift may also be concluded by conduct.

- 840 The dispatch and receipt of a gift and of alms are tantamount to verbal offer and acceptance.

- 841. Receipt in the case of gift is like acceptance in the case of sale. Consequently, if the donor makes his offer by stating that he has given the given by way of gift or by using some similar expression, and the recipient, without signifying his acceptance, merely takes delivery of the thing given, at the time it was offered, the gift thereupon becomes complete.

- 842. The recipient may not take delivery of the thing given by way of if it, unless he has received the permission, express or implied, of the donor.

- 843. The donor, by his offer, is considered by implication to have authorised the recipient to take delivery of the thing given. There is an express authority, however, when the donor makes use of formal words, as when he states that he has given something to someone and invites that person to take it, in the event of the gift being present when the parties meet, or that he has given something to someone and invites him to go and get it, should the gift itself not be there when the parties meet.

- 844. When the donor has given his express authority, the recipient may take delivery of the property bestowed by way of gift either at the meeting place of the parties, or after they have separated. If the authority is merely implied, however, it is only valid so long as the parties are present together. After they have separated, the recipient may not validly take delivery of such property.

  Example:- The donor states that he has bestowed a certain by way of gift. The recipient may validly take delivery of the thing given so long as the parties remain present together, but he may not do so once they have separated. If the donor states that he has made a gift of something belonging to him which is in a certain place, without requesting the recipient to go and get it, the recipient may not validly go to the place where such thing is and take delivery thereof.

- 845. A purchaser may make a valid gift to a third party of a thing he has purchased, even before having taken delivery thereof from the vendor.

- 846. A gift made by the owner of a thing to a person who is already in possession thereof is complete by reason of the mere acceptance of the recipient, without the necessity of any further delivery.

- 847. If a person to whom money is due makes a gift of such money to the person from whom the money is due, or releases the debtor from payment thereof, such gift or release is valid, and the debt is forthwith extinguished, provided that the debtor does not decline to agree thereto.

- 848. Should a person to whom money is due make a gift of the sum due to him to some person other than the person who owes him such money, expressly authorising the recipient to take payment from the latter, the gift is complete as soon as the recipient has received payment.

- 849. The death of the donor or the recipient before the transfer of the gift makes such gift null and void.

- 850. In the case of gift made by a father to a son who is of age, that is, who is of sound mind and who has arrived at the age of puberty, the thing bestowed by way of gift must be delivered by the donor, and delivery must be taken thereof by the recipient.

- 851. A gift made to a minor by his tutor or by the person in charge of his upbringing and education, of such person's property is complete by reason only of the offer of the donor, and the minor becomes absolute owner thereof without any need for taking delivery, whether the thing given is in the possession of the donor, or in the safe keeping of some third person.

- 852. A gift made by a person to a child is complete when the tutor or person in charge of the upbringing or education of the child takes delivery of such gift.

- 853. If the recipient is a minor who is of perfect understanding, the gift becomes complete when the minor himself takes delivery thereof, even though he has a tutor.

- 854. A gift which is to take effect in the future is invalid.

Example:- A donor states that he has made a gift of a certain thing with effect as from the first of next month. The gift is invalid.

- 855. The donor may validly demand some compensation in return for his gift. In such a case the contract is valid and the condition binding upon the recipient.

Examples:-

(1). The donor makes a condition that the recipient shall give him some particular thing in return, or that he shall pay his debt amounting to a certain sum. If the recipient fulfils the condition the gift becomes irrevocable; if not, the donor has the right of revoking it.

(2). A person makes a gift of his real property held in absolute ownership upon condition that the recipient shall make provision for his maintenance for the whole of his life time. If such person changes his mind, he cannot revoke his gift and claim the return of such property so long as the recipient continues to comply with the condition.

SECTION II. CONDITIONS ATTACHING TO A GIFT.

- 856. The thing bestowed by way of gift must be in existence at the time the gift is made. Consequently, if a gift is made of grapes to be produced in a vineyard, or the foal of amre not yet born, such gift is invalid.
- 857. The thing bestowed by way of gift must be the property of the donor. Consequently, if a person makes a gift to some other person of property which is not his own, such gift is invalid. If the owner, however, thereafter ratifies the gift, such gift is valid.
- 858. The thing bestowed by way of gift must be clearly ascertained and defined. Consequently, if the donor makes a gift of a certain portion of his property without specifying which, or if he makes a gift of a horse by telling the recipient that he may take whichever he likes of two horses, and the recipient at the time the gift is made states which one of the two he selects, such gift is valid. If the recipient selects the one he wants after the meeting at which the gift has been made, however, such selection is invalid.
- 859. The donor must be of sound mind and must have arrived at the age of puberty. Consequently, a gift made by a minor, or a madman, or an imbecile is invalid. A gift however, may validly be bestowed upon such person.
- 860. The donor must assent to the gift. Consequently, a gift made as a result of force or constraint in invalid.

CHAPTER II. FUNDAMENTAL RULES RELATING TO GIFT.

SECTION I. REVOCATION OF A GIFT.

- 861. The recipient becomes owner of the property bestowed by way of gift upon taking delivery thereof.
- 862. The donor may revoke the gift of his own accord before delivery thereof is taken.

- 863. If the donor forbids the recipient to take delivery after making an offer of the property, he revokes the gift.

- 864. The donor may revoke the gift or present after delivery has been taken, provided the recipient agrees there to. If the recipient does not agree, the owner may apply to the Court, and the Court may cancel the gift in the absence of any prohibition contained in the following Articles, but not otherwise.

- 865. If the donor takes back the gift after delivery has been taken without the assent of the recipient, or of an order of the Court, he becomes a person wrongfully appropriating property; and if the gift is destroyed or lost while in his possession, he must make good the loss.

- 866. If a person makes a gift of anything to his ascendants or descendants, or to his brother, sister, or to their children or to his uncle and aunt, he may not revoke such gift.

- 867. If the husband or wife, while the marriage stands, gives and delivers something to the other, he or she can no longer go back from it.

- 868. If something is given on account of the gift and is received by the donor, the donor may not revoke such gift. Consequently, If something is given to the donor on account of the gift, whether by the recipient or by some other person, and the donor takes delivery thereof, he may not revoke such gift.

- 869. In cases where something is added to and becomes part of the gift, as where the property bestowed by way of gift consists of land, and the person in whose favour the gift is made erects buildings or plants trees thereon; or where the gift consists of a lean animal and the person in whose favour the gift is made fattens such animal; or where the gift is altered in such a way that its name is changed, as where corn is ground into flour, the gift may not validly be revoked. But an increase which is not part of the gift in no way prevents revocation. Consequently, if a mare which is bestowed by way of gift to a certain person becomes in foal, the gift may not be revoked. But after the mare has foaled, the gift any be revoked. In that case the foal belongs to the person in whose favour the gift has been made.

- 870. If the person in whose favour the gift has been made divests himself of the ownership therein by selling such gift or making a gift thereof, and delivering the same, the donor has no right of revoking the gift.

- 871. If the gift has been destroyed while in the possession of the person in whose favour the gift has been made, such gift may not be revoked.

- 872. In the event of death of either the donor or the person in whose favour the gift has been made, the gift may not be revoked. Consequently, if the person in whose favour the gift has been made dies, the donor may not revoke the gift; and if the donor dies his heirs cannot claim the return of the gift.

- 873. If the creditor makes a gift of a sum owning to him by a person who is indebted to him, he can in no case revoke the gift.(See Article 51 and 848.)

- 874. A gift made by way of alms cannot be revoked once delivery thereof has been taken.

- 875. If a person allows some other person to consume certain food, the latter, after receiving it, may not deal with it in a manner indicative of a right of ownership, as by selling it, or by making a gift of it to some third person. He may, however, eat such food, and the owner cannot later claim the value thereof.

Example:- A eats a quantity of grapes in a vineyard with the permission of the owner thereof. The owner may not later claim the value of such grapes.

- 876. Presents made on the occasion of circumcision or marriage ceremonies belong to those persons for whom they were intended by the owners thereof, whether for the child, or the bride, or the father, or the mother. If they fail to state for whom they were brought and the point cannot be settled by inquiry from them, the question will be dealt with in accordance with local custom.

SECTION II. GIFTS MADE DURING THE COURSE OF A MORTAL SICKNESS.

- 877. If a person who is without an heir makes a gift of the whole of his possession to some other person during the course of a mortal sickness and delivers the same, such gift is valid, and the Treasury has no right of interfering with the estate after his decease.

- 878. If a husband who has no heir apart from his wife, or a wife who has no heir other than her husband, makes a gift of the whole of his or her possessions to the wife or husband respectively during the course of a mortal sickness and delivers the same, such gift is valid, and the Treasury has no right of interfering with the estate of either of them after their decease.

- 879. If any person makes a gift to one of his heirs during the course of a mortal sickness, and then dies, such gift is not valid unless ratified by the other heirs. If the gift, however, is made and delivered to some person other than an heir, and the gift does not exceed one third of the estate, such gift is valid, If it exceeds one third, however, and the heirs do not ratify the gift, such gift is valid in respect to one third of the estate, and the person in whose favour the gift is made must return the balance.

- 880. If a person whose estate is overwhelmed by debts makes a gift of his property during the course of a mortal sickness to his heir, or to some other person, and delivers the same and then dies, the creditors may disregard the gift and may divide such property between them in proportion to their claims.

PROMULGATED BY ROYAL IRADAH 29TH MUHARRAM, 1289.

AL-MAJALLA AL AHKAM AL ADALIYYAH
(The Ottoman Courts Manual (Hanafi))

BOOK VIII. WRONGFUL APPROPRIATION AND DESTRUCTION.

INTRODUCTION.

TERMS OF ISLAMIC JURISPRUDENCE.

- 881. Wrongful appropriation consists of taking and keeping the property of another, without that person,s permission. the person taking such property is called the person wrongfully appropriating the property. The property itself is called the property wrongfully appropriated. The owner of such property is called the person whose property has been wrongfully appropriated.

- 882. Standing value is the value of buildings and trees as they stand in the ground. The value of the land is estimated first together with the buildings and trees and then without the building and trees. The difference between the two valuations is called the standing value of the buildings and trees.

- 883. The building value is the standing value of the buildings.

- 884. The pull-down value is the value of the debris of the buildings after they have been pulled down and of the trees after they have been uprooted.

- 885. The pulling-down value is the pulled-down value after deducting therefrom the cost of pulling down buildings or uprooting trees.

- 886. The minus value of land consists of the difference between the rent of a piece of land before cultivation and after cultivation.

- 887. Direct destruction consists of the destruction of a thing by a person himself. The person destroying the thing is called the actual doer of the act.

- 888. Indirect destruction consists of being the cause of the destruction of a thing. That is to say, to do an act which causes the destruction of another thing in the normal course of events. The person performing such act is called the person causing the destruction.yvT , Examples:-

(1). The cord of a hanging lamp is cut. The lamp falls down and is broken. The person cutting the cord is the direct cause of the destruction of the cord and is the indirect cause of the destruction of the lamp.

(2). A person splits a water-skin in half and oil contained therein escapes and is lost. Such person is the direct cause of the destruction of the water-skin and the indirect cause of the destruction of the oil.

- 889. Prior warning consists of giving warning and recommendation before taking action, with a view to preventing the occurrence of any probable injury.

CHAPTER I. WRONGFUL APPROPRIATION

SECTION I. WRONGFUL APPROPRIATION IN GENERAL.

- 890. If the wrongfully appropriated property exists in its original state, such property must be restored to the owner thereof at the place where it was wrongfully taken. If the owner meets the person who has wrongfully appropriated the property in some other place, and the wrongfully appropriated property is with him, the owner may, if he wishes, demand the return of the property there. If he asks for the property to be handed over at the place where the wrongful appropriation occurred, the expenses occasioned by handing over and transport fall upon the person who has wrongfully appropriated the property.

- 891 If the person who has wrongfully appropriated property destroys the same, he must make good the loss occasioned thereby. He is also liable to make good the loss if such property is destroyed or lost with or without his fault. Thus, he must pay the value thereof if such property is of the sort the like of which cannot be found in the market, as at the time and place at which the wrongful appropriation occurred, and give a similar article if like of it can be found in the market.

- 892. If the person wrongfully appropriating property returns the identical property to the owner thereof at the place where the wrongful appropriation occurred, he is free from all liability to make compensation.

- 893. If the person who has wrongfully appropriated property places such property before the owner thereof in such a way that he can take possession of it, the property is question is deemed to have been restored, even though the owner may not actually have taken delivery thereof.

  If such person places the value of property which has been wrongfully appropriated and which has been destroyed before the owner thereof, he is not free from liability to make good the loss until the owner has taken delivery thereof.

- 894. If the person who has wrongfully appropriated some specific piece of property delivers such property to the owner thereof in a dangerous place, the owner has the right of refusing to accept it. In such case, the person who has wrongfully appropriated the property is not freed from the liability of making good for any loss.

- 895. If the person who has wrongfully appropriated property which has been destroyed, tenders the value thereof to the owner, who refuses to accept the same, such person may apply to the Court for an order for acceptance.

- 896. If the person whose property has been wrongfully appropriated is a minor, the person who has wrongfully appropriated may validly restore such property to the minor, provided the latter is of perfect understanding and capable of preserving the property, but not otherwise.

- 897. If the property wrongfully appropriated consists of fruit and the condition thereof changes while in the possession of the person who has wrongfully appropriated such property, such as by becoming dry, the owner has the option either of claiming the return of the identical property wrongfully appropriated, or of asking for the value thereof to be paid.

- 898. If the person wrongfully appropriating property in any way changes the nature of such property by adding thereto anything of his own, the person whose property has been wrongfully appropriated has the option either of claiming the value of such property, or of asking for the return of the identical property after paying the value of the increase.yvT U Example:- A wrongfully appropriates cloth and dyes the same. The owner thereof has the option either of claiming the value of the cloth or of asking for the return of the cloth itself after paying the price of the dye.

- 899. If the person wrongfully appropriating property alters such property in such a way that the same thereof is changed, he is bound to make good the loss and keep the property himself.yvT * Examples:-

(1). A wrongfully appropriates certain wheat and grinds it into flour. He is obliged to make good the loss and the flour becomes his property.

(2). A wrongfully appropriates wheat and sows it in his own field. He is obliged to make good the loss and the crops becomes his property.

- 900. If the price and the value of a thing decrease after the wrongful appropriation thereof, the owner may not refuse to accept it and claim the value thereof at the time such thing was wrongfully appropriated. But if the value of such thing was wrongfully appropriated. But if the value of such thing decreases by reason of the use thereof by the person who has wrongfully appropriated such property, such loss must be made good. Examples :-

(1). A wrongfully appropriates an animal and restores such animal to its owner in a weakened condition. A is bound to make good the decrease in the value of the animal.

(2). A wrongfully appropriates clothes and tears them, thereby decreasing their value. If the decrease is of small amount, that is to say, if it does not amount to one-fourth of the value of the property wrongfully appropriated, the person wrongfully appropriating such property is liable to make good the loss. But if the decrease in value is of great amount, that is to say, if it is equal to or exceeds one fourth of the value thereof, the person from whom such property has been wrongfully appropriated has the option either of claiming to have the amount of the decrease in value made good, or of abandoning the property to the person wrongfully appropriating it and claiming the full value thereof.

- 901. Any act whereby a person is deprived of his power to deal with his own property and which results in a situation equivalent to that created by wrongful appropriation is considered to amount to wrongful appropriation. Thus, if a person to whom property has been entrusted for safe keeping denies such trust, such act amounts to wrongful appropriation, and if thereafter the property entrusted to him is destroyed without his fault, he is liable to make good the loss.

- 902.If any person is deprived of possession of his property held in absolute ownership without any intention of being so deprived, as where a garden situated upon a mountain subsides and fall upon another garden situated below it, the property which is of lesser value is subject to that which is of greater value. That is to say, the owner of property which is greater in value is bound to indemnify the owner of property which is of lesser value, and becomes owner of such property.

Examples:-

(1). If the value of the garden situated above is worth five hundred piastres and that of the garden situated below is worth one thousand piastres before the collapse of the mountain, the owner of the latter, by paying the owner of the former five hundred piastres, may take over the first garden.

(2). The owner of a pearl worth fifty piastres drops it and it is swallowed by a hen worth five piastres. The owner of the pearl may take the hen upon payment of five piastres. (See Articles 27, 27, and 29.)

- 903. Any increase in the property wrongfully appropriated belongs to the owner thereof. If the person wrongfully appropriating such property consumes such increase, he is bound to make good the loss.yvT , Examples: The milk and young of an animal wrongfully appropriated and which are produced while in the possession of the person wrongfully appropriated them, and the fruit produced in a garden while in the possession of a person who has wrongfully appropriated such garden, are the property of the owner of the things wrongfully appropriated; and if the person wrongfully appropriating them consumes them, he is liable to make good the loss.

- 904. The honey of bees which make their home in a garden belongs to the owner of the garden. If any other person takes and consumes such honey, he is liable to make good the loss.

SECTION II. WRONGFULLY APPROPRIATION OF REAL PROPERTY.

- 905. If the property wrongfully appropriated is real property, the person wrongfully appropriating such property is bound to restore it to the owner thereof without any change or decrease.

If the real property wrongfully appropriated is decreased in value by the act of the person wrongfully appropriating such property, he is bound to make good the decrease in value.yvT [Examples:-

(1). A wrongfully appropriates a house and destroys a part thereof, or ruins it by living in it. If the value thereof decreased, he is bound to make good the amount of such decrease.

(2). If a person wrongfully appropriating a house destroys it by lighting a fire therein, he is bound to make good the building value of such house.

- 906. If the property wrongfully appropriated is land and the person wrongfully appropriating such property constructs building or plants trees thereon, such person shall be ordered to restore such land after uprooting the trees or pulling down the buildings.

If the fact of pulling down the buildings or of uprooting the trees causes injury to the land, the person whose land has been wrongfully appropriated may take possession of such buildings or trees upon paying the pulling-down value thereof.

If the value of the buildings and trees is greater than that of the land, however, and such buildings or trees have been constructed or planted under the belief that there was some legal justification for so doing, the owner of the buildings or trees may claim to be vested with the ownership of the land, upon paying the price thereof.yvT Example:- A inherits a piece of land from his father and erects buildings thereon for a cash expenditure exceeding the value of the land. Thereupon, a person who has a right to that land appears and claims it. A is entitled to take possession of the land upon paying the price thereof.

- 907. If a person wrongfully appropriates a piece of land belonging to another and cultivates it, and the owner obtains the return thereof, the latter is also entitled to be indemnified for any decrease in the value of the land arising out of such cultivation.

  Similarly, if a person who is joint owner with another of a piece of land cultivates that land alone without the permission of the other, such person's co-owner is entitled, upon taking his share of the land, to be compensated, in respect to his share, for any decrease in the value of the land caused by the other co-owner's cultivation.

- 908. If a person wrongfully appropriates a field belonging to another and clears it, and the owner thereafter retakes possession of such field, such person has no right of claiming the cost of clearing the land from the owner thereof.

- 909. If any person occupies a piece of land belonging to another and places sweepings or similar refuse thereon, such person shall be obliged to remove such matter, and to evacuate the land.

SECTION III. WRONGFUL APPROPRIATION FROM A PERSON WHO HAS ALREADY WRONGFULLY appropriated PROPERTY.

- 910. Any person who wrongfully appropriates property from a person who has already wrongfully appropriated such property is considered to be in the same position as the first person wrongfully appropriating the property. Consequently, if property already wrongfully appropriated is again wrongfully appropriated from the first person by some other person and is destroyed by him or while in his possession, the person from whom the property has been wrongfully appropriated has the option of claiming to have his loss made good either by the first or second person who has wrongfully appropriated such property. He also has the option of claiming a portion of the value of the property from the first and a portion from the second person wrongfully appropriating such property. If the first person wrongfully appropriating such property makes good the loss thereof, such person has a right of recourse against the second. If the second person, however, makes good loss, such person has no right of recourse against the first.

- 911. If the second person wrongfully appropriating property restores it to the first person who has wrongfully appropriated such property, the former alone is free from liability in connection therewith. If he returns it to the person from whom the property has been wrongfully appropriated, however, both persons are free from liability.

CHAPTER II. DESTRUCTION OF PROPERTY.

SECTION I. DIRECT DESTRUCTION OF PROPERTY.

- 912. If any person destroys property of another, whether intentionally or unintentionally, and whether in his own possession or in that of some person to whom it has been entrusted, such person must make good the loss occasioned thereby.

  If any person destroys property which has been wrongfully appropriated while in the possession of the person who has wrongfully appropriated it, the owner of the property may claim to have the loss made good by the person who has wrongfully appropriated such property, who in turn has a right of recourse against the person who destroyed the property, or he can claim to have the loss made good by him. The latter, however, has no right of recourse against the person wrongfully appropriating the property.

- 913. If a person slips and falls upon and destroys any property belonging to another, he is bound to make good the loss.

- 914. If any person destroys the property of any other [person under the mistaken belief that it is his own, he must make good any loss occasioned thereby.

- 915. If any person drags the clothes of another and tears them, he must make good the full value thereof. If a person takes hold of the clothes of another, and the owner of such clothes drags them and tears them, however, such person is liable to make good half the value thereof.

  Similarly, if any person sits upon the skirt of another, and the owner, unaware thereof, gets up, and tears his clothes, such person must make good half the value of the clothes.

- 916. If a minor destroys the property of another, he must make good the loss thereof out of his own property. If he is not possessed of any property, payment may be postponed until he is in a position to pay. His tutor may not be called upon to make good the loss.

- 917. If any person causes any diminution in value of the property of another, he must make good the amount of such loss.

- 918. If any person without justification knocks down the real property of another, such as a house or a shop, the owner of such property has the option either of abandoning the debris of such real property to the person who has knocked it down and of claiming the building value thereof from him, or of deducting the value of the debris from the building value of such real property and of claiming the value of the remainder, keeping the debris. If the person wrongfully appropriating such property rebuilds the property and restores it to its original state he is not liable to make compensation.

- 919. Should fire breaks out in any particular place and should any person pull down a house without the permission of the owner thereof, and the fire is stopped, such person is not liable to make good the loss occasioned thereby, provided he has pulled down the house by order of the authorities. If he pulls down the house on his own initiative, however, he must make good the loss.

- 920. If any person without any justification cuts down the trees in the garden of another, the owner has the option of claiming the standing value of such trees and of abandoning them to the person who has cut them down, or of deducting the cut-down value from the standing value and of claiming the balance together with the trees cut down.yvT " Example:- If the value of the garden with the trees standing amounts to ten thousand piastres and without the trees to five thousand piastres, and the value of the trees when cut down to two thousand piastres, the owner has the option of leaving the trees cut down to the person who has felled them, and of taking five thousand piastres, or of taking three thousands piastres, keeping the trees cut down.

- 921. The fact that a person has suffered an injury does not authorise that person to inflict an injury upon another person.yvT I Examples:-

  (1). A destroys the property of B. If B in turn destroys the property of A, both persons are liable to make good the loss they have caused.

  (2). A member of one tribe destroys the property of a member of another tribe. The latter destroys the property of another member of the first tribe. Both persons are liable to make good the loss they have caused.

(3). A is given counterfeited money by B. B may not pass the money on to another person.

SECTION II. INDIRECT DESTRUCTION OF PROPERTY.

- 922. If a person is the cause of the destruction of the property of another, or of any decrease in the value thereof, that is to say, if his own act is the cause leading to the destruction or decrease in value of such property, such person must make good the loss.yvT - Examples:-

  (1). A quarrels with B. During the quarrel A seizes hold of B's c;other, and an object in B's clothes falls to the ground and is destroyed or damaged. A is bound to make good the loss.

  (2). A without any justification cuts off the water in B's field or garden. If the crops and plantations dry up and are destroyed, or if A lets the water overflow into the garden of another and swamps his crops, causing them to be destroyed, A must make good the loss.

  (3). A opens the door of B's stable. An animal therein runs away and is lost. A must make good the loss.

  (4). A opens the door of a cage belonging to B. A bird therein flies away. A must make good the loss.

- 923. If an animal takes fright at a particular person and runs away and is lost, such person is not obliged to make good the loss. But if such person intentionally frightens such animal, he is bound to make good the loss. Similarly, if an animal takes fright at the noise of a gun fired by a huntsman when hunting and runs away, and while doing so, falls and is killed or breaks its leg, the huntsman is not liable to make good the loss. But if the latter fires his gun with the intention of frightening the animal, he is bound to make good the loss. (See Article 93).

- 924. The liability of a person who is the cause of an act, as referred to above, to make good any loss sustained thereby, depends upon such act being of a wrongful nature. That is to sway, the liability of a person who causes an injury to be sustained to make good the loss caused thereby, is dependent upon the act which led to such injury being performed by him without any justification.yvT F Example :- A without permission from any public authority digs a well in the public highway. An animal belonging to B falls therein and is destroyed. A must make good the loss. But if A digs a well in his own land held in absolute ownership and B's animal falls therein and is destroyed, A is not liable to make good the loss.

- 925. If a person performs any act which is the cause of the destruction of a thing and meanwhile some voluntary act supervenes, that is to say, if some other person directly destroys that thing, the author of such voluntary act is liable to make good the loss. (See Article 90.)

SECTION III. MATTERS OCCURRING IN THE PUBLIC HIGHWAY.

- 926. Every person has a right of way on the public highway, subject to the safety of others. That is to say, provided no harm is caused to others in circumstances which can be avoided.yvT O Examples:-

  (1). If a porter drops the load he is carrying on the public highway and destroys the property of another, the porter must make good the loss.

(2). If sparks fly from a blacksmith's shop while he is working iron and set fire to the clothes of a passer-by in the public highway, the blacksmith must make good the loss.

- 927. No person may set up in the public highway for the purpose of buying and selling without the permission of the public authorities, nor may he place or produce any thing there without permission. If he does so, he is bound to make good any injury or loss which may be caused thereby.yvT Examples:-

  (1). A piles up wood or stones in the public highway. B's animal treads thereon, slips and is destroyed. A must make good the loss.

  (2). A drops a slippery substance such as oil on the public highway. B's animal slips thereon and is destroyed. A must make good the loss.

- 928. If a wall belonging to a particular person falls down and causes damage to any other person, the owner of the wall is under no necessity to make good the loss. But if some other person has previously warned the owner to knock down the wall as it is likely to collapse, and sufficient time has elapsed for the wall to be knocked down, the owner is then obliged to make good the loss. Provided always that the person giving such warning has the right to do so. Thus, if the wall has collapsed on to a neighbour's house, the person giving the warning must be one of the inhabitants of that house. A warning given by a person outside is of no effect. If the wall collapses on to a private road, the person giving the warning must be a person having a right of way over such road. If it collapses on the public highway, any person whatsoever has the right of giving the warning.

SECTION IV. INJURY CAUSED BY ANIMALS.

- 929. The owner of an animal is not liable to make good any damage caused by the animal of its own volition. (See Article 94). But if an animal consumes the property of some other person and the owner of the animal is cognizant thereof and takes no steps to prevent the injury, the owner is bound to make good the loss. But if the owner of an animal known to be of a destructive character such as a bull which gores, or a dog which bites, is warned by one of the inhabitants of the district or village to tie up such animal, and the owner nevertheless lets him go loose and he destroys the animal or the property of some other person, the owner is bound to make good the loss.

- 930. If an animal, whether ridden by its owner or not, and while on land owned by him in absolute ownership, injures any other person by striking such person with his fore feet, or with his head, or tail, or by kicking with his hind legs, the owner of such animal is liable to make good the loss.

- 931. If any person causes any animal to enter the property held in absolute ownership belonging to another, having obtained the permission of the owner of such property to do so, such animal is regarded as being on such person's land, and the owner is not liable to make good the loss in respect to any injury caused by such animal, as set forth in the preceding Article. If the owner has caused the animal to enter without such permission, he is liable in any case to make good any damage caused, whether riding, leading or driving, or even when not near to such animal. But if an animal breaks loose and enters the property of another held in absolute ownership and does damage thereon of its own accord, the owner is not liable to make good the loss.

- 932. Every person has a right of way with his animal over the public highway. Consequently, if anyone rides his animal on the public highway, he is not liable to make good any injury or loss which he could not have avoided.yvT o Example: If dirt and mud are scattered about by the hoofs of an animal and another person's clothes are splashed therewith; or if such animal kicks with his hind legs or swishes his tail and inflicts injury thereby, there is no need to make good the loss. But a person riding an animal is responsible for collision or for blows inflicted by the fore feet or the head.

- 933. Any person leading and any person driving an animal in the public highway is considered to be the same as a person riding such animal. That is to say, there are only obliged to make good any loss sustained to the extent that the person riding the animal is so obliged. the public

- 934. No person has the right of stopping or of tying up his animal in the public highway. Consequently, if any person stops his animal or ties it up in the public highway and such animal kicks with his fore or hind legs, or inflicts injuries in any other way, such person is in every case obliged to make good the loss caused by such animal. An exception, however, is made in the case of places specially set aside for animals, such as horse- markets and places for animals sent out on hire.

- 935. If any person turns his animal loose on the public highway he is responsible for any injury caused by such animal.

- 936. If an animal ridden by any person tramples upon anything with either his fore or hind legs, whether upon his own property or upon that of any other person and such thing is destroyed, such person is considered to have directly destroyed it and in every case is bound to make good the loss.

- 937. If the animal does not take the bit, and the rider is unable to hold his head, and injury is caused by such animal, the rider is not responsible therefor.

- 938. If any person ties his animal up in his own property and a second person arrives and likewise ties up his animal there without permission, and the animal belonging to the owner of the property kicks and destroys the animal belonging to such second person, the owner of the first animal need not make good the loss.

  If the animal belonging to the second person destroys the animal of the owner of the property, the second person must make good the loss.

- 939. If two persons have the right of tying up their animals in one place, and having done so, one of them destroys the other, there is no need to make good the loss.yvT - Example:- Two persons who are joint owners of a horse tie up their animals in a certain place in such house and while there the animal belonging to one of them destroys the animal belonging to the other. The owner of the animal inflicting the injury is not liable to make good the loss.

- 940. If two persons tie up their animals in a place where they have no right to do so and the animal belonging to the first person who ties up animal destroys the animal belonging to the second, the first person is not obliged to make good the loss. BUt if the animal belonging to the second person who so ties up his animal destroys the animal belonging to the first, the second person must make good the loss.

PROMULGATED BY ROYAL IRADAH, 23RD RABI UL AKHRA, 1289.

AL-MAJALLA AL AHKAM AL ADALIYYAH
(The Ottoman Courts Manual (Hanafi))

BOOK IX. INTERDICTION, CONSTRAINT AND PRE-EMPTION.

INTRODUCTION.

TERMS OF ISLAMIC JURISPRUDENCE RELATING TO INTERDICTION, CONSTRAINT AND PRE-EMPTION.

- 941. Interdiction consists of prohibiting any particular person from dealing with his own property. After interdiction, such person is called an interdicted person.

- 942. By permission is meant removing the interdiction and destroying the right of prohibition. The person to whom such permission is given is called the permitted person.

- 943. A minor of imperfect understanding is a young person who does not understand selling and buying, that is to say, who does not understand that ownership is lost by sale and acquired by purchase, and who is unable to distinguish obvious flagrant misrepresentation, that is misrepresentation amounting to five in ten, from minor representation. A minor who can distinguish between these matters is called a young person of perfect understanding.

- 944. Lunatics are divided into two classes. The first consists of persons who are continuously mad and whose madness lasts whole times. The second class consists of whose madness is intermittent, that is to say, persons who are sometimes mad and sometimes sane.

- 945. An imbecile is a person whose mind is so deranged that his comprehension is extremely limited, his speech confused, and whose actions are imperfect.

- 946. A prodigal person is a person who by reckless expenditure wastes and destroys his property to no purpose. Persons who are deceived in their business owing to their being stupid or simple-minded are also considered to be prodigal persons.

- 947. A person of mature mind is a person who is able to take control of his own property and who does not waste it to no purpose.

- 948. Constraint consists of wrongfully forcing a person through fear to do something without his consent. (*).(The translation of certain technical terms in this Article has been omitted as having no meaning for the English reader.)

- 949. constraint is divided into two classes. The first class consists of major constraint, whereby the death of a person or the loss of a limb is caused. The second consists of minor constraint whereby grief of pain alone is caused, such as assault or imprisonment.

- 950. Pre-emption consists of acquiring possession of a piece of property held in absolute ownership which has been purchased, by paying the purchaser the amount he gave for it.

- 951. The pre-emptor is the person enjoying the right of pre-emption.
- 951. The subject of pre-emption is real property to which the right of pre-emption is attached.
- 953. The subject matter of pre-emption is the property held in absolute ownership of the pre-emptor is virtue of which the right of pre-emption is exercised.
- 954. A joint owner of a servitude is a person who shares with another is right over property held in absolute ownership, such as a share in water, or a share in road.
- 955. A private right of taking water is a right of taking water from some flowing water reserved for a limited number of persons. But the right of taking water from rivers used by the public does not belong to this class.
- 956. A private road is a road from which there is no exit.

CHAPTER 1. MATTERS RELATING TO INTERDICTION.

SECTION 1. CLASSES OF INTERDICTED PERSONS AND MATTERS RELATING THERETO.

- 957. Minors, lunatics and imbeciles are ipso facto interdicted.
- 958. A person who is a prodigal may be interdicted by the court.
- 959. A person who is in debt may also be interdicted by the court upon the application of the creditors.
- 960. Any disposition of property such as sale and purchase on the part of interdicted persons referred to it in the preceding Articles, is invalid. Such persons, moreover, must immediately make good any loss caused by their own acts.

Example:- If A, even though he may be a young person of imperfect understanding, destroys property belonging to B, he must make good the loss.

- 961. Upon the court declaring a prodigal and a person in debt to be interdicted, the reason for such interdiction must be given, and announced in public.
- 962. It is not essential that the person whom the court intends to interdict should be present. He may validly be interdicted in his absence. Such person must, however, be informed of the interdiction; and the interdiction does not take effect until he has been so informed. Consequently, any contracts or admissions made by him up to that date are valid.
- 963. Provided he has not squandered his property, a person of dissolute character may not be interdicted solely by reason of his dissolute conduct.
- 964. Persons who cause injury to the public, such as an ignorant physician, may also be interdicted. In such cases, however, the object of the interdiction is to restrain them from practice, and not to prohibit them from dealing with their property.
- 965. No person who carries on business or trade in the market may be restrained from carrying on the same by reason of the fact that other persons carrying on such business or trade allege that their

work is being ruined thereby.

SECTION II. MATTERS RELATING TO MINOR, LUNATICS AND IMBECILES.

- 966. A minor of imperfect understanding may not in any manner make any valid disposition of his property, even through his tutor assents thereto.

- 967. Any disposition of property entered into by a minor of imperfect understanding, which is purely for his own benefit, such as the acceptance of gift and presents, is valid, even though his tutor does not assent thereto. Any disposition of property, however, which is purely to his own disadvantage, such as bestowing a thing upon another by way of gift, is invalid, even though the tutor assents thereto. But in the case of contracts where it is not certain whether they will be for his benefit or disadvantage, such contracts are concluded subject to the permission of the tutor. The tutor has the option of giving or withholding his consent. Thus, if he thinks that it is to the advantage of the minor, he will give his consent, and not otherwise.

  Example:- A minor of perfect understanding sells certain property without permission. The execution of the sale is subject to the assent of his tutor, even though he has sold it for a price which is greater than the value thereof, the reason being that the contract of sale is one where it is not certain whether it will be for his advantage or disadvantage.

- 968. Tutor may give a minor of perfect understanding a portion of his property on trial with which to engage in business, and if it turns out as a result that he is of mature mind, he may deliver him the balance of such property. Article

- 969. The repeated conclusion of contracts from which the intention to make profit may be inferred, amounts to permission to engage in business.

  Example:- A tutor tell a minor to engage in business, or to buy and sell property of a certain nature. This amounts to permission to engage in business. But if he merely authorises him to conclude a single contract, as where he states that certain things are to be found in the market and tells him to buy them, or tells him to sell a certain thing, such act does not amount to permission to engage in business, but the tutor is considered to have employed such minor as agent in accordance with custom.

- 970. Permission given by the tutor may not be made subject to any condition as to time and place, or limited to any particular type of business.

  Example:-

  (1). The tutor gives permission to a minor of perfect understanding for a period of one day or one month. The minor has full and absolute permission, and may act for all time, until the tutor makes him interdicted.

  (2) The tutor tells the minor to engage in trade in a certain market. The minor may engage in trade anywhere.

  (3). The tutor tell the minor to buy and sell property of a particular sort. The minor may buy and sell any sort of property.

- 971. Permission may be given explicitly or by implication.

  Example:- A minor of perfect understanding engages in business with the knowledge of his tutor, who makes no comment thereon and does not prohibit him from so doing. The tutor has given him permission by implication.

- 972. When permission is given to a minor by his tutor, such minor is considered to have arrived at the age of puberty in respect to the matters included in the permission. Contract such as those relating to sale and hire are valid.

- 973. A tutor who has given permission to a minor may later revoke such permission by making the minor interdicted, but the interdiction must take the same from as the permission. Example:- A tutor gives a general permission to a minor to engage in business. After this permission has become known to people in the market, he wishes to make the minor interdicted. The interdiction must in the same way be made general, and must be made known to the majority of the people in the market. It is not enough for him to be made interdicted in his own house in the presence of two or three persons.

- 974. The tutor of a minor in this connection is
  (1) His father.
  (2). If his father is dead, the guardian chosen, that is to say, the guardian chosen and appointed by the father during his lifetime.
  (3). If the guardian chosen is dead, then the guardian appointed by him during his life time.
  (4). The true ancestor, that is to say, the father of the father of the minor, or the father of the father of his father.
  (5). The The guardian chosen and appointed by such ancestor during his lifetime.
  (6). The guardian appointed by such guardian.
  (7). The court, or the guardian appointed, that is to say, the guardian appointed by the court.

  Any permission given by a brother, or an uncle, or other relative who are not guardians, is invalid.

- 975. If the Court deems it in the interest of a minor that he allowed to dispose of property, and a senior tutor of such minor refuses to give permission, the Court may give the minor permission to do so, and no other tutor may under any circumstances make such minor interdicted.

- 976. In the event of the death of a tutor who has given permission to a minor, thee permission which he has given becomes void. BUt the permission given by the Court does not becomes null and void by reason of the death or dismissal of the judge.

- 977. A minor who has been granted permission by the Court may be interdicted by such Court or by the successor of the judge who granted such permission. The father, or any other tutor, however, may not make the minor interdicted after the death or dismissal of such judge.

- 978. An imbecile is considered to be a minor of perfect understanding.

- 979. Lunatics who are continuously mad are considered to be minor of imperfect understanding.

- 980. Acts of disposition over property by lunatics who are not continuously mad, and performed during a lucid interval, are like acts of disposition over property performed by the sane person.

- 981. When a young person arrives at the age of puberty, there should be no undue haste in handing his property to him, but his capacity should be put to test. and if it turns out that he is of mature mind, his property should then be given to him.

- 982. If a young person who is not of mature mind arrives at the age of puberty, his property should not be handed to him and he should be prohibited as previously from dealing with the, until it has been proved that the is of mature mind.

- 983. If property is handed by a guardian to a minor before it has been proved that he is of mature mind, and such property is lost while in the possession of the minor, or the minor destroys the same, the guardian must make good the loss.

- 984. If property is handed to a minor upon his reaching the age of puberty, and if is later proved that he is a prodigal, such person shall be interdicted by the Court.

- 985. Puberty is proved by the emission of seed during dreams, by the power to make pregnant, by, menstruation, and by the capacity to conceive.

- 986. The commencement of the age of puberty in the case of males is twelve years completed and in the case of females nine years completed. The termination of the age of puberty in both cases is fifteen years completed. If a male on reaching twelve have not arrived at the age of puberty, they are said to be approaching puberty until such time as they do in fact arrive at the age of puberty.

- 987. Any person who upon reaching the termination of the age of puberty, shows no signs of puberty, is considered in law to have arrived at the age of puberty.

- 988. If any young person who has not arrived at the commencement at the age of puberty brings an action to prove that he has in fact arrived at the age of puberty, such action shall not be heard.

- 989. If a male of female approaching the age of puberty admit in Court that they have arrived at the age of puberty, and the condition of their bodies shows that their admission is false, such admission shall not be confirmed. If, however, the condition of their bodies shows that their admission is true, their admission should be confirmed, and that their contracts and admissions are executory and valid. If such persons later state that at the time they made the admission they had not arrived at the age of puberty, and seek to annul any disposition they may have made over their property, no attention shall be paid thereto.

SECTION III. INTERDICTED PRODIGALS.

- 990. An interdicted prodigal is, as regards his civil transactions, like a minor of perfect understanding. The court alone, however, may be the tutor of the prodigal. The father, ancestor and guardians have no right of tutorship over him.

- 991. Any disposition of property by the prodigal after interdiction as regards his civil transactions are invalid. Any such dispositions made prior to the interdiction are the same as those of other people.

- 992. Any expenditure necessary for the interdicted prodigal or for those dependent upon him for support may be made from his own property.

- 993. If the interdicted prodigal sells property, such sale is not executory. If the court thinks that any benefit may be derived therefrom, however, it may validate such sale.

- 994. An admission made by an interdicted prodigal of a debt due to another is absolutely invalid, that is to say, any admission made in respect to property in existence at the time the interdiction was declared, or accruing thereafter, is without effect.

- 995. Any claim which any person may have against an interdicted prodigal shall be paid from the prodigal's property.

- 996. If an interdicted prodigal borrows money and uses it for his personal expenditure, and the amount thereof is not excessive, the Court shall repay such money from the prodigal's property. If it is excessive, however, the Court shall estimate the amount necessary for his maintenance and disallow the rest.

- 997. If the interdicted prodigal reforms, the interdiction may be removed by the Court.

SECTION IV. INTERDICTION OF DEBTORS.

- 998. If it is clear to the Court that the debtor is putting off paying his creditors, although he is able to pay, and the creditors ask the court to sell the property of the debtor and pay his debts therefrom, the Court shall prohibit the debtor from dealing with his property.

  Should the debtor himself refuse to sell his property and pay his debts therefrom, the Court shall do so. The Court shall begin by selling those things which are most advantageous to the debtor.

  The Court shall first deal with the cash assets and if these are not sufficient the merchandise, and if that is not sufficient, the real property of the debtor.

- 999. If the debtor is bankrupt, that is to say, if his debts are equal to or exceed his property, and the creditors fear that his property will be lost by trading, or that he will dispose of his property in fraud of his creditors, or that he will make it over to some other person, they may make application to the Court and ask for such person to be prohibited from dealing with his property or admitting a debt to some other person, and the Court shall then declare the debtor to be interdicted and shall sell his property and divide the proceeds among the creditors. One or two suits of clothes shall be left for the debtor. If the debtor's clothes, however, are expensive, and it is possible to do with less expensive clothes, such clothes shall be sold and a suit of cheap clothes shall be bought from the sum realised and the balance should be paid to the creditors. Again, if the debtor has a large country house and a smaller one is sufficient for him, such country house shall be sold and a suitable dwelling purchased from the sum realised, and the balance given to the creditors.

- 1000. Any expenditure necessary for the maintenance of an insolvent debtor during the period of his interdiction, or for persons dependent upon him for support, shall be paid from the debtor's property.

- 1001. Interdiction on account of debt only applies to property of the debtor in existence at the time the interdiction was declared. It does not apply to any property accruing to the debtor after the interdiction.

- 1002. The interdiction applies to anything likely to destroy the rights of the creditors, such as making gifts and bestowing alms and selling property at less than the estimated value. Consequently, any contracts entered into by a bankrupt debtor which are prejudicial to the rights of creditors, and other dispositions of property and gifts, are invalid in respect to property which existed at the time the interdiction was pronounced. They are valid, however, in respect to a debt relating to any property in existence at the time the interdiction was pronounced. They are valid, however, in respect to property acquired after the interdiction was pronounced. Any admission made to any other person in respect to a debt relating to any property in existence at the time the interdiction was pronounced, is invalid. After the interdiction has been removed, however, the admission is valid, and he is liable to make payment thereof. If he acquires property after the interdiction has been pronounced, an admission that he will make payment therefrom is executory.

CHAPTER II. CONSTRAINT.

- 1003. The person who causes constraint must be capable of carrying out his threat. Consequently, the threat of any person who is unable to put such threat into execution, is considered to be of no effect.

- 1004. The person who is the subject of constraint must be afraid of the occurrence of the event with which he is threatened. That is to say, he must have become convinced that the person causing the constraint would carry out his threat in the event of his failing to do what he was being constrained to do.

- 1005. Constraint is considered to be effective if the person who is the subject of such constraint performs the act he has been forced to do, in the presence of the person causing constraint, or of his representative. But if he performs such act in the absence of the person causing the constraint or of his representative, such act is not considered to have been caused by constraint since he has performed the act freely after the cessation of the constraint.

  Example:- A brings constraint to bear on B to oblige him to sell property to C. B sells the property to C. in the absence of A or of his representative. The sale is considered to be valid and the constraint ineffective.

- 1006. Contracts of sale, purchase, hire, gift, transfer of real property, settlement in regard to property, admission, release, postponement of debt and renunciation of a right of pre-emption, if entered into as a result of effective constraint, are invalid, whether caused by major constraint or minor constraint. If the person subject to constraint ratifies the contract after the cessation of the constraint, such contract is valid.

- 1007. Major constraint applies not only to cases of formal dispositions of property as referred to above, but also to dispositions of property by conduct. Minor constraint, however, only applies to formal dispositions of property and not to dispositions of property by conduct. Consequently, if a person tells another to destroy the property of a certain person or he will murder him, or destroy one of his limbs, and the person who is subject of such constraint does destroy the property, the constraint is effective and the person responsible for the constraint alone may be called upon to make good the loss. But if a person tells another to destroy property of a certain person, or he will strike him or imprison him and he does destroy such property, the constraint is not effective, and the person destroying such property alone may be called upon to make good the loss.

CHAPTER III. PRE-EMPTION.

SECTION 1. DEGREES OF PRE-EMPTION.

- 1008. There are three causes of pre-emption.

  (1). Where a person is the joint owner of the property sold itself. As where two persons jointly own an undivided share of real property.

  (2). Where a person is part of a servitude in the thing sold. As where a person shares is a private right of taking water or in a private road. (see 3rd at the end of Examples)

Examples:-

(1) One of several gardens each having shares in a private right of taking water is sold. Each of the owners of the other gardens obtains a right of pre-emption, whether they are adjoining neighbours or not.

(2) A house opening on to a private road is sold. Each of the owners of the other houses giving on to the private road obtains a right of pre-emption, whether they are adjoining neighbours or not.

But if a house taking water from a river which is open to the use of the public or the doors of which give on to a public road is sold, the owners of the other houses taking water from such river, or which give on to the public road, do not possess any right of pre-emption.

(3) Where a person is adjoining neighbour to the thing sold.

- 1009. The right of pre-emption belongs:
First, to the person who is a joint owner of the thing sold.
Second, to the person who is a joint owner of the servitude over the thing sold.
Third, to the adjoining neighbour.

If the first person claims his right of pre-emption, the others lose theirs. If the second person claims his right of pre-emption, the third person loses his.

- 1010. If a person is not a joint owner of the thing sold, or if, being a joint owner, he has renounced his right of pre-emption, and there is a person who has a share in a servitude in the thing sold, such person possesses a right of pre-emption. Should there be no person having a servitude in the thing sold, or, should there be one, and such person renounces his right thereto, the right of pre-emption accrues to the adjoining neighbour.

q Example:- A sells real property which he owns in absolute ownership to the exclusion of any other person, or A, being a joint owner of real property, sells his undivided jointly owned share therein and his partner relinquishes his right of pre-emption to such real property, and there is a person enjoying a private right of taking water who is part owner is a servitude over a private road. The right of pre-emption belongs to such person. Should there be no such person, or, in the event of there being such a person, that person relinquishes his right thereto, the right of pre-emption accrues to the adjoining neighbour.

- 1011. Where the upper portion, that is, the top storey belongs to one person and the lower portion, that is the lower storey of a building belongs to another, such persons are considered to be adjoining neighbours.

- 1012. Where a person is joint owner of the wall of a house, he is considered to be joint owner of such house. And if, while not being joint owner of the wall, the beams of his own house rest upon his neighbour's wall, he is considered to be an adjoining neighbour. The mere fact, however, that such person enjoys the right of putting the ends of his beams upon such wall does not entitle him to be considered as a joint owner or as a person sharing in a servitude over such property.

- 1013. Should there be several persons enjoying a right of pre- emption, they are dealt with according to their numbers and not according to the number of parts, that is shares, which they hold.

Example:- A holds a half share in a house, and B and C hold a third and sixth share respectively.

In the event of the owner of the half share selling such share to another person, and of B and C claiming the right of pre-emption, the half share is divided between them equally. B, the owner of the share of one third, may not claim to have a larger share granted to him on the basis of his prior holding.

- 1014. Where two classes of persons having joint shares in a servitude come together, the particular take precedence over the general.

Example:-

(1). Where a person who is the owner of a garden owned in absolute ownership, situated on land enjoying the right of taking water from a creek opening from a small river to which a right of taking water is also attached sells such garden, those persons having a right of taking water from the creek have a prior right of pre-emption. But if a person who is owner of a garden owned in absolute ownership situated on land enjoying the right of taking water from such river,sells his garden, all persons enjoying the right of taking water, whether from the river, or from the creek, possess a right of pre-emption.

(2). A person who is the owner of a house held in absolute ownership the door of which opens on to a blind alley which branches off from another blind alley, sells such house. Those persons the of whose houses open on to the branch blind alley possess a right of pre-emption. But if the owner of a house the door of which opens on to the principal blind alley sells such house, all persons having a right of way, whether over the principal or branch blind alley, possess a right of pre-emption.

- 1015. If the owner of a garden possessing a private right of taking water sells such garden without the right of taking water, those persons who share in the right of taking water cannot claim a right of pre-emption. The same principle is applied in the case of a private road.

- 1016. A right of taking water is preferred to a right of way. Therefor, if upon the sale of a garden in respect of which one person is the joint owner of a private right of taking water and another of a private right of way attaching thereto, the owner of the right of taking water is preferred to the owner of the right of way.

SECTION II. CONDITIONS ATTACHING TO THE RIGHT OF PRE-EMPTION.

- 1017. The property to which the right of pre-emption attaches must be real property held in absolute ownership. Therefore, no right of pre-emption can attach to a ship or other movable property, nor to real property which has been dedicated to pious purposes, nor to state land.

- 1028. The property on account of which the right of pre-emption is claimed must also be held in absolute ownership. Consequently, upon the sale of real property held in absolute ownership, the trustee or tenant of adjacent real property which has been dedicated to pious purposes cannot claim a right of pre-emption.

- 1019. No right of pre-emption may be claimed in respect to trees and buildings held in absolute ownership and situated on land dedicated to pious purposes, or on state land, since these are regarded as movable property.

- 1020. In the event of a piece of land held in absolute ownership being sold together with the trees and buildings standing thereon, such trees and buildings, since they follow the land, are also subject to the right of pre-emption. But if such trees and buildings alone are sold, no right of pre-emption can be claimed.

- 1021. Pre-emption can only be established by a contract of sale.
- 1022. A gift subject to compensation is regarded as a sale. Consequently, if a person who is the owner of a house in absolute ownership bestows such house upon another by way of gift subject to compensation and gives delivery thereof, this adjoining neighbour has a right of pre-emption.
- 1023. No right of pre-emption attaches to real property given to others in absolute ownership without payment, as in cases of gift without right of compensation, inheritance, or bequest.
- 1024. The person claiming the right of pre-emption must not have agreed to the sale which has been concluded, either expressly or by implication.

Examples:-

(1). If A, upon hearing of the conclusion of the sale expresses his concurrence therein, he loses his right of pre-emption, and he may not thereafter claim any such right.

(2). If A, after having heard of the conclusion of the sale, seeks to buy or to hire the property to which the right of pre-emption attaches from the purchaser, he loses his right of pre-emption.

Similarly, no right of pre-emption can be claimed by a person who has sold real property as agent for some other person. (see Article 100).

- 1025. The price must consist of property the amount of which is clearly ascertained. Consequently, there is no right of pre-emption is respect of real property transferred in absolute ownership for a price which does not consist of property.

Examples:-

(1). A sells a house which he owns in absolute ownership for the rent accruing from the letting of a bath. No right of pre-emption can be claimed because in this case the price of the house in not clearly ascertained, but in rent which is in the nature of an interest.

(2). There is no right of pre-emption in respect to real property held in absolute ownership and which is given as a marriage portion.

- 1026. The vendor must have divested himself of his absolute ownership in the thing sold. Consequently, in the case of a voidable sale, so long as the vendor retains the right to demand the return of the thing sold, there is no right of pre-emption. In the case of sale subject to an option, however, there is a right of pre-emption if the person possessing the option is the purchaser only. If the vendor has a right of option, however, there is no right of pre-emption until the vendor has divested himself of his right of option. But the existence of an option for defect or for inspection is no bar to the assertion of a right of pre-emption.
- 1027. There is no right of pre-emption upon the division of real property.

Example:- If the joint owners of a house jointly owned divide such house among themselves, the adjoining neighbour has no right of pre- emption.

SECTION III. THE CLAIM OF PRE-EMPTION.

- 1028. Three claims must be made in cases of pre-emption.

  (1). A claim made immediately upon hearing of the sale;

  (2). A claim made formally and in the presence of witnesses;

  (3). A claim that the person alleging the right of pre-emption is entitled to bring an action and to be granted absolute ownership of the property.

- 1029. The person claiming the right of pre-emption must at the moment he heard of the conclusion of the sale, make a statement showing that he claims the right of pre-emption, as by saying that he is the person who has the right of the property sold subject to pre-emption, or that he claims the property by way of pre-emption. The claim is referred to as the claim made immediately upon hearing of the sale.

- 1030. After having made a claim immediately upon hearing of the sale, the person claiming the right of pre-emption must make a claim formally and in the presence of witnesses.

  Thus, such person must say in the presence of two witnesses, and by the side of the property sold, that such and such a person has bought the real property in question, or, being by the side of the purchaser, must say that such person has bought such and such a piece of real property or, if the property sold is still in the possession of the vendor, must say by the side of the vendor that the latter has sold the real property in question to such and such a person, but that he has a right of pre-emption thereto, and that he calls such person to witness that he has made a further claim at that moment.

  If the person claiming the right of pre-emption is in some distant place and is not in a position personally to make a claim formally and in the presence of witnesses, he may appoint a person as his agent to do so. If he is unable to find an agent, he may send a letter.

- 1031. After having made a claim formally and in the presence of witnesses, the person claiming the right of pre-emption must make a claim before the court and bring a action. This is called a claim to bring an action and to be granted absolute ownership of the property.

- 1032. If the person claiming the right of pre-emption delays in making his claim immediately upon hearing of the sale, he loses his right of pre-emption at the moment he hears of the sale, but behaves in a manner tending to show that he does not intend to pursue his claim such as dealing with some other matter, or engaging in conversation regarding a different subject, or if he goes away without making any claim to pre-emption whatsoever, such person loses his right of pre-emption.

- 1033. If the person claiming the right of pre-emption delays in making his claim formally and in the presence of witnesses for any time longer that is necessary for him to act, even though it be by letter, such person loses his right of pre-emption.

- 1034. If the person claiming the right of pre-emption delays without any legal excuse, as where he is in some other country, for more than one month in making a claim formally and in the presence of witnesses, such person loses his right of pre-emption.

- 1035. The tutor of an interdicted person may claim the right of pre-emption of behalf of such person. If a tutor fails to claim a right of pre-emption on behalf of a minor, such minor is not entitled to claim by way of pre-emption after he has reached the age of puberty.

SECTION IV. THE EFFECT OF PRE-EMPTION.

- 1036. The person who is entitled to a right of pre-emption becomes owner of the property to which such right attaches, either by the purchaser handing over such property as the result of mutual agreement, or by virtue of a judgement issued by the court.

- 1037. The act of taking over property held in absolute ownership, by way of pre-emption, is equivalent to buying such property in the first instance.

  Consequently, rights which are valid in the case of original purchase, such as the option of inspection and the option for defect, are also valid in the case of pre-emption.

- 1038. If the person claiming the right of pre-emption dies after having made both the immediate and formal claims, but without becoming the owner of the property to which the right of pre-emption attaches owing to such property having been handed over by the purchaser either by way of mutual agreement or as the result of a judgement of the court, the right of pre-emption is not transferred to his heirs.

- 1039. If the person claiming the right of pre-emption sells the property by virtue of which he holds a right of pre-emption after having made the two claims a set out above, but without having become owner of the property to which the right of pre-emption attaches, such person loses his right of pre-emption.

- 1040. If a piece of real property held in absolute ownership adjoining property subject to the right of pre-emption is sold before the person claiming the right of pre-emption attaches as set out above, such person person cannot claim a right of pre-emption in the second piece of real property.

- 1041. Pre-emption does not admit of division. Consequently, the person claiming the right of pre-emption has no right to reject a portion of the property to which the right of pre-emption attaches and take the rest.

- 1042. None of the holders of a right of pre-emption may bestow their right upon other holders by way of gift. If they do so, their right of pre-emption is lost.

- 1042. If any holder of a right of pre-emption relinquishes such right prior to the judgement of the court, any other person possessing a right of pre-emption may take the whole of the real property to which the right of pre-emption attaches. If any holder of a right of pre-emption relinquishes his right of pre-emption after judgement by the court, such person's right does not accrue to any other person holding a right of pre-emption.

- 1044. If the purchaser adds something to the building to which the right of pre-emption attaches, such as paint, the person possessing the right of pre- emption has the option either of leaving such building or of taking it and paying the price of such addition, together with the price of the building. If the purchaser has erected buildings upon the real property to which the right of pre-emption attaches, or has planted trees thereon, the holder of the right of pre-emption has an option of leaving such real property, or of taking it and paying the price thereof together with the value of such buildings and trees. If he does not do so, he cannot force the purchaser to pull down the buildings and uproot the trees.

PROMULGATED BY ROYAL IRADAH, 16TH REBI UL AKHIR, 1290.

AL-MAJALLA AL AHKAM AL ADALIYYAH
(The Ottoman Courts Manual (Hanafi))

BOOK X. JOINT OWNERSHIP.

INTRODUCTION

TERMS OF ISLAMIC JURISPRUDENCE.

- 1045. Joint ownership consists of a thing itself belonging absolutely to more than one person, so that such persons enjoys a special position in relation to such thing. It is also customary to apply this expression to the contract whereby the state of joint ownership is brought about, and it is used in this sense in technical legal phraseology. Consequently, joint ownership is generally divided into two classes. The first consists of joint ownership of property held in absolute ownership brought about by one of the modes of acquiring property,such as purchase, or the acceptance of a gift. The second consists of joint ownership as a result of contract brought about by the offer and acceptance of the joint owners, the details concerning both of which are dealt with in the relevant Chapters. Another class consists of gratuitous joint ownership which is brought about by the joint acquisition of ownership by the public of things which are free and themselves belong absolutely to no particular person, such as water.

- 1046. Partition means to split up. The description and definition thereof will be given in the relevant Chapter.

- 1047. By wall is meant any wall, or partition made of boards or a fence of brushwood.

- 1048. By passers-by is meant generally those who pass along and across the public highway.

- 1049. By water channels is meant pipes and underground channels for conducting water.

- 1050. By dam is meant any boundary or water dam and the sides of any water channel.

- 1051. By vivification is meant cultivation whereby land is made fit for agriculture.

- 1052. By fencing is meant putting stones and other matter round land in order that other persons may not take possession thereof.

- 1053. By expenditure is meant disbursing property.

- 1054. Maintenance consists of the expenditure of money, goods and provisions for upkeep and sustenance.

- 1055. By accepting responsibility is meant undertaking to do and carry out any particular piece of work.

- 1056. Partners with equal shares are those who form a partnership with equal shares.

- 1057. By capital is meant money invested in anything.

- 1058. profit consists of interest and benefit.

- 1059. Where one person supplies capital to another on condition that the whole of the profit is to belong to him, the capital is called the invested capital: The person supplying such capital is called the investor and the person taking such capital is called the person employing capital.

CHAPTER I. JOINT OWNERSHIP OF PROPERTY OWNED IN ABSOLUTE OWNERSHIP.

SECTION I. DESCRIPTION AND CLASSIFICATION OF JOINT OWNERSHIP OF PROPERTY OWNED IN ABSOLUTE OWNERSHIP.

- 1060. Joint ownership of property owned in absolute ownership is brought about when more than one person join in the ownership on any particular thing, that is to say, where such thing belongs to them, as where ownership therein is acquired by any of the causes of acquiring ownership such as purchase, or taking by way of gift, or by acceptance of a bequest, or inheritance or by mixing or causing to mix one property with another, that is to say, by uniting them in such a way that they cannot be distinguished or separated the one from the other. Examples:-

(1). Two persons buy a piece of property, or a person bestows property upon them by way of gift or by bequest and they accept the same: or two persons take a piece of property by way of inheritance. such property is jointly owned by them and they become joint owner in that property, and each one participates therein with the other.

(2). Two persons mix their corn together, or their corn becomes mixed together; by reason of there being holes in the sacks. The corn mixed together in this way becomes joint property.

- 1061. If a gold coin belonging to one particular person is mixed with two other gold coins of the same type belonging to some other person in such a way that it cannot be distinguished from them, and two of them are lost, the remaining gold coin becomes the joint property of the two persons, in the proportion of one third and two thirds, the two thirds belonging to the owner of the two gold coins, the one third belonging to the owner of the one coin.

- 1062. Joint ownership of property owned in absolute ownership is divided into voluntary and obligatory joint ownership.

- 1063. Voluntary joint ownership is joint ownership brought about by the acts of the joint owners themselves, as where it arises through purchase, or acceptance of a gift, or by accepting a bequest, or mixing property together as referred to above.

- 1064. Obligatory joint ownership is joint ownership brought about be some cause other than the acts of the joint owners, as where it arises through inheritance or through two properties being mixed together.

- 1065. The joint responsibility of various persons to whom a thing has been entrusted for safe keeping is in the nature of voluntary joint ownership. But if a gust of wind carries away a person's garment, and it falls in a house which is jointly owned, the joint responsibility of the owners of the house for the preservation of the garment is in the nature of obligatory joint ownership.

- 1066. Joint ownership of property owned in absolute ownership is also divided into joint ownership of specific property and joint ownership of debt.

- 1067. Joint ownership of specific property consists of joint ownership of some specific property which is in existence, as where two persons have undivided joint ownership of a sheep or of a flock of sheep.

- 1068. Joint ownership of debt consists of joint ownership of something to be received, as where two persons ore joint owners of a certain sum of money owing to them by some other person.

SECTION II. THE MANNER OF DEALING WITH SPECIFIC PROPERTY JOINTLY OWNED.

- 1069. The joint owners of property held in absolute ownership may by agreement deal with their property in any way they wish, in the same way as a single owner of such property.

- 1070. The joint owners of a house may dwell together in such house. If one of them, however, wishes to introduce a stranger into the house, the other can prevent him from doing so.

- 1071. One of the joint owners of property held in absolute ownership may deal with such property alone, with the permission of the other. He may not, however, deal with it in such way as to cause injury to the other joint owner.

- 1072. Neither of the joint owners may force the other to sell or purchase his share. If the property held in absolute ownership jointly by them is capable of division, and the joint owner is not absent, such property may be divided. If it is not capable of division they may share the usufruct thereof. Details are given in Chapter II.

- 1073. The produce of property jointly owned in absolute ownership may be divided among the owners in accordance with their shares. Consequently, any stipulation that the milk of an animal which is jointly owned, or the young thereof shall go to one of the joint owners in excess of his share is invalid.

- 1074. The property in the young of animals follow the mother.

Examples:-

(1) A stallion belonging to A covers a mare belonging to B. The foal belongs to the owner of the mare.

(2). A owns male and B female pigeons. The young belongs to the owner of the female pigeons.

- 1075. The joint owners of property held in absolute ownership are strangers to one another as regards their shares. Neither; is the agent of the other. Consequently, neither joint owner may deal with the share of the other without the latter's permission. But in the case of dwelling in a house which is jointly owned and as regards matters pertaining thereto, such as coming in and going out, each of the joint owners is considered to be an absolute owner of such property.

Examples:-

(1). One of the owners of a jointly owned horse lends or gives such horse on hire without the permission of the other, and it is destroyed while in the possession of the borrower or of the person taking it on hire. The second joint owner may claim to have the loss of his share made good by the first.

(2). One joint owner rides a jointly owned horse, or places a load upon him without the permission of the other, the horse is destroyed while being ridden or driven. The second joint owner may claim to have the loss of his share made good by the first.

(3). One joint owner uses a horse for a certain period so that it becomes weak and its value decreases. The other joint owner may claim to have the decrease in value which is represented by his share made good.

(4). One of two joint owners of a house lives in such house for a certain period without obtaining the permission of the other. He is considered to be living in his own property held in absolute ownership, and he cannot be called upon by the other joint owner to pay rent corresponding to his share. If the house is burnt down by accident, he is likewise under no obligation to make good any loss.

- 1076. If one of the two joint owners of land cultivates such land, the other may not claim a share of the produce thereof in accordance with local custom, such as a third or a fourth. If the value of the land is decreased by reason of the cultivation, however, he may claim to have the amount of the decrease in value of his share made good by the joint owner cultivating the land.

- 1077. If one of two joint owners of lets such property on hire and receives the rent thereof, he is obliged to pay the other his share thereof.

- 1078. If one of the joint owners of property owned in absolute ownership is absent, the one who is present may take the usufruct of such property to the extent of his share thereof, provided the consent of other is given by implication, as is set forth in the following Articles.

- 1079. The absent joint owner is considered to have given his consent by implication to enjoyment of the usufruct by the joint-owner who is present, if the latter causes no harm in so doing to the jointly owned property held in absolute ownership.

- 1080. There can be no consent by implication to the enjoyment of the usufruct of jointly owned property held in absolute ownership where such property is changed by use by the particular person using it. Consequently, one of two joint owners of a piece of clothing cannot wear such clothing in the absence of the other. Again, one of two joint owners may not ride a jointly owned horse in the absence of the other. He may do so, however, up to the extent of his share in cases where there is no change by use of the particular person using it, such as carrying burdens, or ploughing land. again, where one of two joint owners is absent, the other may, every other day, enjoy the services of a servant who has been taken into their joint service.

- 1081. Habitation of a house is not changed by a change of persons dwelling therein. Consequently, if one of two joint owners of a house held in common in equal shares is absent, the other may use such house for a period of six months and leave it for six months. If members of such person's household are numerous, however, their dwelling in the house is of such a nature as to change it by reason thereof, and the absent joint owner cannot be held to have assented thereto by implication.

- 1082. In the event of the shares of a house jointly owned by two persons, one of whom is absent, being separated the one from the other, the joint owner who is absent. If there is danger of the house falling into disrepair, however, by reason of it being left vacant, the Court may let such separate part on hire and keep the rent of behalf of the absent joint owner.

- 1083. Partition of usufruct can only be had and is only valid after being settled by an action at law. Consequently, if one of the owners of a joint owned house lives alone in such house for a certain period without paying any rent is respect to the share of the other, the latter cannot claim rent in respect to his share for that period, or claim that he will dwell in it for a corresponding period. He may however, divide such house if it is capable of partition, or he may cause the usufruct thereof to be divided so that it may be valid thereafter. But if one of the joint owners is absent, and the other, as stated in the preceding Article, dwells therein for a certain period, and the absent joint owner returns, he may dwell in such house for a corresponding period.

- 1084. One of the owners of a jointly owned house who is present may validly let such house on hire, taking his own share of the rent and keeping the share of the absent joint owner. On the return of the latter, he may obtain his share from the former.

- 1085. Should one of the joint owners of land be absent, and it is known that cultivation will be beneficial to such land and will not result in any decrease in the value thereof, the joint owner who is present may cultivate the whole of such land. If the absent joint owner returns he may cultivate the land for a corresponding period. If it is known that cultivation of the land will result in a diminution of the value thereof and that leaving the land fallow will be beneficial thereto and will result in the increased fertility thereof, the absent joint owner cannot be held to have agreed by implication to the cultivation of such land. Consequently, a joint owner who is present may only cultivate the amount of his own share of such land. For example, if such land is jointly owned in equal shares, he may cultivate a half thereof. Should he cultivate the land again in the following year, he may only cultivate his own half. He may not cultivate one half in one year and the other half in the following year. If he cultivates the whole of such land and the absent joint owner returns, he may make good to him the decrease in value of his share of his land.

The details as set out above apply, if the joint owner who is present does not make any application to the Court. Should he apply to the Court, However, the Court shall give permission for him to cultivate the whole of such land in order that the tithe and land tax shall not be lost. In such a case, should the absent joint owner return, he may not bring an action on account of any decrease in the value of the land.

- 1086. If one of the joint owners of an orchard is absent, the owner who is present stands in the place of the absent joint owner, and when the fruit ripens may take and consume his own share. He may also sell the share of the absent joint owner and set aside the price thereof. The absent joint owner, on return, has the option of either ratifying the sale and taking the price set aside, or of rejecting the sale and claiming to be given the value of his share.

- 1087. The share of one of the joint owners is considered to be deposited for safe keeping with the other. Consequently, if one of them, on his own initiative, deposits the jointly owned property with some other person for safe keeping and such property is destroyed, he must make good the loss of the share of the other joint owner. (See Article 790.)

- 1088. One of the joint owners may, if he wishes, sell his share to the other joint owner, or he may also sell it to some other person without the permission of the joint owner. (See Article 215.) In the case of mixed property, however, as mentioned in section I, no person may sell his share of mixed property to another unless he has obtained the permission of the joint owner.

- 1089. If some of a number of heirs to land which has devolved upon them by way of inheritance sow seed therein which is their joint property with the permission of the other heirs, or if such other heirs are minors, with the permission of their guardians, the whole of the resulting produce is jointly owned by all of them. If one of them sows his own seed, the resulting produce is his own.

He must, however, make good any loss accruing to the share of the other heirs by reason of any decrease in the value of the land caused by the cultivation thereof. (See Article 907.).

- 1090. If one of a number of heirs, without the permission of the others, takes and uses a quantity of money belonging to the estate prior to the division thereof, he must bear any loss occasioned thereby, but is entitled to keep the profits obtained by such transaction.

SECTION III. JOINTLY OWNED DEBTS.

- 1091. If two or more persons are owed a sum of money by some other person and that debt arises from single cause, debt is a debt jointly owned by the two creditors. If the debt does not arise from a single cause, it is not a joint debt. These matters will be dealt with in the following Articles.

- 1092. Any Specific property left by a deceased person is jointly owned by his heirs in proportion to their shares. In the same way, sums owing to him by any other person are jointly owned by the heirs in proportion to their shares.

- 1093. A debt owed by a person and arising by reason of such person having to make good loss caused by the destruction by him of property jointly owned, is jointly owned by the owners of such property.

- 1094. If two persons who jointly own a certain sum of money lend such money to some other; person, the debt is jointly owned by such two persons. If two persons lend money separately to some other person, each one becomes a separate creditor, and the debts are not jointly owned by the two persons.

- 1095. if property jointly owned is sold en bloc, and the share of none of the joint owners is mentioned at the time of the sale, the sum of money to be paid by the purchaser becomes a debt jointly owned. If the amount of the share of the price of the thing sold of each one of them is mentioned at the time of the sale, or the nature thereof, as for example, where it is stated that the share of one of them consists of so much money and the share of the other of so much, or where the share of one is said to consist of sound coin and the share of the other of base coin, whereby their shares are defined, the vendors do not jointly own the price of the thing sold, but each becomes a separate creditor. Similarly, if one on them sells his undivided share to some other person, and the other also sell his undivided share to that person separately, such persons do not jointly own the price of the thing sold, but each of them becomes a separate creditor.

- 1096. If two persons each sell their property en bloc to some other person, as, for example, when one sells a horse and the other a mare at one and the same time, for a certain sum of money, the amount in question becomes a debt jointly owned by the vendors. If each one of them names the price of his own animal as being so much, they each becomes separate creditors, and the total value of their animals does not become a debt jointly owned. Again, if two persons each separately sell property to some other person, the total value of the things sold does not become jointly owned, but each one becomes a separate creditor.

- 1097. If two persons in their capacity as guarantors pay the debt of some other person from property which they jointly own, the amount which they are entitled to recover from the principal debtor is a debt jointly owned.

- 1098. If a person gives an order to two other persons to pay a debt amounting to certain some and the latter pay such debt from property which they jointly own, the sum which they are entitled to receive from such person is a debt jointly owned. If the money they have paid is not jointly owned by them, and the share of each of them is in fact clearly distinguished, the mere fact that they have paid at one and the same time does not make the amount they are entitled to claim from such person a debt jointly owned.

- 1099. If the debt is not jointly owned, each of the creditors may demand payment separately from the debtor of the sum he is entitled to receive and whatever sum either of them receives, is credited to such person's account. The other creditor is not entitled to share therein.

- 1100. If the debt is a joint one, each of the creditors may demand and receive payment of his own share from the debtor separately. If one of the creditors applies to the Court in the absence of the other and asks for payment of his share from the debtor, the Court shall make an order to this effect.

- 1101. Whatever sum is received by one of the creditors is respect to a joint debt is jointly owned by him and the other creditors who receives such sum may not deduct it from his own share alone.

- 1102. If one of the creditors receives his share of a joint debt and disposes of it, the other joint creditor may claim to have the loss he has suffered made good.

    Example:- One of two persons who are joint creditors in equal share for a sum of one thousand piastres receives his share of five hundred piastres from the debtor and disposes of it. The other joint creditor may claim from him the sum of two hundred and fifty piastres for the loss he has suffered. The five hundred piastres still remaining due continues to be owned by the two creditors.

- 1103. If one of the joint creditors while receiving nothing in respect to the joint debt buys goods from the debtor against his share, the other does not becomes a joint owner of the goods. He may,however, claim to have his share made good by the other creditor out of the price of the goods. if they come to an agreement as to their shares, the goods are held jointly between them.

- 1104. If one of the joint creditors comes to a settlement with the debtor as to his share in the joint debt, as for example, where he agrees to accept from the debtor a certain quantity of cloth and does in fact do so, he may either to the other joint creditor an amount of cloth corresponding to the latter's share, out of the cloth he has received, or he may deliver him a sum of money corresponding to the amount of the share of the joint debt which he has forgone.

- 1105. If one of the creditors, as mentioned above, receives a part of the whole of a joint debt, or if he buys property to the value of his share, or if he comes to a settlement with the debtor as to certain property against his claim, the other creditor in any case has the option of either adopting the transaction of the other joint creditor, when, as is set forth in the preceding Articles, He has the right of receiving his share from, or of refusing to adopt the transaction and claiming his share from the debtor. If he fails to obtain anything from the debtor, he has a right of recourse against the creditor who has obtained his share, and the fact that he has not previously adopted the transaction is no bar to his right of recourse.

- 1106. If one of the creditors receives his share of the joint debt from the debtor, and it is accidentally destroyed while in his possession, he is not liable to make good the loss to the other joint creditor in respect to the amount represented by such joint creditor's share therein. The amount remaining to be paid by the debtor belongs to the joint creditor.

- 1107. If one of the creditors employs the debtor for a wage to be reckoned against his share of the joint debt, the other joint creditor may call upon the former to make good to him the amount represented by his share therein.

- 1108. If one of the joint creditors receives a pledge from the debtor in respect to his own share, and the pledge is destroyed while in his possession, the other joint creditor may call upon the former to make good to him the amount represented by his share therein.

  Example:- The amount of the joint debt held in equal shares is one thousand piastres. One of the creditors receives a pledge in respect to his share of five hundred piastres. The pledge is destroyed while in his possession. The other creditor may call upon the former to make good to him a sum of two hundred and fifty piastres, since half the joint debt has been lost.

- 1109. If one of the creditors obtains a guarantor from the debtor in respect to his share to some other person, any sum obtained by such creditor from the guarantor or the person to whom the transfer has been made is shared by the other creditor.

- 1110. If one of the debtors makes a gift of his share in the joint debt to the debtor or releases him therefrom, such gift or release is valid. He is not liable on that account to the other creditor in respect to his share.

- 1111. If one of the joint creditors is respect to a joint debt is responsible for the destruction of the property of the debtor, and the sum represented thereby is set off against the debt, the other joint creditor has the right of receiving his share from him in respect thereto. But if one of the joint creditors was in the debt of the debtor in respect to a debt which came into existence prior to the joint debt in respect to which he has a claim, the two claims are set off one against the other and the other joint creditor cannot claim from him anything in respect thereto.

- 1112. Neither of the joint creditors may extend the due date of postpone the joint debt without the permission of the other.

SUPPLEMENT.

- 1113. If any person sells any property to two other persons, he may claim his share from each one of them separately. He may not claim the amount owing by one of them from the other, unless they are guarantors of each other.

CHAPTER II. PARTITION.

SECTION I. NATURE AND CATEGORIES OF PARTITION.

- 1114. Partition consists of defining an undivided share. That is to say, to distinguish and separate shares from each other by means of some standard, such as a measure of capacity, or of weight, or of length.

- 1115. Partition is effected in two ways. The first consists of specific objects owned jointly, that is, numerous and jointly owned things being separated into parts, the divided shares belonging to each individual being united in one part. This is called partition by units, as where thirty sheep which are jointly owned between three persons are divided up into tens.

  The second consists of dividing a specific thing owned jointly and of allotting a part in respect to the undivided shares relating to each portion. This is known as partition by allotment, or individual partition, as where a piece of land is divided into two parts.

- 1116. Partition consists on the one hand of separation and on the other of exchange. Examples:-

  (1). The two persons own a kile of corn jointly in equal shares. Each has a half share in each grain. When it is divided into two parts, the division is by partition by units, one part being given to one and the other part to the other joint owner. Each one is then considered to have separated his half share and to have exchanged his own half with the half share of the other.

  (2).Two persons are joint owners of a piece of land which they hold in equal shares in respect to every part. The land is divided into two by partition by allotment, and a part is given to each one of them. Each one is considered to have separated his own half share and to have exchanged it with the half share of the other joint owner.

- 1117. Separation is preferred in the case of things the like of which can be found in the market. Consequently, each joint owner of jointly owned things the like of which can be found in the market may take his own share in the absence of the other and without his permission. The division, however, is not complete until the share of the absent joint owner has been handed over to him. If the share of the absent joint owner is destroyed before being handed over, the share which has been received by the other joint owner is jointly owned between them.

- 1118. In the case of things the like of which cannot be found in the market, exchange is preferred. Exchange may take place by agreement of the parties or may be made as the result of a judgement by the Court. Consequently, one of the joint owners may not take his share of any specific object the like of which cannot be found in the market, in the absence of the other and without his permission.

- 1119. Things estimated by measure of capacity, things estimated by weight and things measured by enumeration and which closely resemble one another, such as walnuts and eggs, are all things the like of which can be found in the market. But things estimated by weight and which change in accordance with the difference of craftsmanship, such as hand-made pottery, are things the like of which cannot by found in the market. Things which are similar to each other, though of a different nature, and which are mixed together in such a way that they cannot be distinguished and separated from each other, such as barley and corn, are things the like of which cannot be found in the market.

  Things measured by length are also things the like of which cannot be found in the market. But things measured by length and sold at so much per yard, there being no difference between the undivided units thereof, such as cloth of a particular type, and linen goods produced by a process of manufacture, are things the like of which can be found in the market.

  Things measured by enumeration and which are dissimilar from each other and is respect to which there is a difference in value as regards the undivided units thereof, such as animals, melons and water melons, are things the like of which cannot be found in the market.

  Books written by hand are things the like of which cannot be found in the market. Printed books are things the like of which can be found in the market.

- 1120. Partition by units and partition be allotment are each divided into two categories. The first is partition by consent. The second is partition by order of the Court.

- 1121. Partition by consent consists of a partition made by agreement of the two joint owners of property held in absolute ownership, whereby they mutually agree to a division between them, or whereby the Court makes a division with the assent of all parties.

- 1122. Partition by order of the Court consists of a partition which is obligatory and has the force of law, and which is made upon the application of certain of the owners of the jointly owned property.

SECTION II. CONDITIONS ATTACHING TO PARTITION.

- 1123. The thing divided must be some specific object. Consequently, any partition of a debt jointly owned prior to being received is invalid.

Example:- A deceased person has various sums of money owing to him. The allocation of so much money owing to him by A to one of his heirs and so much owing to him by B to another of his heirs is invalid. Should one of the heirs obtain any sum of money in this way, the other heirs become joint owners therein. (See Chapter i, Section iv).

- 1124. NO partition is valid until the shares have been identified and separated.

Example:- One of the joint owners of a heap of corn requests the other joint owner to take one half of the heap, adding that he will take the other. The partition is invalid.

- 1125. The thing divided must be the property of the joint owners held in absolute ownership at the time of partition. Consequently, if some person appears who is entitled to the whole of the property after the partition has been made, such partition becomes null and void. Similarly, if someone appears who is entitled to an undivided share therein such as a half or a third, the partition is invalid and the property must be divided again. Again, if someone appears who is invalid, and the remainder is jointly owned by the other persons holding shares in the property. If someone appears who is entitled to some specific part of a share only, or an undivided part, the owner of such undivided share has the option of either cancelling the partition, or of agreeing thereto, and of exercising a right of recourse against the other joint owner in respect to the amount short.

Example:- A piece of land measuring one hundred and sixty ARSHUNS is divided into two equal shares. Someone appears who is entitled to a half of one share. The owner of such share may, at his option, cancel the partition, or may exercise a right of recourse against the other; joint owner to the extent of a quarter of his share, that is to say, he may take from his share a portion measuring twenty ARSHUNS. If someone appears who is entitled to a specific part of each share, the partition cannot be cancelled if it has been made in equal shares. If one has received less and the other more, the greater amount only is held to be valid, the matter being regarded as though only one person had appeared entitled to a fixed portion of one share. The person to whose share the greater amount is attributed as stated above has the option either of cancelling the partition, or of having recourse against the other joint owner in respect to the amount which he has lost.

- 1126. Partition by an unauthorised person is subject to ratification, which may be oral, or in writing, or by conduct.

Example:- A divides jointly owned property on his own initiative. The partition is neither permissible nor executory. But if the owners ratify by signifying their assent, or if they deal with their separate shares by way of absolute ownership, that is to say, if they perform any act indicative of a right of ownership, such as sale or hire, the partition is valid and executory.

- 1127. The partition must be equitable. That is to say, it must be made in accordance with the shares due to each joint owner, and no one may in any way be deprived of the full amount to which he is entitled. Consequently, an action for flagrant misrepresentation will lie in a case of partition. If the person in whose favour the partition has been made, however, admits that he has received what he is entitled to, his admission is a bar to an action for flagrant misrepresentation.

- 1128. In the partition by consent, the consent of each of the persons sharing in the partition must be given. Consequently, if one of them is absent, partition be consent is invalid. If one of them is a minor, the tutor or guardian stands in his place. In the absence of tutor or guardian, the partition is subject to the order of the Court, which will appoint a guardian through whom the partition will be carried out.

- 1129. Partition made by order of the Court is subject to a request being made to that effect. Any compulsory partition made by the Court in the absence of any request made by one of the parties is invalid.

- 1130. If some of the joint owners apply for partition and others oppose such application, the Court shall make a compulsory partition if the property jointly owned is capable of partition, as is set forth in Section 3 and Section 4. Otherwise no partition shall be made.

- 1131. Capable of partition refers to jointly owned property which is fit for partition. Thus, the benefit to be derived from such property must not be lost by the partition.

SECTION III. PARTITION BY UNITS.

- 1132. Specific objects which are jointly owned and which are of one type, are subject to partition by order of the court. That is to say, the Court will order the partition of such property upon the application of some only of the joint owners, whether the property in question consists of things the like of which can be found in the market or not.

- 1133. In the case of partition of things the like of which can be found in the market, and which are of one type, each of the joint owners receives what he is entitled to and becomes absolute owner thereof, since there is no defers between the various undivided units thereof, and partition cannot injure any one of the joint owners. Thus, upon the partition of a quantity of corn jointly owned by two persons, in accordance with their shares, each of them receives what he is entitled to, and becomes the independent owner of the corn falling to his share. The same applies in the case of a number of dirhems of bar gold, or of a number of okes of bar silver, or of bar copper or iron, or of a number of pieces of woollen cloth of one type or of a number of pieces of linen or a quantity of eggs.

- 1134. If a difference exists between things the like of which cannot be found in the market, and which are of one type, but such difference is so small that it may be said not to exist at all, such things are considered to be capable of partition as referred to above.

Example:- Five hundred sheep owned jointly by two persons are divided between them in accordance with their shares. Each one is considered to have received the identical things to which he is entitled. The same thing applies in the case of so many hundreds of camels and so many hundreds of cows.

- 1135. Specific objects which are jointly owned and which are of different types, are not subject to partition by the Court, Whether consisting of things the like of which can be found in the market or not. That is to to say, the Court will not give an order for their compulsory division by units upon the application of one of the joint owners only.

Example:- An order of the Court for the partition of property whereby one of the joint owner receives so many kiles of corn, and another so many kiles of barley, as being equivalent thereto; to one so many sheep, to another so many camels or cows, as being equivalent thereto; to one a sword, to the other a set of saddlery; to one a country house, to the other a shop or a farm,is invalid. But if the joint owners agree thereto, a partition by order of the Court, as mentioned above, is valid.

- 1136. Pots which differ in accordance with the craftsmanship are considered to be different types, even though made from metal of one type.

- 1137. Ornaments, large pearls and jewellery are also specific objects of different types. But small jewels not differing from each other in value, such as tiny pearls and small diamonds known as counting stones, are considered to be of the same type.

- 1138. A number of country houses, shops and farms, are also of different types and cannot be divided by partition by units.

Example:- One of a number of country houses may not be given to one joint owner and another to a second in pursuance of an order for partition given by the Court. Each of them may be divided by partition by allotment as set out below.

SECTION IV. PARTITION BY ALLOTMENT.

- 1139. Any specific piece of property which is jointly owned is capable of partition, provided such partition does not injure any of the owners thereof.

Examples:-

(1). A piece of land is divided and buildings erected on each portion, trees are planted and wells sunk. In this way, the benefit to be divided from the land is preserved.

(2). A country house is divided into men's and women's quarters, so that it becomes two separate houses. The benefit to be derived from the country house, which was to dwell therein, is not lost. Each of the joint owners becomes the independent owner of a separate house. Consequently, both in the case of the land and of the country house, a division by order of the Court is valid. That is to say, if one of the owners desires partition and the other does not, the Court may give an order for compulsory partition.

- 1140. Should the partition of some specific piece of property jointly owned be advantageous to one of the owners thereof, and disadvantageous to the other, that is to say, should the benefit to be derived therefrom be lost to him, and should the person deriving some advantage therefrom desire partition, the Court may give an order for partition.

Example:- A house is jointly owned and the share of one of the joint owners is so small that after partition he is unable to derive benefit therefrom by dwelling therein. The joint owner holding the greater share desires partition. The Court will give an order fro partition.

- 1141. Partition may not be ordered by the Court of some specific property which is jointly owned in cases where such partition would be injurious to each of the joint owners of such property.

Example:- If a mill is divided, it can no longer be used as a mill, and for this reason the benefit to be derived therefrom is lost. Consequently, the Court will not order partition of the mill upon the application of one of the joint owners only. It may, however, be divided by consent. Baths, wells, water pipes, a small room, a wall between two houses, are of the same type. Merchandise such as a horse and a carriage, a saddle, a cloak, the stone for a ring, which must be broken or split, are also of this nature. In no case may division be ordered by the Court.

- 1142. The partition of the pages of a book jointly owned is invalid: and the partition volume by volume of a book in several volumes is likewise invalid.

- 1143. If one of the joint owners of a road owned by two or more person to which no other person has the right of access desires partition, and the others object, it must first be ascertained as to whether, if partition is effected, each of the joint owners will have a road. If so, the road will be divided. If not, no order will be made for compulsory partition. Nevertheless, if each one has a separate road and entrance, partition may be made.

- 1144. A right of flow jointly owned is similar to a road jointly owned. If one of the owners desires partition and the other objects, and there is sufficient room for each one for the flow of water after partition, or there is some other place to which the water may flow, the partition may be made, but not otherwise.

- 1145. A person may sell a road which he owns in absolute ownership, subject to his retaining a right of way thereover, in the same way that upon the partition of a piece of real property jointly owned by two persons, the absolute ownership of a road jointly owned may be retained by one, and the other may be given a right of the way thereover only.

- 1146. Upon the partition of a house, a wall separating the two shares may remain in the joint ownership of the owners thereof, or such house may be divided in such manner that the wall becomes the property in absolute ownership of one of them only.

SECTION V. METHOD OF PARTITION.

- 1147. If property jointly owned is estimated by measure of capacity, it is divided by such measure; if it is estimated by weight, it is divided by weight; if it estimated by number, it is divided by number; if it is estimated by length, it is divided by length.

- 1148. Land being measured by length, is divided by length. But trees and buildings situated thereon are divided by estimating the value thereof.

- 1149. Should it be found upon the partition of a country house that the building represented by one share is more valuable that the building of the other, land in addition is taken from the site of the other share, if this course is possible, equivalent to the difference in value, and added thereto. If this is not possible, a proportionate amount of money is added.

- 1150. If two persons who are joint owners of a house desire partition thereof so that one receives the upper portion and the other the lower portion, both the upper and the lower portions are valued, and the partition is made on the basis of the value.

- 1151. If a country house is to be divided, the person carrying out the partition must first make a plan thereof on paper, must measure the land upon which it is built, value the buildings thereof, and make a settlement and adjustment in accordance with the shares of the owners thereof. If possible he must divide any right of way, or right of taking water, or right of flow, so that they are completely independent the one from the other. They must be called share number one, two and three respectively. Afterwards, lots must be drawn. The first name turned up gets the first share, the second name gets the second share, and the third name gets the third share. If there are more than three, the same procedure is followed.

- 1152. If taxes levied by the State are for the protection of the interests of the people, they must be levied in accordance with the amount of the population. Women and children are not included in the register. If they are levied for the protection of property, they are levied in accordance with the amount of such property, because, as is mentioned in Article 87, disadvantage is an obligation accompanying enjoyment.

SECTION VI. OPTIONS.

- 1153. An option conferred by contract, an option of inspection, and an option for defect are attached to the various types of partition, as in the case of sale.

Example:- Property jointly owned is divided by agreement between the owners thereof. One receives so many kiles of corn and the other so many kiles of barley, or one of them receives so many sheep and the other so many cows. If one of the joint owners has a contractual option, he may, during that period, either agree to the partition, or cancel it. If one of them has not yet seen the divided property, he similarly has an option upon seeing it. If the share of one of them proves to be defective he may either accept it or reject it.

- 1154. An option conferred by contract, an option of inspection, and an option for defect are also attached to things the like of which cannot be found in the market, upon the partition thereof.

Example:- Upon the partition of one hundred sheep among the owners thereof in proportion to their shares, one of the owners may, if he has stipulated therefor by contract, exercise an option of accepting or rejecting the partition within a period of so many days. If he has not yet seen the sheep, he similarly may exercise an option upon seeing them. If a defect of long standing is revealed in the sheep which fall to the share of one of them, he likewise has an option and may either accept them or reject them.

- 1155. Upon the division of things the like of which can be found in the market, and which are of the same type, no option is conferred by contract or upon inspection. An option, however, exists for defect.

Example:- A heap of corn belonging to two persons jointly is divided. An option conferred by contract to be exercised within a certain number of days is invalid. If one of them has not seen the corn, he cannot exercise an option upon seeing it. But if one of them is given the upper part and the other the lower, and the lower portion proves to be rotten, the owner has the option of rejecting or accepting it.

SECTION VII. CANCELLATION AND RESCISSION OF PARTITION.

- 1156. When the lots have all been drawn, the partition is complete.
- 1157. When the partition has been completed, there cannot be any withdrawal therefrom.

- 1158. If one of the joint owners wishes to withdraw while the partition is being carried out, as for example, where the majority of the lots have been drawn and there remains one only, the withdrawal is valid if the partition is one made by consent. It is invalid, however, if it is made by order of the Court.

- 1159. If the joint owners cancel and rescind the partition by agreement after such partition has been carried out, they may again become joint owners of the property as heretofore.

- 1160. If flagrant misrepresentation is apparent during the partition, the partition is cancelled, and an equitable partition is made afresh.

- 1161. If after the partition of an estate if proves that the deceased person was in debt, the partition is cancelled. Nevertheless, if the heirs pay debt, or if the creditors relinquish their claims, or if there is other property belonging to the deceased and the debt is satisfied therefrom, the partition is not cancelled.

SECTION VIII. eFFECT OF PARTITION.

- 1162. Each of the joint owners becomes the independent owner of his own share after partition. No one has any further interest in the share of the other. Each one of them may deal with his own share precisely as he wishes, as will be set forth in Chapter III. So that if a house jointly owned by two persons is divided, one of them obtaining the buildings and the other the vacant land, the owner of the land may dig well wells, or make a channel for water, or erect a building of any height he wishes, even to the extent of depriving the owner of the building of air or sun-light, and the latter is powerless to prevent the former from doing so.

- 1163. Upon the partition of land, trees are included therein without being mentioned. Upon a farm being partitioned, trees and buildings are also included without being mentioned. That is to say, the trees and buildings belong to the person to whose share they fall. There is no need for the inclusion of any particular statement or of any general expressions, such as that the partition includes all rights or all appurtenances.

- 1164. Upon the partition of either lands or farms, crops and fruits are not included therein unless specifically mentioned and they remains jointly owned as heretofore, and this, whether any general expression was used when the partition was carried out, such as that the partition includes all rights, or not.

- 1165. Any right of way or of flow over adjoining lands attaching to the partitioned property is in every case included in the partition. That is to say, the right is question belong to the person who obtains the share to which they are attached, and this, whether at the time the partition is carried out, the partition is stated to include all rights or not.

- 1166. If at the time the partition is carried out, it is stipulated that there shall be a right of way or right of flow over another share, the stipulation is valid.

- 1167. If the road belonging to one share exists in the other share, and no stipulation is made for the retention thereof at the time of the partition, and it is possible to place the road elsewhere, this shall be done, whether at the time of partition the partition was stated to include all rights or not. If the road cannot be placed elsewhere, however, and at the time of the partition, all rights were stated to be included, the road shall be included in the partition without any change. If so such expression of a general nature has been included, the partition shall be cancelled.

In this connection, the right of flow follows the same rule as the right of way.

- 1168. If a person has a right of way through a house jointly owned by two other persons, and the two joint owners desire to partition such house, the owner of the right of way cannot prevent them from so doing. The joint owners, however, upon carrying out the partition, must leave the road intact. If all three agree to sell the house together with the road and the road is jointly owned between the three, the price is divided between them. If the absolute ownership of the road belongs to the owners of the country house, and such person merely possesses a right of way, each one takes what he is entitled to receive. Thus, if the land is valued on one occasion with the right of way and on another without, the difference between the two belongs to the owner of the right of way. The balance belongs to the owners of the house.

  The same rule applies in the case of a right of flow. That is to say, if one person has a right of flow over the house of another which is jointly owned and the owners of the house desire the partition of such house, the right of flow remain undisturbed.

- 1169. If a person owns a dwelling situated in the courtyard of a country house, and possesses a right of way over the courtyard, and the owners of the country house desire to partition the dame, the owner of the dwelling cannot prevent them from doing so. Upon carrying out the partition, however, they are obliged to leave him a road as wide as the breadth of the door of the dwelling.

- 1170. If a country house is divided into two and there is a wall separating the two parts, and the ends of the beams of the wall of one part project on to the wall which is jointly owned, and at the time of the partition a stipulation has been made that the beams shall be removed, such beams shall be removed, but not otherwise. The same rule applies when a partition is made subject to the condition that the wall separating the two parts shall belong to one joint owner is absolute ownership, and the beams the ends of which rest upon such wall belong to the other.

- 1171. The branches of trees situated in one part and which project into the other part may not be cut off unless a condition has been made to that effect at the time the partition was made.

- 1172. Upon the partition of a house jointly owned having a right of way over a private road, each of the joint owners may construct doors and open windows looking on to such road. The other owners of the road may not prevent them from so doing.

- 1173. If one of the joint owners of a piece of property held in absolute ownership which is capable of partition erects a building for himself without the permission of the other, and the other joint owner asks for partition, such partition shall be made. If the building falls to the share of the person who built it, such building shall remain intact. If the building falls to the share of the other joint owner he may have such building pulled down.

SECTION IX. PARTITION OF USUFRUCT.

- 1174. Partition of usufruct consists of the division of benefits.

- 1175. There can be no partition of usufruct in the case of things the like of which can be found in the market. partition of usufruct may be had in the case of those things the like of which cannot be found in the market, the usufruct of which may be enjoyed, while the identical things remain intact.

- 1176. Artesian of usufruct is of two categories. The first category consists of a partition of usufruct limited by time.

Examples:-

(1). Two persons are joint owners of land which they hold subject to the condition that one shall cultivate such land one year, and the other the second year.

(2). Each of the joint owners of a country house own such house on the terms that they shall each dwell therein in turns for a period of one year.

The second category consists of a partition of usufruct limited as to place.

Examples:-

(1). Two persons are joint owners of land subject to the condition that one shall cultivate the first half and the other the second half.

(2). The joint owners of a country house agree to live one in one part and the other in the other part thereof, or one in the upper part and the other in the lower part thereof.

(3). Two persons own two houses jointly. They agree to live one in one house and the other in the other.

- 1177. The joint owners of an animal may validly agree to share the usufruct thereof by using such animal in turns. They may also agree to share the usufruct of two animals by one using one of them and the other the other.

- 1178. Partition of usufruct limited by time is in the nature of an exchange. Thus, one of the joint owners is considered to have exchanged his share of the benefit accruing to his turn for that of the share of the benefit accruing to the turn for that of the share of the benefit accruing to the turn of the other. From this point of view, partition of usufruct limited by time is in the nature of hire. Consequently, in partition of usufruct limited by time, a period of time must be mentioned, such as so many days or months.

- 1179. Partition of usufruct limited by place is in the nature of separation. Thus, the usufruct accruing to two joint owners of a country house is undivided, that is to say, it embraces every part of such house. Upon partition, the usufruct of one of the joint owners is considered to be concentrated in one part of such country house, and the usufruct of the second joint owner in the other part thereof. Consequently, there is no necessity to mention a period of time in the case of partition of usufruct limited as to place.

- 1180. In the case of partition of usufruct limited as to time, the commencement of the period, that is to say, determining who of the joint owners is to enjoy the usufruct first, is decided by drawing lots. Similarly, in the case of a partition of usufruct limited as to place, the place is determined by drawing lots.

- 1181. If one of the joint owners of several things jointly owned desires a partition of the usufruct thereof, and the other joint owner objects thereto, a partition will be enforced if the usufruct of the jointly owned property is of the same type. If the usufruct is of a different type, the partition will not be enforced.

Example:- One of the joint owners of two houses jointly owned desires a partition of the usufruct whereby he shall live in one and the other joint owner is the other; or in the case of two animals jointly owned, one of the joint owners desires a partition of the usufruct whereby one of them shall use one animal, and the other the other. If the other joint owner objects thereto the partition may be enforced. But if one them desires partition whereby one is to live in one house and the other is to be let on hire as a bath, or whereby one is to live in one house and the other is to cultivate land, such partition is valid if it is by consent; but if one of the joint owners objects thereto, the division of the usufruct cannot be enforced.

- 1182. If one of the joint owners of property which is capable of partition desires partition, and the other desires partition of the usufruct, the claim to partition will be upheld. If none of the joint owners desires partition, but one of them desires partition of the usufruct and the other objects, partition of the usufruct will be enforced.

- 1183. If one of the joint owners of some specific object which is not capable of division desires partition of the usufruct and the other objects, partition of the usufruct will be enforced.

- 1184. The rent of real property jointly owned, such as a ship, mill, a coffee-shop, an inn, and a bath, which are let on hire to the public, is divided between the joint owners in accordance with their shares. If one of the joint owners objects to giving his share on hire, partition of the usufruct will be enforced. If the rent accruing to the share of one of the joint owners during his turn is disproportionately large, the amount in excess is divided among the joint owners.

- 1185. Each joint owner may, after a partition of usufruct limited as to time has been carried out, make personal use of the real property jointly owned, when his turn comes, and in the case of a partition of usufruct limited as to place, may make personal use of the part falling to his own share. He may also obtain rent therefore by giving it on hire to some third party.

- 1186. If after a partition of usufruct has been made, the joint owners give their respective shares on hire, and the revenue accruing thereby to one of them is greater than the other, the latter does not share in such excess.

But if a partition of usufruct arising out of profit is made, as, for example, whereby one of the joint owners receives the rent of a house for one month and the other for another month, any excess amount is jointly held. But if a partition of usufruct is made whereby the profit arising out of one of two houses is to go to joint owner and the other to the other, and the profit arising out of one is greater than that of the other, the latter does not share therein.

- 1187. There may be no partition of usufruct in the case of any specific property.

Example:- The partition of the usufruct of the fruit of trees jointly owned, or of the milk or wool of animals jointly owned, on the terms that one joint owner shall gather the fruit of a certain number of such trees and the other the fruit of some other; number of trees, or that one shall take the milk and wool of one flock of sheep, and the other the milk and wool of the other, is invalid, since they relate to specific property.

- 1188. If the joint owners divide the usufruct of their shares by consent, one of them alone may subsequently cancel such partition. If one of them, however, has given his share on hire to some other person, the other cannot cancel the partition of usufruct until after the termination of the period of hire.

- 1189. one of the joint owners alone may not cancel a partition of usufruct carried out by order of the Court. The whole of the joint owners, however, may cancel such partition by consent.

- 1190. If one of the joint owners wishes to sell his share or to divide it, he may cancel the partition of usufruct. But any partition of usufruct which is sought to be cancelled without any due cause and whereby the jointly owned property will merely return to its former state, will be disallowed by the Court.

- 1191. A partition of usufruct continues to be valid after the death of one or all of the joint owners.

CHAPTER III. WALLS AND NEIGHBOURS.

SECTION I. RULES OF LAW RELATING TO PROPERTY OWNED IN ABSOLUTE OWNERSHIP.

- 1192. Any person may deal with his property owned in absolute ownership as he wishes. But if the rights of any other person are concerned therein, the owner of such property may not deal with it as though he were the independent owner thereof.

Example:- The upper storey of a building is owned in absolute ownership be A and the lower storey similarly by B. A has a right of support from B and B has a right to be protected from sun and rain. Neither may perform any act which will prejudice the other without obtaining permission from him, and neither may pull down his part of the building.

- 1193. If there is one door giving on to the street for both the upper and lower storeys, both owners may make use thereof. Neither may prevent the other from coming in or going out thereby.

- 1194. Whoever owns a piece of land in absolute ownership is likewise owner of what is above it and what is below it. That is to say, he may deal with it as by erecting buildings on a piece of land he owns in absolute ownership, and raising it as high as he wishes. He may also dig the ground and make store-rooms therein and dig wells as deep as he wishes.

- 1195. No person may extend the eaves of a room which he has constructed in his house, over his neighbour's house.

If he does so, the amount which so extends over his neighbour's house may be removed.

- 1196. If the branches of trees in any person's garden extend into the house or garden of his neighbour, the owner may be made by the neighbour to tie up such branches and thus bring them back into his own garden, or to cut them down and thus obtain a clear current of air. He may not, however, cut down the tree on the grounds that the shadow of such tree is injurious to the cultivation in his garden.

- 1197. No person may be prevented from dealing with his property which he owns in absolute ownership. Nevertheless, if such person by so doing causes great injury to any other person, he may be prohibited therefrom, as will be set forth in Section II.

SECTION II. RELATIONS OF ONE NEIGHBOUR TO ANOTHER.

- 1198. Any person may raise the wall of his property owned in absolute ownership to any extent he wishes, and may do anything he desires, and, providing that he does not cause his neighbour any great injury thereby the latter cannot prevent him from doing so.

- 1199. Great injury consists of anything which causes damage to a building, that is to say, which weakens it and causes it to collapse or makes it impossible for it to be put to the use for which it was originally intended, as in the case of a dwelling house.

- 1200. Great injury, caused in any way whatsoever, must be removed.

Examples:-

(1). A forge or a mill is erected adjacent to a house. The house is weakened by the hammering from the forge, or the turning of the mill wheel; or it becomes impossible for the owner of such house to dwell therein by reason of the great quantity of smoke given off by a furnace or a linseed oil factory, erected in close proximity thereto. These acts amount to great injury, which must be removed.

(2). A constructs a water channel on a piece of land adjoining B's house. Water is brought along it to a mill and the walls of B's house are weakened: or A makes a rubbish heap at the foot of the neighbour's wall and throws sweepings there and the walls becomes rotten. The owner of the house may have the injury removed.

(3). A construct a threshing floor near to B's house and the dust coming therefrom makes it impossible for B to dwell in his house. B may have the injury removed.

(4). A erects a high building near a threshing floor belonging to B and thereby cuts off the flow of air to the threshing floor. This act amounts to great injury and may be stopped.

(5). A opens a cook shop in the cloth merchants' market. The smoke therefrom is deposited on his neighbours goods and causes great injury thereto. The injury may be stopped.

(6). The sewer in A's house is broken and sewage flows into his neighbour's house. This amounts to great injury, and upon the neighbour bringing an action, A must repair the sewer and put it in order.

- 1201. Any interference with benefits which are not fundamental necessities, such as cutting off the air or the view of a house, or preventing the entrance of sunlight, does not amount to great injury. If light is entirely cut off, however, this amounts to great injury.

Consequently, if a person erects a building and cuts off the light from the window of a room belonging to his neighbour, the room being darkened to such an extent that it is impossible to read anything written therein, the act amounts to great injury and may be stopped; and it may not be argued that light can come in through the door, since the door must be kept closed on account of the cold and for other reasons. If the room has two windows, however, and a building is erected and the light of one of them is cut off as mentioned above, such act does not amount to great injury.

- 1202. The fact that places which are frequented by women, such as a kitchen, the head of a well, and the courtyard of a house are overlooked, is considered to amount to great injury. Consequently, if a person constructs a new window in his house whereby he overlooks quarters frequented by the women of an adjoining neighbour, or of the owner of a house on the other side of the street, or if he overlooks them from a window in a nearby built house, an order shall be given for the removal of such injury. Such person may also be obliged to remove such injury by building a wall or constructing a partition in such a way that the women cannot be forced to close up the window. If quarters occupied by women can be seen through the interstices of a wall made of brushwood, the owner of the wall may be ordered to close such interstices. He may not, however, be obliged to tear the brushwood down and build a wall. (See Article 22)>

- 1203. If a window is constructed in a place which is of the same height as a man, a neighbour of the person constructing such window may not have it removed by alleging that it is probable that he will overlook the women's quarter of his neighbour by placing a ladder there. (See Article 74).

- 1204. A garden is not considered to be women's quarters. Consequently, if a person is unable to see the women,s quarters of his neighbour,s house, but is able to see his garden, and consequently the women, but merely on the occasions when they go out into the garden, his neighbour may not demand that his view into the garden shall be stopped.

- 1205. If a person climbs up the fruit trees in his garden, and thereby overlooks the women's quarters of his neighbour, such person must give information that he intends to climb such trees, in order that the women may cover themselves. Should he fail to give such information, the Court may forthwith prohibit him from climbing such trees.

- 1206. If upon the partition of a country house jointly owned by two persons, the share falling to one overlooks the women's quarters of the other, the joint owners shall be ordered to construct a joint partition.

- 1207. If any person deals with property owned in absolute ownership in some manner authorised by law, and some other person constructs a building by the side thereof whereby he suffers injury, he himself alone must remove such injury.

Examples:-

(1). The women's quarters in a house newly constructed ore overlooked by the windows of an old house. The owner of the newly constructed house must himself remove the injury. He may not call upon the owner of they old house to do so.

(2). A person constructs a house on apiece of land adjoining a blacksmith's forge, and alleges that the hammering in the forge has caused great injury to his house. He cannot stop the forge from working.

(3). A person builds a house in a place where a threshing floor has been established for some time past and alleges that the dust is being deposited in his house. He cannot call upon the owner of the threshing floor to stop work.

- 1208. If a person who owns an old house with windows looking on to a piece of vacant land belonging to his neighbour has such house destroyed by fire, and the neighbour builds a house on the land in question, and thereafter the owner of the old house has it rebuilt in its former state and from the windows thereof overlooks the women's quarters of the new house, the injury must be removed by the owner of the new house himself. He cannot oblige the owner of the old house to remove the injury.

- 1209. If a person constructs new windows in his house and is unable to overlook the women's quarters of his neighbour by reason of the latter having constructed a high room between, and the room is later pulled down by the neighbour with the result that the women's quarters of the latter can be seen, the neighbour cannot call upon such person to stop the view from the windows, or to close them up, but must remove the injury himself.

- 1210. One of the joint owners of a wall may not raise such wall without the permission of the other, nor may he erect a kiosk thereon or any similar thing, whether causing injury to the or not. But if one of them wishes to place beams on the ground in order to build a room, that is to say, if he wishes to place them upon the edges of the beams on the wall, he may not be prevented from doing so. The other joint owner, however, has the right of placing the same number of beams. He may not, however, put more than half the total number of beams which can be supported and may not exceed that number. If both of them originally had an equal number of beams upon such wall, and one of them increases his number of beams, the other may prevent him from so doing.

- 1211. One of the joint owners of a wall may not have the position of the beams on such wall changed to the right or left or up or down. If the beams, however, are placed in an elevated part of the wall, he may put them on a lower part thereof.

- 1212. If any person constructs a cesspit or a sewer near a well of water belonging to some other person, and contaminates the water thereof, he may be made to remove the injury. If it is impossible to remove the injury, he may be made to close up the cesspit or sewer. Again, if any person constructs a sewer near to a water channel, and the dirty water from such sewer flows into the channel and causes great injury thereto, and no other way can be found to remove such injury than by closing it, the sewer shall be closed.

- 1213. If any person who owns a house on either side of a street wishes to construct a bridge from the one to the other, he shall be prevented from doing so. If he does so, and the bridge causes no injury to the passers by, such bridge shall not be pulled down. There is, however, no right to permanency in the case of bridges and resting places constructed over the public highway. Consequently, if after a bridge constructed over the public highway as mentioned above has been pulled down, and the owner wishes to construct another such bridge, he may again be prevented from so doing.

- 1214. anything which causes great injury to passers by on the public highway may be removed, such as low projecting balconies and resting places, even though they have been there for a long period of time. (See Article 7).

- 1215. Any person who wishes to repair his house may make quickly on one side of the road for use on his building, provided that he does not thereby cause any injury to the passers by.

- 1216. When necessary, the property of any person held in absolute ownership may be taken for its value by order of the authorities and made part of the road. He may not be deprived of ownership thereof, however, until he has been paid the price. (See articles 251 and 262).

- 1217. Provided no injury is done to passers by, any person may obtain any surplus land on the highway by paying its estimated price to the Government, and attach such land to his house.

- 1218. Any person whatsoever may construct a door giving on to the public highway.

- 1219. No person who is not the owner of a right of way in a private road may construct a door looking thereon.

- 1220. A private road is like the jointly owned property held in absolute ownership of persons having a right of way. Consequently, none of the owners of a private road may make any fresh construction therein without the permission of the other, whether such construction is prejudicial or not.

- 1221. One of the owners of a private road may not allow water to flow from a house which he has newly built, on to such road, without the permission of the other owners.

- 1222. If any person closes up a door giving on to a private road, he does not thereby lose his right of way thereover. Consequently, if he sells his house at some later date, the purchaser may again construct the door.

- 1223. Persons passing along the public highway have the right, if there is a great crowd of people therein, of entering a private road. Consequently, the owner of a private road may not sell it by agreement among themselves, nor may they divide it among themselves, nor may they close up the entrance thereto.

SECTION IV. RIGHT OF WAY, RIGHT OF AQUEDUCT, RIGHT OF FLOW.

- 1224. In case of right of way, right of aqueduct and right of flow, ancient rights shall be observed. That is to say, rights acquired in the remote past are left as they were, because, as is laid down in Article 6, things which have been in existence from time immemorial shall be left as they were; and until some proof to the contrary is produced, they shall not be changed. But anything existing from time immemorial which is contrary to law is invalid. That is to say, if any act which has been performed was originally illegal and has existed from time immemorial, such act is invalid, and, if it causes great injury, shall be removed (See Article 27).

  Example:-If the dirty water of a house has flowed from time immemorial into the public highway, and causes injury to the passers by, the ancient rights are disregarded, and the injury must be removed.

- 1225. If any person has a right of way over the land of another;, the owner of the land cannot prevent him from passing and crossing over the land.

- 1226. A person who has given something for nothing, to be consumed, has a right to revoke the gift. If injury is inflicted by consent, such consent may be withdrawn. Consequently, If a person who has no right of way over the land belonging to another exercises a right of way thereover for a certain period, with the permission of the owner of such land only, the latter may, whenever he wishes, prevent him from exercising the right.

- 1227. If any person has right of way over a defined pathway on the land of some other person, and the owner of the land erects a building on such pathway with the permission of the owner of the right of way, the latter loses his right of way, and has no right of disputing the matter with the owner of the land. (See Article 51).

- 1228. If a cutting or a water channel belonging to one person runs by right across the land of another, the owner of the land may not endeavour to prevent the former from exercising his right in the future. If such cutting and water channel are in need of improvement and repair, the owner thereof shall be allowed access thereto, if this is possible, and may make such improvements and repairs, however, without entering upon the land, and the owner of the land will not give the necessary permission, the Court shall oblige him either to grant permission for entry on the land, or to carry out the repairs.

- 1229. If the rain water of a house has flowed on to the house of a neighbour from time immemorial, the latter may not thereafter seek to prevent such flow.

- 1231. No person may cause the water from a newly constructed room to flow into the house of some other person.

- 1232. The owner of a house which is burdened by a right of sewage may not stop the right of flow, nor any person who purchases such house.

- 1233. The owner of sewer the sewage of which flows through the house of some other person must, if the sewer becomes full, or breaks, thereby causing great injury to the owner of the house remove such injury.

CHAPTER IV. JOINTLY OWNED PROPERTY WHICH IS FREE.

SECTION I. THINGS WHICH ARE FREE AND THINGS WHICH ARE NOT FREE.

- 1234. Water, grass and fire are free. The public are joint owners of these three things.
- 1235. Water flowing under ground is not the absolute property of any person.
- 1236. Wells which have not been made by the labour of any particular person, the benefit of which may be enjoyed by the public, are the jointly owned and free property of the public.
- 1237. Seas and large lakes are free.
- 1238. Rivers which belong to the State and are not the property owned in absolute ownership of any person, are those rivers the bed of which does not pass through the property of a group of persons owned in absolute ownership. All such rivers are free. Examples of such rivers are the Nile, the Euphrates, the Danube and the Tonja.
- 1239. Rivers which are the property of individuals owned in absolute ownership, that is to say, rivers which, as stated above, flow through the property of persons owned in absolute ownership are of two categories.

  The first category consists of rivers the water of which is divided between the joint owners of the land through they flow, but is not completely exhausted and continues its course through vacant land which is free to public. Rivers of this class are called public rivers, since they are at the disposal of the public. No right of pre-emption attaches to these rivers.

  The second category consists of private rivers, the water of which are divided between the land belonging to a limited number of persons, and which, upon arriving at the limits of such land, disappear and do not flow in vacant land. A right of pre-emption attaches to such land.

- 1240. Mud brought down by a river and deposited upon a person's land becomes such person's property owned in absolute ownership, and no other person may interfere therewith.
- 1241. Grasses which grow wild in places having no owner are free. So also are grasses which grow in any person's property owned in absolute ownership, without being planted. But if such person is the indirect cause of their growing, as when he waters the land or digs a creek round it, thereby preparing it and making it fit for vegetation to grow in, the vegetation produced becomes his property and no other person has any right thereto. If any other person takes them and consumes the same, he must make good the loss.
- 1242. Grasses consist of vegetation which has no truck, and consequently does not include trees. Mushrooms are considered to be grasses.
- 1243. Trees which grow wild on mountains which are not yet passed into the possession of anyone, are also free.

- 1244. Trees which grow wild in property owned by anyone in absolute ownership belong to such person. No person may cut them down for firewood without the owners permission. If he does so, he must make good the loss.

- 1245.If any person grafts a tree, the shoots coming from the graft are his property held in absolute ownership, including the fruit thereof.

- 1246. All produce arising from seeds sown by any person for himself is such person's property, and no one may interfere therewith.

- 1247. Game is free.

SECTION II. ACQUISITION OF OWNERSHIP OF THINGS WHICH ARE FREE.

- 1248. There are three means of acquiring absolute ownership. The first consists of the transfer of property held in absolute ownership from one owner to another, such as sale or gift. The second consists of one person succeeding another, such as inheritance. The third consists of obtaining a thing which is free and which has no owner. The latter is either actual, as where someone in fact appropriates such thing, or constructive, as where someone puts out a receptacle to collect rain water, or sets a trap to catch game.

- 1249. Any person who obtains possession of a thing which is free, becomes the independent owner thereof.

  Example:- A, by means of a receptacle such as a jug or a can obtains water from a river and stores it therein. The water becomes the property of A. No other person may make use of it without A's permission. If any other person takes and consumes it without A's permission, he must make good the loss.

- 1250. Taking possession must be coupled with intention. Consequently, if any person puts out a receptacle with the object of catching rain water, the rain water caught in the receptacle becomes that person's property. Again, water is collected in a receptacle not intentionally put in any particular place, does not become the property of the owner thereof. Any other person may take it and consume it. (See Article 2).

- 1251. In taking possession of water, the flow thereof must be interrupted. Consequently, possession cannot be taken of water from a well which oozes out from the sides thereof and if a person takes and uses the water, he is not liable to make good the loss thereof, even though the owner has not made a free gift thereof for consumption. Similarly, possession cannot be taken of water the flow of which is regulated, that is to say, water which leaves one side of a tank in the same quantity as it enters the other side.

- 1252. Possession may be taken of wild grasses by collecting them and by cutting them and making them into bunches.

- 1253. Trees growing in a state of nature of mountains which are property of no one, may be cut down for firewood by any person whatsoever. And by merely cutting them down such person becomes the owner thereof. There is no need to tie them into bunches.

SECTION III. GENERAL CONDITIONS ATTACHING TO THINGS THAT ARE FREE.

- 1254. Any person may make use of any thing that is free provided that is doing so no injury is inflicted upon any other person.

- 1255. No person may prevent any other person from taking and obtaining possession of anything that is free.

- 1256. Any person may pasture his beasts on wild grasses growing in places that have no owner. He may take and obtain possession of as much thereof as he pleases.

- 1257. Although wild grasses growing on the property of a person owned is absolute ownership, and on which such person is not the indirect cause, are free, the owner, nevertheless, may prevent any other person from entering on his property.

- 1258. If any person gathers wood from mountains which are free, and leaves such wood there and some other person takes it, the former may demand the return thereof.

- 1259. The fruit of trees having no owner and which are found in mountains that are free, and in valleys and pasture lands having no owner, may be gathered by any person whatsoever.

- 1260. If any person hires any other person to gather wood or to catch game for him from uncultivated country, the wood gathered or game caught by such person belongs to the person employing him.

- 1261. If a person lights a fire in his own property owned in absolute ownership, he may prevent any person from entering thereon and taking advantage thereof. But if any person lights a fire in a desert place belonging to no one, other persons may take advantage thereof. They may warm themselves by it. may sew by the light thereof, and may light their lamps therefrom. The owner of the fire may not prevent them from so doing. No one, however, may take a live coal from the fire without the owner's permission.

SECTION IV. RIGHTS OF TAKING WATER AND RIGHT OF DRINKING WATER.

- 1262. By watering is meant taking one's turn in making use of water to water crops and animals.

- 1263. The right of drinking consists of the right of drinking water.

- 1264. Any person may make use of air and light and of seas and big lakes.

- 1265. Any person may water his lands from rivers which are not owned in absolute ownership by any particular person, and, in order to irrigate them and to construct mills, may open a canal or water channels, provided that he does not thereby inflict injury on any other person. Consequently, if the water overflows and causes injury to the public, or the water of the river is entirely cut off, or boats cannot be navigated, such injury must be stopped.

- 1266. All persons and animals have a right of drinking from water, possession of which has not been taken by any other person.

- 1267. The right of taking water from rivers which are privately owned, that is to say, the course of which are privately owned, belongs to the owners thereof. Other persons have a right of drinking therefrom. Consequently, no person may, without permission, water his land from a river which is appropriated to a group of persons, or from a water course, or a water pipe, or a well, He may, however, drink water therefrom, since he has a right of drinking water. He may also water his animals, by reason of the large number thereof, from such river, water-course, or water-pipe, provided there is no danger of destroying the same. He may also bring the water to his house or to his garden by means of jugs or buckets.

- 1268. Any person having in his property which he owns in absolute ownership a tank, a well, or a river, from which water alternatively enters and leaves, may prevent any person who wishes to drink water from entering his property. If however, there is no free water to be had in the neighbourhood, the owner of the property is obliged either to draw off water, or to give such person permission to enter his property and take it. If he does not draw off the water, such person has the right of entering and taking it, subject, however, to no injury being caused, that is to say, provided that no injury is done, such as destroying the edge of the tank, or of the well, or of the river.

- 1269. A person who is joint owner of a river may not open up another therefrom, unless he has obtained the permission of the other joint owners. neither may he alter the old established order in which he has his right of taking water. Nor may he divert his share of the water from such river on to other land not enjoying a right of taking water. If the other joint owners agree to such things, either they, or their heirs, may denounce such agreement at any subsequent date.

SECTION V. THE VIVIFICATION OF DEAD LAND.

- 1270. Dead land consists of land which is not the property of anyone in absolute ownership, nor the grazing ground of any town or village, nor a place where wood can be gathered, and which is remote from civilisation. That is to say, a place where the voice of a person who is shouting from the outskirts of a town or village cannot be heard.

- 1271. Land which is near to civilisation is left to the public for grazing grounds, threshing floors, and for cutting wood. such land is called land left to the public.

- 1272. If any person, after obtaining Imperial sanction vivifies and cultivates any place consisting of dead land, such person becomes the absolute owner thereof. If the Sultan of his representative gives permission to any person to vivify land on the terms that he shall merely make use of such land without becoming owner thereof, such person may deal with the land in the way he has been authorised to do, but does not become the absolute owner thereof.

- 1273. If a person vivifies a piece of land and leaves the rest, he becomes the absolute owner of the part he vivifies, but not of the remainder. But if in the middle of the part he has cultivated he leaves a portion vacant, such portion becomes his.

- 1274. If a person vivifies a piece of dead land and thereafter some other persons arrive and vivify the land situated on all four sides thereof, a road shall be made in the land of the last comer for the former. That is to say, there shall be a road for him there.

- 1275. Vivification consists of sowing seed, planting trees, ploughing the land, watering it, or opening water-channels or canals, in order to irrigate it.

- 1276. If any person builds walls round dead land, or with a view to protecting it from flooding, makes a dam round it by raising the sides thereof, such land is considered to have been vivified.

- 1277. The placing of stones, or thorns, or the dead branches of trees so that they surround the four sides of land, or clearing away the grasses on such land, or burning the thorns on it, or sinking wells thereon, does not amount to vivification. This is enclosing land.

- 1278. If any person cuts down the grasses of thorns on dead land, puts them round such land and puts earth thereon, but does not complete it in such a way that they form a dam preventing the flow of water, such act does not amount to vivification, but is considered to be enclosing the land.

- 1279. If any person encloses a piece of dead land, he possesses a stronger right to such land than any other person, for a period of three years. If he fails to vivify it during the period of three years, he loses such right. It may be given to some other person to vivify.

- 1280. If any person digs a well in dead land with Imperial permission, such person becomes the absolute owner of such well.

SECTION VI. OWNERSHIP OF LAND SURROUNDING WELLS SUNK, WATER BROUGHT, AND TREES PLANTED WITH IMPERIAL PERMISSION IN DEAD LAND.

- 1281. The land attaching to the ownership in a well amounts to forty ARSHINS.

- 1282. The land attaching to springs of water is five hundred ARSHINS from each side.

- 1283. The land attaching to the two sides of a big river which does not require continually to be cleaned amounts to one half the breadth of the river. The amount of land attaching to both sides of the river is equal to the breadth of the whole river.

- 1284. The land attaching to small rivers which continually require to be cleaned, that is to say water courses, canals and underground channels, consists of an amount large enough for the stones and mud to be thrown upon when being cleaned.

- 1285. The land attaching to water in channels running along the surface of the ground amounts to five hundred ARSHINS, as in the case of springs.

- 1286. The land attaching to wells is the absolute property of the owner of the wells. No other; person may deal therewith in any way whatsoever. If any other person sinks a well in such person's land, he can cause it to be closed. The same rule applies to land attaching to springs, rivers and water channels.

- 1287. If any person, with Imperial sanction, digs a well in the vicinity of land attaching thereto on the other side amounts to forty ARSHINS. He may not, however, trespass upon the land attaching to the first well.

- 1288. If any person digs a well outside the land attaching to some other well, and the water from the first well flows into the second well, no liability is incurred. Similarly, if a person opens a shop next door to the shop of some other person and the business of the latter declines, the former cannot be obliged to shut his shop.

- 1289. The land attaching of trees planted in dead land with Imperial sanction is five ARSHINS on each side. No other person may plant trees within this distance.

- 1290. The banks of a water channel, the water of which flows into the land of some other person, belong to the owner of such channel, on each side, to the amount necessary to hold the water. If the banks are raised on both sides, the raised land also belongs to the owner of the channel. If banks are not raised, and there is no evidence to prove that either the owner of the land or of the water channel has taken possession thereof, as by planting trees therein, the banks belong to the owners of the land. The owner of the channel, however, has the right, when cleaning his channel, of throwing mud therefrom on both sides.

- 1291. No land attaches to a well dug by a person in his own land owned in absolute ownership. His neighbour may dig a well next to it in his own land owned in absolute ownership and the former may not seek to prevent the latter from doing so by alleging that he is attracting water away from his well.

SECTION VII. FUNDAMENTAL CONDITIONS AFFECTING HUNTING.

- 1292. Game may be hunted with implements which inflict wounds, such as a lance or a gun, or with things such as a net or a trap, or with savage animals, such as a trained dog, or with birds of prey, such as a trained hawk.
- 1293. Game consists of wild animals which are afraid of man.
- 1294. Domestic animals may not be hunted, nor wild animals which have been tamed. Consequently, if any person catches a pigeon or a hawk with a ring on its leg, or a stag with a collar on its neck, from which it may be inferred that they are not wild, they are considered to be lost property, and the person who has taken them must make known that he will restore them to their owners upon application made by them.
- 1295. Game must be in a position to flee from mankind. That is to say, must be able to get away and escape by means of its legs or its wings. If it is unable to escape and flee, for example, where a stag falls into a well, it loses its quality of game.
- 1296. Any person who deprives game of its quality of game is considered to have caught it.
- 1297. Game belongs to any person who catches it.

Example:- A shoots at game and wounds it so that it cannot escape. The game becomes the property of A. But if A wounds it slightly so that it can escape, he does not become the owner thereof and if any other person hits or catches it in any other way, the latter becomes the owner thereof.

- 1298. If two persons shoot at game and both hit it, the game in question is divided in equal shares between the two.
- 1299. If two persons each let trained dogs chase after game and both catch an animal, such animal similarly becomes the joint property of the owners of the dogs.

If each of them catch an animal, their masters become owners of such animal.

Again, if two persons each let trained dogs chase after game and one of them brings down the animal and the other kills it, the master of the first dog becomes owner of the animal, if the dog has so treated it that it could not get away and escape.

- 1300. If any person catches fish found in a water channel or canal belonging to some other person, which cannot be caught without fishing for them, such person becomes the owner thereof.
- 1301. If any person prepares a place for fishing by the water side, and a large number of fish come there, and on account of the water decreasing the fish can be taken without the need of fishing for

them, such fish belong to that person. But if by reason of the large quantity of water in that place it is necessary to catch the fish,such fish do no become the property of that person, but, if fished for and caught by some other person, become the property of the latter.

- 1302. If game enters the house of any person, and such person closes the door and catches the game, the game becomes his property.

  If he closes the door, however, But fails to obtain possession of the game, he does not become owner thereof, and if any other person catches it, such person becomes owner thereof.

- 1303. If any person put down anything such as a net or a trap in a particular place in order to trap game, and catches such game therewith, such person becomes the owner thereof. But if any person puts out a net in a particular place to dry and game is caught therewith, such game does not become his property. Again, if game falls into a hole in land belonging to a particular person, any other person may take it and thereby become the owner thereof. But if the owner of the land dug the hole for the purpose of catching game, he has a prior right over any other person to such game. (See Article 1250).

- 1304. If a wild bird builds its nest in any person's garden and lays eggs therein, it does not become the property of such person. Any other person may take its eggs, or its young, and the owner of the garden may not demand their return. But if such person has prepared his garden so that a wild bird may lay its eggs, and bring forth its young there, such person may take the eggs and the young of such bird and becomes the owner thereof.

- 1305. If bees select a place in any person,s garden and make a hive there, the honey is considered to be one of the perquisites of the garden and becomes the property of such person, and no other person may interfere therewith, A tithe, however, must be paid to the treasury.

- 1306. Bees which gather in a hive belonging to any particular person are considered to be property of which he has obtained possession. The honey produced by them also becomes the property of that parson.

- 1307. If a swarm of bees leave the hive of one particular person and settle in the house of another and such person appropriates them, the owner can demand the return thereof.

CHAPTER V. JOINT EXPENSES.

SECTION I. REPAIRS TO JOINTLY OWNED PROPERTY AND EXPENSES CONNECTED THEREWITH.

- 1308. If property jointly owned in absolute ownership is in need of repairs, the joint owners must jointly repair such property in proportion to their shares.

- 1309. If one of the joint owners spends a reasonable sum of his own money with the permission of the other of the repair of the jointly owned property, he may have recourse against the other joint owner for his share. That is to say, he may recover from the joint owner whatever part of the expenditure falls to his share.

- 1310. If one of the owners of the property jointly held in absolute ownership which requires repairs is absent, the other may apply to the Court for permission to effect such repairs. Permission given by the Court is equivalent to permission given by the absent joint owner. That is to say, upon the joint owner who is present carrying out the repairs of the jointly owned property by order of the Court, he is considered to have obtained the permission of the absent joint owner and has a right of recourse against him for his share of the expenses.

- 1311. If any person carries out repairs to property jointly owned in absolute ownership on his own initiative without obtaining the permission of the other joint owner, or of the Court, he is considered to have carried out such repairs free of charge. That is to say, he has no right to claim an amount corresponding to the share of the other joint owner, whether such jointly owned property is capable of partition or not.

- 1312. If any person wishes to carry out repairs to property jointly owned in absolute ownership which is capable of partition, and the other joint owner objects thereto, such person is considered to have carried out the repairs free of charge. That is to say, he cannot have recourse against the other joint owner for his share. If upon the refusal of the joint owner in this manner, such person applies to the Court, no order can be made for repairs, in view of the terms of Article 25. An order may, however, be given for partition. After partition has been effected, such person may do what likes with his share.

- 1313. If property jointly owned in absolute ownership such as a hill or a bath, which is not capable of partition, is in need of repairs and one of the joint owners wishes to carry out such repairs and the other refuses to agree, the former, after obtaining an order from the Court, may expend a reasonable amount of money on such repairs. He becomes a creditor of the other joint owner for a portion of the expenses occasioned by the repairs corresponding to his share. He may obtain payment of the sum owing to him by letting the jointly owned property on hire and taking the rent. If he carries out the repairs without obtaining an order from the Court, he can only obtain payment of a sum, as laid down, corresponding to the value of the building at the time the repairs were carried out, notwithstanding what he may actually have paid.

- 1314. If things jointly owned in absolute ownership which are not capable of partition, such as mill and a bath, are totally destroyed, so that only the land upon which they were erected remains, and one of the owners wishes to erect a building thereon and other refuses to agree, the latter cannot be obliged to build, but the land shall be divided.

- 1315. If a building owned in absolute ownership is destroyed or burnt, the upper storey belonging to one person and the lower storey to another. either of them may restore his portion of such building to its original state. neither can prevent the other from so doing. If the owner of the upper storey requests the owner of the lower storey to repair his part so that he may build his portion thereon, and the owner of the lower storey refuses, the owner of the upper storey may apply to the court for an order empowering him to reconstruct both lower and upper storeys and upon doing so, he may prevent the owner of the lower storey from dealing therewith until he has paid his share of the expenses.

- 1316. If a wall jointly owned by two neighbours is destroyed and things are resting upon it, such as a kiosk or the ends of beams belonging to the two, and one of them rebuilds the wall and the other refuses to do so, the one who rebuilds can prevent the other from placing anything on such wall until he has paid his half of the expenses.

- 1317. If a wall separating two houses is destroyed, and the women's quarters of one of them can be overlooked from the other, and the owner of one of the houses wishes the wall to be rebuilt jointly and the owner of the other refuses, he may not be forced to do so. The Court, however, may order them to build jointly a screen made of wood or some other material.

- 1318. If a wall jointly owned by two neighbours becomes weak and it is feared that it will collapse, and one of them wishes to knock it down and the other refuses to agree thereto, he shall be obliged to knock down such wall together with the other joint owner.

- 1319. If real property jointly owned by two minors, or which is situated between two properties which have been dedicated to pious purposes, is in need of repair, and injury will result thereto if it is left in its present state, and injury will result thereto if it is left in its present state, and one of the two guardians, or one of the two administrators of the pious foundations wishes to carry out the repairs and the other does not, the latter shall be obliged to do so.

Examples:-

(1). A jointly owned wall separates the houses of two minors and it is feared that it will collapse. one of the guardians wishes to repair the wall and the other refuses. The court will then send a reliable person to investigate the matter. If as a result it proves that injury will result to the minor if the wall is left in its present state, the guardian who refuses shall be forced to repair such wall jointly with the other guardian from the property of the minor.

(2). A house which is the joint property of two pious foundations is in need of repairs. One of the administrators wishes to carry out the repairs and the other does not. The latter will be forced to do so be the Court from the property of the pious foundation.

- 1320. If two persons are joint owners of an animal, and one of them refuses to feed him and the other applies to the Court, the Court shall order the joint owner who refuses to feed him either to sell his share, or feed the animal jointly with the other owner.

SECTION II. THE CLEANING AND IMPROVEMENT OF RIVERS AND WATER COURSES.

- 1321. The cleaning and improvement of rivers which do not belong to any particular person in absolute ownership in incumbent upon the Treasury. If it is not in the power of Treasury to do so, the public may be forced to do so.

- 1322. The cleaning of rivers jointly owned in absolute ownership is incumbent upon the owners thereof, that is to say, upon those who have the right of taking water therefrom. The owners of a right of drinking water may not be called upon to share in the expenses of cleaning and improvement.

- 1323. If some of the owners of a right of taking water from a jointly owned river desire to clean such river and the others refuse to do so, the persons who refuse will be made to clean such river jointly with the others, if it is a public river. If it is a private river, those persons who wish to clean it may, by order of the Court, proceed to do so, and may prevent those who refuse from making use of the river until such time as they have paid the amount which falls to their share of the expenses.

- 1324. Should all the owners of a right of taking water refuse to clean a river which is jointly owned, they may be forced to do so, if it is a public river, but not if it is a private river.

- 1325. If any person owns land on the banks of a public river, whether such river is absolute ownership or not, and there is no other road for satisfying such needs as drinking water or improving the river, the public may pass over such land the owner cannot prevent them from so doing.

- 1326. Expenses connected with the cleaning and improvement of a jointly owned river begin from above. First of all, the whole of the joint owners must share therein, beginning with the joint owner whose land comes last, the reason being that disadvantage is an obligation accompanying enjoyment.

  Example:- A river jointly owned by ten persons is being cleaned. The expenses connected with the joint owner's land which is highest up must be borne by the whole of the joint owners and thereafter by the nine others. The same procedure is then followed in the case of the land of the second joint owner, the expenses being divided among the eight others. This procedure is then followed in the case of the land of the second joint owner, the expenses being divided among the eight others. This procedure is then continued until the joint owner's land which is lowest down is reached, who shares in the expenses of all. The last joint owner does his share alone. In this way, the expenses of the joint owner who is highest up are the least of all, and the expenses of the joint owner who is lowest down are the greatest of all.

- 1327. The expenses occasioned by the cleaning of a jointly owned sewer begin from below. Thus, all the joint owners contribute towards the payment of the expenses of the portion of the sewer which is situated on the land of the joint owner who is lowest. On proceeding higher up, the latter has no further expenses to pay, and so on until they have all paid their shares, the joint owner who is highest up paying the expenses connected with his share alone. In this way, the expenses of the joint owner who is lowest down are lower than those of any other, and the expenses of the joint owner who is highest up greater than those of the rest.

- 1328. The repair of a private road, like a sewer, begins from below. The entrance is considered to be the lowest part, and the termination the highest part. A joint owner who is at the entrance shares in the expenses of repairing connected with his share alone. The joint owner who is at the termination of the private road, besides sharing in the expenses attaching to the shares of all the joint owners, pays his own share alone.

CHAPTER VI. PARTNERSHIP.

SECTION I. DEFINITION AND CLASSIFICATION OF PARTNERSHIP.

- 1329. A contract of partnership consists of a contract for joint ownership whereby two or more persons jointly share in capitol and profit.
- 1330. The basis of a contract of partnership consists of offer and acceptance, express and implied.

  Examples:-

  (1). A informs B that he has become his partner whereby they will carry on business with a certain amount of capital. B agrees. An express partnership has been formed by offer and acceptance.

  (2). A gives a thousand piastres to B, requesting B to give a thousand piastres also and buy certain property. B does so. A partnership has been formed by his implied acceptance.

- 1331. Contractual partnership is divided into two categories:

(1). Partnership with equal shares. A partnership with equal shares is a partnership which is formed when the partners enter into a contract of partnership stipulating for complete equality between them, and, after they have contributed the property which is to form the capital of the partnership, they maintain equality in the amount of their capital, and their shares of the profit. Similarly, if a person dies, and his sons take over the whole of his property left to them and make it their capital on the terms that they may buy and sell property of all kinds and share the profit equally between them, they may thereby form a partnership with equal shares. Formation of a partnership of this type, where there is complete equality, however, is rare.

(2). Partnership with unequal shares. A partnership with unequal shares is formed when a contractual partnership is concluded without stipulating for complete equality.

- 1332. A partnership, whether one of equal or of unequal shares, is either a partnership in property, or a partnership in work or a partnership on credit. Thus if the partners contribute a quantity of property to be the capital either jointly, or separately, or absolutely, and from a partnership with a view to trading and sharing the profits between them, such partnership is a partnership in property. If they agree that their labour shall be their capital and that they shall undertake to do work for some other person, and that the remuneration they receive shall be divided between them and form a partnership to that effect, such partnership is a partnership of work. A partnership of this nature is also called a personal partnership, or an artisans partnership, or a partnership of wage-earners, as, for example, where one tailor goes into partnership with another tailor, or a tailor goes into partnership with the dyer. If a partnership is concluded in which there is no capital and the partners buy and sell on credit on the terms that they shall divide the profits, such partnership is a partnership on credit.

SECTION II. GENERAL CONDITIONS AFFECTING A CONTRACTUAL PARTNERSHIP.

- 1333. Every contractual partnership includes a contract of agency. Thus, each of the partners is the agent of the other to deal with property, that is to say, to buy or sell, or to work for a wage for some other person. Consequently, in all partnership there is a condition that the partners shall be of sound mind and perfect understanding, as in the case of agency.

- 1334. A partnership with equal shares also includes a contract of guarantee. Consequently, the partners must be competent to conclude a contract of guarantee.

- 1335. A partnership with unequal shares includes a contract of agency only and does not include a contract of guarantee. Consequently, if at the time of the conclusion of the contract there has been no mention of a guarantee, the partners are not guarantors of each other. Consequently, a minor who has received authority may also enter into a partnership with unequal shares. But if at the time of the conclusion of a partnership with unequal shares, the contract of guarantee has been mentioned, the partners are guarantors of each other.

- 1336. It must be stated in what way the profit is to be divided among the partners. If this is vague or unknown, the partnership is voidable.

- 1337. The shares of the profit to be divided between the partners must consist of undivided parts such as a half, a third, or a quarter. If a contract is made whereby one of the partners is to receive a fixed amount of the profit, the partnership is null and void.

SECTION III. CONDITIONS AFFECTING A PARTNERSHIP IN PROPERTY.

- 1338. The capital must be some kind of cash.

- 1339. Copper coins which are in current use are considered by custom to be cash.

- 1340. If it is customary among people to transact business with gold and silver which has not been coined, such gold and silver is considered to be cash. If not, it is considered to be merchandise.

- 1341.The capital must consist of some specific object. a debt, that is to say, a sum due to be received from anyone, cannot be the capital of a partnership.

  Example:- Two persons cannot form partnership with capital consisting of something due from some other person. If the capital of one consists of some specific property and of the other of a debt, the partnership is invalid.

- 1342. A partnership may not be validly concluded with regard to property which is not considered to be cash, such as merchandise or real property. That is to say, it cannot be the capital of the partnership. Nevertheless, if two persons desire to make the capital of the partnership out of property which is not in the nature of cash, each of them may sell the half of his property to the other, and after they have become joint owners thereof, they may conclude a partnership in respect to the jointly owned property. Similarly, if two persons mix together property of theirs the like of which can be found in the market, as, for example, a quantity of wheat, they then become joint owners of property owned in absolute ownership, and they can conclude a partnership with the mixed property as their capital.

- 1343. A partnership formed whereby one person provides a horse and the other the harness on the terms that the money obtained by letting the horse on hire is to be shared between them is voidable, and the money obtained belongs to the owner of the horse; and since the harness is a necessary of the horse, the owner thereof is not entitled to a share of the money received but may only claim an estimated sum for the harness.

- 1344. If two persons enter into partnership whereby one who is the owner of an animal loads the goods of the other on to such animal, such partnership is voidable, and the profit earned belongs to the owner of the goods. The owner of the animal is entitled to an estimated payment. If two persons enter into partnership whereby one of them sells his goods in the shop of the other on the terms that the profit shall be shared between them, the partnership is voidable and the profit derived from the good belong to the owner. The owner of the shop is entitled to receive as estimated rent for the shop.

SECTION IV. RULES RELATING TO A CONTRACTUAL PARTNERSHIP.

- 1345. Work becomes possessed of specific value when the value thereof is estimated. That is to say, labour is valued when the worth thereof is assessed. The work of one person may be proportionately more valuable than the work of some other person.

  Example:- Two persons are partners in a partnership of unequal shares. Their capital is subscribed in equal shares and it is stipulated that both of them shall work in the business. It may validly be agreed that one of them shall have a greater share of the profits than the other since the skill of one in trading may be greater and his output of work larger and more valuable.

- 1346. A liability for work is in the nature of work. Consequently, a contract of partnership in work may validly be made whereby a person puts an artisan in his shop and has the work which he has undertaken to do performed by him on the terms that they are to divide the profit equally between them. The right of the owner of the shop to a half share accrues merely by reason of having guaranteed and undertaken the work, and this includes his right to make use of the shop.

- 1347. The right to profit may arise out of property, or work, or, as is shown in Article 85, by liability in respect thereto. Thus, in a case where one supplies the capital and the other the labour, profit is earned by property being supplied by the owner thereof and the labour furnished by the person who undertakes to work. An artisan may also engage an apprentice and validly cause such apprentice to perform work which he has undertaken to do for half the normal wages. The apprentice is entitled to half the wage received from the employers by reason of the work he has performed, and his master is entitled to the other half, since he is liable for the work being properly performed.

- 1348. If none of the three elements mentioned above, that is to say, property, work, and liability are present, there is no right to profit.

  Example:- A asks B to trade with his property and share the profit with him. No partnership is formed, and A cannot thereby take a share of the profit.

- 1349. The right to profit is entirely limited by the terms of the contract of partnership. It is not in proportion to the business done. Consequently, even though the partner who is bound to do certain work fails to do so, he is presumed to have done such work.

  Example:- It is stipulated in a valid partnership that the two partners shall both perform certain work and one of them does so and the other with some excuse, or with out any excuse, fails to do so, the latter, by reason of his being the agent of the former, is considered to have performed the work, and the profit is divided between them in the manner agreed upon.

- 1350. Partners are trustees the one for the other, and the property of the partnership in the possession of either is considered to be property entrusted for safe keeping. If the property of the partnership is destroyed while in the possession of one of them without any fault or negligence on his part, he is not liable to make good the loss to the share of his partner.

- 1351. In a case of partnership in property, the capital may be subscribed in equal or unequal shares by the partners. But if in a case where one supplies the capital and the other the labour, it is agreed that the profit shall be shared jointly between them, the partnership is one where one partner subscribes the capital and the other furnishes the labour. This type of partnership will be dealt with in the relevant Chapter. Should the profit go entirely to the workman, it is a loan; and if it is stipulated that the profit shall go entirely to the owner of the capital, such capital, while in the possession of the workman, is called invested capital and the workman is called a person employing capital. If he is such, he is considered to be an agent working for nothing, and profit and loss fall upon the owner of the property.

- 1352. The death of one of the partners, or his affliction by permanent madness, causes the dissolution of the partnership.

  But if there are three or more partners, the dissolution of the partnership only affects the one who dies or goes mad and the partnership subsists as regards the others.

- 1353. The partnership may also be dissolved by one of the partners, provided the others are informed thereof. Cancellation by one without the knowledge of the others does not bring about the dissolution of the partnership.

- 1354. If the partners dissolve the partnership on the terms that the cash in hand is to go to one of them and debts due to the other, the division is invalid;and any sums received in this way from cash in hand by one of them is jointly owned with the other. Debts due are jointly owned in the same way. (See Article 1123).

- 1355. If one of the partners receives a quantity of the partnership property and dies while dealing with it in a manner unknown to the other partner, the share of the latter shall be paid out of the estate of the deceased.(See Article 801).

SECTION V. PARTNERSHIP WITH EQUAL SHARES.

- 1356. As is stated in Section II, partners with equal shares are guarantors the one of the other. Consequently, an admission with regard to the other. If one of them makes an admission with regard to a debt, the person in whose favour the admission is made may demand payment from whichever of the partners he wishes. Any loan contracted, of any nature whatsoever, by one of the partners on account of the business transactions of the partnership, such as sale, purchase, or hire, is binding on the other also. Anything sold by one of them containing a defect may be returned to the other, and anything bought by one of them may be returned by the other on account of defect.

- 1357. Any food, clothing and other necessaries bought by one of the partners with equal shares for himself and his family are his property and his partner has no right therein. The vendor, however, may claim the price thereof from the other partner by virtue of the guarantee also.

- 1358. In partnership in property with equal shares, the shares of the partners must be equal in respect to capital and to profit. Neither of the partners may introduce any property by way of capital, that is to say, cash or property in the nature of cash, in excess of the capital of the partnership. The quality of shares, however, is not affected if one of the partners introduces property which cannot become capital of the partnership in excess of the partnership capital, that is to say, merchandise, or real property, or debts due from some other person.

- 1359. If it is agreed in a partnership for work that each of the partners may undertake work of any nature whatsoever, and that they are liable for the work equally, and that they shall be equal as regards profit and loss, and that the one is the guarantor of the other for anything which may happen to the partnership, such partnership is a partnership with equal shares. Consequently, the wages of an employee and the hire of a shop may be claimed from any one of them, and if any person claims goods from them and one of them admits the claim, the admission is binding even though the other; denies such claim.

- 1360. If two persons conclude a partnership whereby they agree to buy and sell property on credit and that the property purchased and the price received and the profit shall be jointly owned by them in equal shares and that each one shall be guarantor of the other, a partnership on-credit is formed with equal shares.

- 1361. Upon the formation of a partnership with equal shares, either the actual word denoting equal shares must be used on the whole of the terms of such partnership must be enumerated. If a contract for partnership is made in general terms, such partnership is one with unequal shares.

- 1362. If one of the conditions as mentioned above in this Section is absent, a partnership with equal shares is changed into a partnership with unequal shares.

  Example:- In the case of a partnership in property with equal shares, one of the partnership in property with equal shares, one of the partners acquires possession of property by way of inheritance or gift. If such property is capable of being used as the capital of the partnership, such as cash, the partnership is changed into a partnership with unequal shares. If it is property, however, which cannot become the capital of the partnership, such as merchandise or real property, no injury is caused to the partnership with equal shares.

- 1363. Any condition essential to the validity of a partnership with unequal shares is also essential to the validity of a partnership with equal shares.

- 1364. Any act performed by partners in a partnership with unequal shares may also be performed by partners in a partnership with equal shares.

SECTION VI. PARTNERSHIP WITH UNEQUAL SHARES

SUB-SECTION I. PARTNERSHIP IN PROPERTY.

- 1365. It is not essential to the validity of a partnership with unequal shares that the partners should subscribe the capital in equal shares.

  The capital of one may be greater than the capital of another. None of them is obliged to subscribe the whole of his money to the capital fund, but may form a partnership with regard to the whole of their property or a portion thereof. For this reason, they may have property as for example money, apart from the capital of the partnership, and which may become capital of the partnership.

- 1366. A contract of partnership may be entered into both with regard to commerce in general, and any particular branch of commerce, as, for example, the provision trade.

- 1367. Any condition which has been laid down with regard to the division of profit in a valid partnership must be observed.

- 1368. In a voidable partnership, the profit must be divided in accordance with the amount of the shares of capital. If a stipulation has been made that more shall go to one than the other, no effect shall be given thereto.

- 1369. Any damage suffered without any fault or negligence shall in any case be divided in proportion to the amount of the shares of capital. If any stipulation has been made to the contrary, no effect shall be given thereto.

- 1370. If the partners agree that the profit shall be divided among them in proportion to the amount of their shares of capital, such agreement is valid, whether the capital has been subscribed in equal or unequal shares, and the profit shall be divided between them in the manner agreed upon, in accordance with the amount of their shares of capital, and that, whether it has been agreed that both of them or only one of them shall work therein. If it is stipulated, however, that only one of them shall work therein, the capital of the other; is considered to be invested capital in such person's possession.

- 1371. If the capital subscribed by the partners is equal and it is stipulated that a larger share of the profit, for example, two thirds, shall go to one than to the other, and it is also stipulated that both shall work therein, both the partnership and the stipulation is valid.(See Article 1345). If it is stipulated that only one of them shall work therein, and it has been agreed that the work shall be performed by the partner whose share of the profits is greater, the partnership is valid and the effect shall be given to the condition, the partner being entitled to a share of the profits arising out of the capital by reason of the amount he has subscribed to the business, and also to an additional amount on account of his work. The partnership, however, resembles a partnership where capital is furnished by one and labour by another, since the capital of the other partner in such person's possession is in the nature of capital subscribed to such a partnership. If it is stipulated that the work shall be performed by the partner whose share in the profits is smaller, such stipulation is invalid, and the profit shall be divided between them in proportion to the amount of capital, the reason being that if the profit is divided as agreed, the additional amount to be received by the partner who performs no work is not sufficient to compensate for property, work and liability. If thee is a right to profit it is only in respect to one of these three things. (See Articles 1347 and 1348.)

- 1372. If the shares of the partners are unequal, for example, if the capital of one amounts to one hundred thousand piastres and of the other to one hundred and fifty thousand piastres, and it has been agreed that the profits shall be divided among them in equal shares, such agreement resembles the case of a partnership where the shares of the partners are equal, a stipulation having been made for greater share of the profits too be given to one of them, the reason being that it has been agreed that the partner with the lesser capital shall have a share of capital. Consequently, if it has been stipulated that both the partners whose share of profits is greater, that is to say, whose capital is greater, shall do the work, the partnership is valid and effect shall be given to the condition. If it has been stipulated that only the partner whose share of profits is smaller, that is to say, whose capital is greater, shall perform the work, such stipulation is invalid, and the profit shall be divided among them in proportion to the amount of their shares of the capital.

- 1373. Each of the partners may sell the partnership property for ready money or on credit, for any price he thinks fit.

- 1374. Property may be bought for the partnership either with ready money or on credit by whomsoever of the partners is in possession of the capital of the partnership. But if he buys the property as the result of flagrant misrepresentation, such property becomes his own and is not the property of the partnership.

- 1375. No partner who is not in possession of the capital of the partnership may buy property for the partnership. If he does so, such property becomes his own.

- 1376. If one of the partners buys anything which is not of the type used in their branch of commerce with his own money, such property is his own and his partner cannot claim a share therein. But if one of he partners while in possession of the capital of the partnership buys property of the type used in their branch of commerce with his own money it becomes the property of the partnership.

Example:- One of two persons who have entered into a partnership to carry on the business of cloth merchants buys a horse with his own money. The horse becomes his own property, and his partner cannot claim a share in such horse. But if he buys cloth, it becomes the property of the partnership, and he has no right of maintaining that he has bought the cloth for himself and that his partner has no share therein. He owns the cloth jointly with his partner.

- 1377. Contractual rights belong to the contracting party only. Consequently, if one of the partners takes delivery of property he has purchased and pays the price thereof, the transaction is binding on him alone. Thus, any claim made by any person as to the price of the property purchased may be made against such partner only, and may not be claimed from the other partner. Again, if one of the partners sells property, he alone is entitled to receive the price thereof. Thus, if the purchaser gives the price to the other partner, he is only liberated in respect to the share of the partner who has received the price, but is not released in respect to the share of the partner with whom he contracted. Moreover, if the partner who has concluded the contract appoints some other person to be his agent to receive the price of the property sold, such person's partner cannot dismiss the agent. But the partner may remove an agent appointed by the other in respect to contracts of sale, purchase and hire.

- 1378. The right of rejection on account of defect being a contractual right, one of the partners may not reject property purchased by one of the other partners on account of defect. Property sold by one may not be returned to another on account of defect.

- 1379. Each of the partners may deposit the partnership property son safe keeping, may give it to some other person on condition that he obtains the whole of the profit, may place it in a business where one person supplies the capital and the other the labour, and may conclude contracts of hire, for example, he may take a shop on hire and pay wages to persons for the preservation of the partnership property. he may not, however, mix the partnership property with his own property or enter into a partnership with some other person without the consent of the other partner. If he does so and the partnership property is lost, he must make good the loss suffered by his partner.

- 1380. No partner may lend the partnership property to any other person without the permission of the other. He may, however, obtain property on loan on behalf of the partnership. Any sum of money borrowed by one partner is a debt for which the other is jointly liable.

- 1381. If one of the partners leaves for some other country on behalf of the business of the partnership, the expenses are a charge of the partnership property.

- 1382. If each of the partners authorises the other to act in accordance with his own judgement or to do as he likes, each of them may perform the work falling to his branch of commerce. Thus, each of them may pledge the partnership property, or take a pledge in respect thereto, or proceed to some other country with the partnership property, or mix it with his own property, or conclude a partnership with some other person. He may not, however, destroy the partnership property of confer the absolute ownership therein upon some other person without consideration, unless he obtains the express permission of his partner.

  Example:- One partner men not lend or make a gift of the partnership property to any other person without the express permission of the other partner.

- 1383. If one of the partners forbids the other to proceed to some other country with the partnership property, or to sell on credit, and the latter nevertheless does so, he is bound to make good any loss occasioned thereby.

- 1384. Any admission of debt made by one of the partners in respect to the operations of a partnership with unequal shares does not bind the other. Thus, if he admits that the debt has arisen solely in connection with his own contracts and transactions, he himself is responsible for the whole of the debt. If he admits that the debt has arisen in connection with a transaction carried out in conjunction with his partner, he must pay half thereof. If he admits that the debt has been incurred solely on account of some transaction carried out by his partner, he is not obliged to pay anything.

SUB-SECTION II. PARTNERSHIP FOR WORK.

- 1385. A partnership for work consists of the conclusion of a partnership with a view to undertaking work. Thus, the partners enter into a partnership whereby they undertake and hold themselves ready to perform any work which they may be commissioned to perform by those who employ them. and that whether they are liable equally for the performance of the work or not. That is to say, whether they have concluded a partnership whereby they undertake to be responsible equally for the performance of the work, or whether, for example, one of them undertakes to be responsible for one third and the other for two thirds.

- 1386. Each of the partners may enter and perform work. One of them may obtain work and the other may perform it. One of the tailors who are partners in a partnership of skilled workmen may accept and cut the material and the other; may sew it.

- 1387. Each partner is the agent of the other for the purpose of undertaking work. Any work so undertaken by one of them must be performed both by him and by his partner. Consequently, the liability for the performance of work in the case of a partnership for work in unequal shares is considered to be that of a partnership in equal shares, since the employer may require the performance of the work by any one of the partners he selects, and each of the partners is obliged to perform such work. No partner may refuse to perform the work by alleging that his partner undertook to do it.

- 1388. A partnership for work in unequal shares is like a partnership in equal shares as regards the right to wages. That is to say, each of the partners may claim the whole of the wages due from the employer and on paying any one of them the employer is discharged from all liability.

- 1389. The partner who actually undertakes to do work is not obliged personally to perform such work. He may perform such work himself if he so desires, or he may cause his partner or some other person to do so. If the employer, however, makes a condition that the partner shall perform the work himself, he must then perform the work personally. (See Article 571.)

- 1390. The earnings of the partners are divided in the manner agreed. That is to say, if it has been agreed that the wages shall be divided in equal shares they shall be so divided. If it has been agreed that the wages shall be divided in equal shares they shall be so divided. If it has been agreed that the wages shall be divided in unequal shares, for example, one third or two thirds, they shall be divided accordingly.

- 1391. It may validly be agreed that work shall be in equal shares, but that the wages shall be unequal.

  Example:- The partners may validly agree that the work shall be performed in equal shares and that the wages shall be divided in the proportion of two thirds and one third, the reason being that one may be more expert in his craft, and his work corresponding it better.

- 1392. The partners are entitled to their wages by reason of their liability to perform the work. Consequently, if one of them performs no work, as, for example, or remains idle, and his partner alone performs such work, the earnings and wages must nevertheless be divided in the manner agreed upon.

- 1393. If one of the partners causes the destruction or damage of property delivered to be worked upon, the other partner is jointly liable with him to make good the loss, and the employer may call upon whichever one he likes to make good the loss to his property, such loss being divided among the partners in accordance with the amount of the loss they have to make good.

- Example:- The partners enter into a partnership whereby they undertake to perform the work in equal shares. They must make good any loss in equal shares. If they enter into a partnership whereby one undertakes to perform one third and the other two thirds, the loss also must be made good in the proportion of two thirds and one third.

- 1394. Porters may validly agree to enter into a partnership whereby they undertake jointly to perform work.

- 1395. Two persons, one of whom owns a shop and the other tools and implements, may validly enter into a partnership whereby they undertake to do work.

- 1396. Tow persons may validly enter into a partnership to do skilled work whereby one supplies the shop and the other the labour. (See Article 1346).

- 1397. Two persons may validly enter into a partnership for work whereby they undertake on equal terms to transport property, one supplying a mule and other a camel. The earnings and wages shall be divided equally between them. The fact that the load of the camel is the greater is of no importance, since in a partnership for work the partners are entitled to their wages by reason of their liability to perform the work. But if no partnership is concluded for undertaking work, but the partners agree to let their mule and camel on hire as such and to divide the earnings between them, the partnership is voidable and the amount of hire paid in respect to the hiring of either the mule or camel belongs to the owner thereof. If one of them helps the other in loading and transport, he is entitled to an estimated wage for his services.

- 1398. Any person who, together with his son living in his household, carries on any skilled work, is entitled to the whole of the earnings. The son is considered to be an assistant. Again, if a person plants a tree and is assisted by his son, the trees belong to such person and the son has no right therein.

SUB-SECTION III. PARTNERSHIP ON CREDIT.

- 1399. It is not essential that the partners should have equal shares in the property purchased.

  Example:- The property purchased may be divided between them in shares of one half, two thirds, and one third.

- 1400. In a partnership on credit, the right to profit arises out of the liability to make good any loss.

- 1401. The liability to make good any loss in respect to the price of the property bought is in proportion to the share of the partners therein.

- 1402.The share of the profit accruing to each of the partners in in proportion to their share of the property purchased.

  If one of the partners makes a stipulation that he shall receive more than his share in the property purchased, such stipulation is void; and the profit shall be divided between them in proportion to their share in the property purchased.

Example:- An agreement is made that the property purchased shall be divided between them in equal shares. The profit must also be divided between them in equal shares. If they agree to divided the property purchased in the proportion of two thirds and one third, the profit shall also be in the same ratio. But if it is agreed that the property purchased shall be divided in equal shares and that the profits shall be divided in proportions of one third and two thirds, the latter condition is invalid, and the profit shall be divided between them equally.

- 1403. Any loss shall be divided between the partners in any case in proportion to their shares in the property purchased and this whether the contract for purchase was made jointly, or by one of them alone.

Example:- Two persons who are partners in partnership on credit suffer loss in their business. The loss must be shared by them equally if they entered into the partnership on the terms that the property purchased should be divided between them equally. If the partnership was concluded on the terms that they should share in the property purchased in the proportion of one third and two thirds, the loss must be divided between them in the same ratio, and this whether the property with regard to which the loss has been suffered was bought by the partners jointly or by one of them on behalf of the partnership.

CHAPTER VII. PARTNERSHIP OF CAPITAL AND LABOUR.

SECTION I. DEFINITION AND CLASSIFICATION OF PARTNERSHIP OF CAPITAL AND LABOUR.

- 1404. A partnership of capital and labour is a type of partnership where one party supplies the capital and the other the labour. The person who owns the capital is called the owner of the capital and the person who performs the work is called the workman.

- 1405. The basis of a partnership of capital and labour is offer and acceptance.

Example:- A person possessing capital asks some other person to take the capital and use it and to share the profits between them equally, or in the ratio of two thirds and one third, or says something indicative of an intention to form a partnership of Capital and Labour, as when he asks such person to take so much money and use it as capital and share the profits with him in a certain ratio and the latter accepts. A partnership of capital and labour has been concluded.

- 1406. Partnership of capital and labour are of two categories:

(1). Absolute partnerships of capital and labour;

(2). Limited partnership of capital and labour.

- 1407. An absolute partnership of capital and labour is one where there is no limitation as to time or place, or any particular type of commerce, or any particular vendor or purchaser. If there is any limitation in respect to any of these matters, the partnership is a limited partnership.

Example:- It is stipulated shall be bought at a certain time, or a certain place, or shall be of a certain type, or that business shall be done with certain persons or with the inhabitants of a certain place. A limited partnership of capital and labour has been concluded.

SECTION II. CONDITIONS AFFECTING A PARTNERSHIP OF CAPITAL AND LABOUR.

- 1408. The owner of the capital must possess the requisite capacity to appoint an agent. The person supplying the labour must possess the requisite capacity to be appointed an agent.

- 1409. The capital must consist of property which can be made the capital of a partnership. (See section III of the Chapter dealing with the contract of partnership). Consequently, merchandise, real property and debts due to be paid may not be used as capital in a partnership of capital and labour. But if the owner of the capital hands over to the person applying the labour certain merchandise and asks him to sell the same and trade with the proceeds thereof by way of a partnership of capital and labour and the person supplying the labour and accepts and takes delivery of the merchandise and sells the same, applying the proceeds thereof to the capital and trades therewith, the partnership of capital and labour is valid. Likewise, if the owner of the capital asks the person supplying the labour to receive a sum due by a certain person and use the same in the partnership business and the person supplying the labour agrees, the partnership is valid.

- 1410. The capital must be delivered to the person supplying the labour.

- 1411. In a partnership of capital and labour the capital must be definitely stated, as in the case of a contractual partnership, and an undivided part must be fixed of the shares in the profits of the two contracting parties, such as a half or a third. If the partnership is defined in general terms, however, as, for example, that the profit shall be shared between the partners, such partnership is regarded as being in equal shares. The profit is divided by halves between the owner of the capital and person supplying the labour.

- 1412. If any of the conditions mentioned above is absent, as, for example, where the shares of the two contracting parties, being in undivided parts, are not mentioned, and one of them has been given a certain sum of money from the profits, the partnership is voidable.

SECTION III. EFFECT OF A PARTNERSHIP OF CAPITAL AND LABOUR.

- 1413. The person supplying the labour is a trustee. While in his possession, the capital is considered to be trusted to him for safe keeping. He is the agent of the owner of the capital in respect to any dealing with the capital. If he makes any profit, he is the joint owner thereof.

- 1414. In an absolute partnership of capital and labour, the person supplying the labour is authorised to perform any act connected with the partnership, whether fundamental or necessary, solely by virtue of the contract. Thus, he may perform the following acts:

(1). He may buy property with a view to selling it at a profit. But if he buys property as a result of flagrant misrepresentation, he is considered to have bought it for himself. It is not entered to the account of the partnership;

(2). He may sell at high or low prices, whether for cash or on credit, but he must give a period for payment which is customary among merchants. He may not sell for a long period of time not recognised by merchants;

(3). He may accept payment of the price of the goods by means of a transfer of debt;

(4). He may authorise some other person to act as his agent for buying and selling;

(5). He may deposit the partnership property for safe keeping, or invest it, or give it on pledge, or take a pledge in respect to it, or give or take it one hire;

(6). He may proceed to some other place in order to carry on business.

- 1415. In an absolute partnership of capital and labour the person supplying the labour may not mix his own property with the partnership property and give it to the partnership solely by virtue of the contract of partnership. If there is a custom of the town, however, for partners to mix their own property with the partnership property, a partner is an absolute partnership of capital and labour may do the same.

- 1416. If the owner of the capital in an absolute partnership of capita; and ;labour tells the person supplying the labour to act as he thinks fit, or has authorised him to act in accordance with his own opinion in the affairs of the partnership he may in any case mix his own property with the partnership property and can give it to the partnership. He may not, however, unless he is specially authorised, bestow any of the partnership property by way of gift, or give it on loan, or contract debts to an extent greater than the capital, without the express permission of the owner of the capital.

- 1417. If the person supplying the labour mixes the partnership property with his own property, the profits realised are divided in accordance with the amount of the capital. That is to say, he takes the profit arising out of his own capital, and the profit arising from the partnership property is divided between him and the owner of the capital on the terms agreed upon.

- 1418. Property bought on credit with the permission of the owner of the capital, and which is in excess of the capital, is jointly owned between the two partners as though it were a partnership on credit.

- 1419. If the person supplying the labour leaves the town in which he is and proceeds to some other town on the business of the partnership, he may claim such expenses as are customary from the partnership property.

- 1420. In a limited [partnership of capital and labour the person supplying the labour must observe whatever conditions are laid down by the owner of the capital.

- 1421. If the person supplying the labour exceeds the limit of his authority or acts in contravention of the conditions laid down, he becomes a person wrongfully appropriating property, in which case he is entitled to any profit and responsible for any loss arising out of his business transactions. If the partnership property is destroyed, he must make good the loss.

- 1422. If the owner of the capital forbids the person supplying the labour to go with the partnership property to any particular place, or to sell property on credit, and the latter in contravention of the prohibition proceeds to such place with the partnership property, and such property is destroyed, or if he sells property on credit, and the money is lost, he must make good the loss.

- 1423. If the owner of the capital fixes the period for the termination of the partnership at some particular date, the partnership is cancelled when such date is passed.

- 1424. If the owner of the capital dismisses the person who supplies the labour, he must notify such dismissal to him. Any act performed by him up to the time his dismissal was notified to him is valid. He may not deal with any cash assets in his possession after his dismissal has been notified to him. If he has any property in his possession other than cash, he may sell such property and convert it into cash.

- 1425. The person supplying the labour is only entitled to profit in respect to his work, such work being possessed of value solely by virtue of the contract. Consequently, in a contract of capital and labour, the person supplying the labour is entitled to a share of the profits in accordance with what has been stipulated in the contract.

- 1426. The owner of the capital is entitled to profit in virtue of the capital subscribed. Consequently, in a voidable partnership of capital and labour the owner of the capital is entitled to the whole of the profit, and since the portion of the person supplying the labour is equivalent to that of an employee of the owner of the capital, he is entitled to an estimated wage. Such wage may not, however, exceed the amount agreed upon at the time of the conclusion of the contract. If there is no profit, he is not entitled to an estimated wage.

- 1427. If any of the partnership property be destroyed, the amount thereof is first deducted from the profit and may not be made a charge of the capital. If the quantity destroyed exceeds the amount of the profit and is made a charge on the capital, the person supplying the labour need not make good the loss, and this whether the partnership is valid or voidable.

- 1428. Any damage or loss must in any case be borne by the owner of the capital. If it has been stipulated that the person supplying the labour shall be jointly liable with him such stipulation is invalid.

- 1429. If either the owner of the capital or the person supplying the labour dies, or is afflicted with madness without any lucid interval, the partnership is cancelled.

- 1430. If the person supplying the labour dies and it is not known what has become of the capital, the loss must be made good from his estate. (See Articles 801 and 1355.)

CHAPTER VIII. PARTNERSHIP IS LAND AND WORK AND PARTNERSHIP IS TREES AND WORK.

SECTION I. PARTNERSHIP IN LAND AND WORK.

- 1431. A partnership in land and work is a type of partnership where one party supplies the land and the other work. that is to say, cultivates the land, on terms that the produce is to be divided between them.

- 1432. The basis of a partnership is land and work is offer and acceptance. Thus, if the owner of the land informs the person supplying the labour, that is, the cultivator, that he has given him the land to be cultivated on condition that he shall receive a certain share of the produce and the latter states that he agrees thereto, or is contended therewith, or makes some statement from which his agreement may be inferred, or if the latter informs the owner of the land that he is ready to cultivate such land on those terms and the owner of the land agrees thereto, a partnership in land and work has been concluded.

- 1433. In a partnership in land and work the contracting parties must be of sound mind. They need not have reached the age of puberty. Consequently, a minor who has received authority may also enter into a partnership of land and work.

- 1434. The nature of what is to be sown must be stated, or it must be known that the cultivator may sow what he likes.

- 1435. At the time of the conclusion of the contract the share of the cultivator in the produce must be stated, such as an undivided part consisting of a half or a third. If the share is not fixed, or if it is decided that something other than the produce shall be given, or if it is stated that so many KILES shall be given from the produce, the partnership in land and work is invalid.

- 1436. The land must be fit for cultivation and must be handed over to the cultivator.

- 1437. If any of the conditions mentioned above are absent the partnership in land and work is voidable.

- 1438. In a valid partnership in land and work the produce shall be divided between the two contracting parties in the manner agreed upon.

- 1439. In a voidable partnership in land and work the whole of the produce belongs to the owner of the seed. If the other party is the owner of the land, he is entitled to a rent for the land. If he is the cultivator, he is entitled to an estimated wage.

- 1440. If the owner of the land dies while crops are green, the cultivator shall continue to work until the crops are ripe. The heirs of the deceased cannot prevent him from so doing. If the cultivator dies, his heir stand in his stead, and may, if he wishes, continue the work of cultivation until the crops are ripe, and the owner of the land may not prevent him from so doing.

SECTION II. PARTNERSHIP IN TREES AND WORK.

- 1441. A partnership is trees and work is a type of partnership whereby one party supplies the trees and the other; tends them on the terms that the fruit produced is to be shared between them.

- 1442. The basis of a partnership in trees and work is offer and acceptance. Thus, if the owner of the trees informs the cultivator that he has given him so many trees to tend on the terms that he shall be entitled to a certain share of the fruit and the cultivator, that is, the person who is to tend such trees, agrees thereto, a partnership in trees and work has been concluded.

- 1443. The contracting parties must be of sound mind. They need not have reached the age of puberty.

- 1444. In a partnership in trees and work the shares of the two contracting parties must be stated, that is an undivided part, such as a half or a third, as in a partnership in land and work.

- 1445. The trees must be handed over to the cultivator.

- 1446. In a valid partnership in trees and work, the fruit must be divided between the two contracting parties as agreed.

- 1447. In a voidable partnership in trees and work, the fruit produced belongs entirely to the owner of the trees. The cultivator is entitled to an estimated wage.

- 1448. If the owner of the trees dies while the fruit is unripe, the cultivator may continue to work until the fruit is ripe. The heirs of the deceased cannot prevent him from so doing. If the cultivator dies, his heir stands in his stead and may, if he so wishes, continue to work. The owner of the trees cannot prevent him from so doing.

PROMULGATED BY ROYAL IRADAH 16TH JUMADI-UL-AKHIRA 1291.

AL-MAJALLA AL AHKAM AL ADALIYYAH
(The Ottoman Courts Manual (Hanafi))

BOOK XI. AGENCY.

INTRODUCTION.

TERMS OF THE ISLAMIC JURISPRUDENCE.

- 1449. Agency consists of one person empowering some other person to perform some act for him, whereby the latter stands in the stead of the former in regard to such act. The first person is called the principal, the person who stands in his stead is called the agent, and the act is called the authorised act.

- 1450. Messengership consists of the transmission of information by one person to some other person by means of some third person who is not privy to the matter in question. The person transmitting the information is called the messenger. The person who sends the message is called the person transmitting information. The person to whom the information is transmitted is called the recipient of the information.

CHAPTER I. FUNDAMENTAL BASIS AND CLASSIFICATION OF AGENCY.

- 1451. The basis of appointment of a person as agent is offer and acceptance. Thus, if the principal informs the agent that he has appointed him agent for a certain matter and the latter states that he has accepted, or uses some other expression importing acceptance, a contact of agency is concluded. Similarly, if the agent remains silent, but attempts to act in the matter referred to by the principal, he is considered to have accepted the agency by implication and his acts are valid. But if the agent refuses after the offer is made, the offer is of no effect. Consequently, if the principal informs a person that he has appointed him agent for a certain matter, and such person declines, but later begins to deal with the matter, all his acts in that respect are invalid.

- 1452. Permission and ratification amount to an authority to act as agent.

- 1453. Subsequent ratification has the same effect as a previous authorisation to act as agent.

  Example:- A, without authority, sells property belonging to B,and informs B thereof. B ratifies the sale, and A is considered to have performed the act as though he had previously been appointed agent by B.

- 1454. Messengership is not of the same nature as agency.

  Examples:-

(1). A sends his servant to fetch him money which his banker is going to lend him. The servant is A's messenger, not his agent to borrow money.

(2). A sends B to a horse-dealer to buy a horse. B tells the horsedealer that A wishes to buy a certain horse from him. The horsedealer informs B that he has sold A the horse for so much money and asks B to inform A of this fact, and to deliver the horse to him. B does as requested and hands the horse over to A. A accepts forthwith. A sale has been concluded between A and the horsedealer. B has merely been a messenger and intermediary between the two, and not an agent.

(3). A asks the butcher to give his servant who does the marketing so many okes of meat every day. The butcher does so. The servant is his master's messenger and not his agent.

- 1455. An order is sometimes is the nature of agency and sometimes in the nature of messengership.

Example:- A servant acting on orders from his master, buys property from a merchant. The servant is his master's agent for purchase. But if the master does business with a merchant, and sends his servant to fetch and bring the property purchased, the servant in his master's messenger and not his agent.

- 1456. The basis of an authority to act as agent is sometimes absolute. That is to say, it is not dependent upon a condition, or made with reference to any particular time or subject to any limitations.

The basis of an authority to act as agent is sometimes conditional.

Example:- A informs B that he has made him his agent to sell his horse in the event of a certain merchant coming to his place, B agrees. The authority to act as agent is concluded subject to the merchant coming to such place. If he comes, the agent can sell the horse, but not otherwise.

The basis of an authority to act as agent is sometimes subject to certain time.

Example :- A informs B that he has made him his agent to sell his animals in the month of April and B accepts. B can sell the animals as agent when the month of April comes or thereafter, but not before.

The basis of an authority to act as agent is sometimes subject to a limitation.

Example:- A informs B that he has appointed him his agent to sell his watch for a thousand piastres. B's authority to act as agent is subject to the limitation that he may not sell for less than a thousand piastres.

CHAPTER II. CONDITIONS ATTACHING TO AGENCY

- 1457. The principal must be able to perform the act which is the subject matter of the agency. Consequently, any authority to act as agent conferred by a minor of imperfect understanding, or a lunatic, is invalid. A minor of perfect understanding may not confer any power to act as agent upon any other person in such matters as bestowal of property by way of gift, or giving alms, which can only be to the disadvantage of the minor, even though his tutor authorises him to do so. A minor may, however, authorise some other person to act as agent for him for the purpose of accepting such things as gifts or alms, which can only be for his advantage even without the permission of his tutor. As regards dispositions of property which may either be to his advantage or disadvantage such as sale and purchase, the minor may authorise some other person to act as agent, if he has been authorised to engage in trade. If not, the authorisation to act as agent in dependent upon ratification by the tutor.

- 1458. The agent must be of sound mind and perfect understanding. He need not have arrived at the age of puberty. Consequently, a minor of perfect understanding, may become an agent. The rights under the contract, however, do not effect him, but his principal.

- 1459. Any person may appoint any other person his agent to perform any act which he can himself perform, or to fulfil any obligation, or to acquire any right, in respect to any transaction to which he himself is liable or entitled.

Example:- A may validly appoint B his agent for buying and selling, giving and taking on hire, giving and taking on pledge, giving and receiving for safe keeping, bestowing and receiving by way of gift, settlement, discharge, admission, instituting an action at law, claiming a right of pre-emption, partition, paying and receiving payment of debts and taking delivery of property. The subject matter of the agency, however, must be known.

CHAPTER III. ESSENTIAL ELEMENTS OF AGENCY.

SECTION I. GENERAL.

- 1560. A contract concluded by an agent must be made by reference to his principal in the case of gift, loan for use, pledge, deposit for safe keeping, lending money, partnership, partnership of capital and labour, and settlement by way of denial. If the matter is not so referred to the principal, it is invalid.

- 1461. A contract concluded by an agent need not be made by reference to his principal in the case of sale and purchase, hire, and settlement by way of admission. Such contract is valid if merely concluded by the agent alone, ownership passes to the principal alone. Should the contract be made without reference to the principal, however, the rights under the contract belong to the contracting party, that is to say, the agent. if the contract is made with reference to the principal, the rights under the contract belong to the principal. In that case, the position of the agent is similar to that of a messenger. Examples:-

(1). An agent for sale concludes the contract without reference to his principal, but merely with reference to himself, and, upon selling the property of his principal, must deliver the property sold to the purchaser. He may claim and receive the price from the purchaser. Should any person appear who is entitled to the property purchased, obtain judgement therefor, and seize the same, the purchaser may have recourse against the agent for sale, that is to say, may claim the price which he has given to him.

(2). An agent for purchase concludes a contract in this way without reference to his principal. He may take delivery of the property purchased, and, even though he has not received the price of the property purchased from his principal, he is obliged to pay it to the vendor from his own property. Should some defect of long standing appear in the property purchased the agent has the right of bringing an action to secure its return.

(3). An agent concludes a contract with reference to his principal, as where he states that he has sold or thought an agent for A. In this case, the contractual rights referred to above belong to the principal, the position of the agent being similar to that of a messenger.

- 1462. In the case of messengership, the rights under the contract belong to the person sending the messenger. The messenger is in no way concerned therewith.

- 1463. Property in the possession of an agent which he has received in his capacity as agent for sale, or purchase, or paying or receiving payment of debt, or receiving any specific property, is considered to be property deposited with him for safe keeping. If it is destroyed without fault or negligence, the loss need not be made good. Property in the possession of a messenger in virtue of his duties as messenger is also considered to be property deposited for safe keeping.

- 1464. If a debtor sends the sum of money he is owing to his creditor and it is destroyed while in the possession of the messenger before being received by the creditor, the debtor must bear the loss if the messenger is his. If the messenger is the creditor's, however, it is the creditor's property which is destroyed and the debtor is free from the debt.

- 1465. If any person appoints two persons simultaneously to be his agent, one of them alone may act as agent. One of them, however, may act alone in actions at law, or for the return of things deposited for safe keeping, or for paying a debt. But if one person has been appointed agent for any particular matter and the other has also been directly appointed agent for the same matter, either of them may act as agent.

- 1466. A person who has been appointed agent for any particular matter may not appoint any other person as agent. Nevertheless, if his principal has authorised him to do so, or to act as he thinks fit, the agent can appoint some other person as agent. The person whom the agent authorises to act as agent in this way becomes the agent of the principal, and not the agent of the agent. Thus, if the first agent is removed or dies, the second agent remains as agent.

- 1467. If upon the appointment of the agent, it has been agreed that a salary shall be paid to him, the agent is entitled to such salary upon fulfilling the terms of the agency. if no stipulation has been made for payment, and the agent is not one of those persons who work for a wage, his services are free, and he cannot demand payment.

SECTION II. AGENCY FOR PURCHASE.

- 1468. In accordance with the terms of the last paragraph of Article 1459, the subject matter of the agency must be sufficiently well known to enable it to be carried out. Thus, the principal must state the nature of the thing to be purchased. If there are various sorts of things of that nature, it is not enough merely to state the nature of such thing, but the particular sort or price of such thing must be mentioned. If the nature of the thing to be bought is not stated, or if it is stated, and there are various sorts of that nature and the particular sort or the price thereof is not mentioned, the agency is invalid, unless the authority to act as agent is of a general nature.

Example:- A appoints B his agent to purchase a horse. The appointment is valid. A appoints B his agent to purchase cloth for making into clothes. A must state the nature thereof, that is to say, whether he wants striped cloth or cloth of any other nature. He must also state the sort of cloth he wants, such as Damascus or Indian cloth, or state the price thereof, such as so many piastres for the roll. If the nature is not stated, as where the principal merely asks for the purchase of a piece of cloth, or where, for example, he asks for the purchase of striped cloth without stating the sort or price thereof, the appointment as agent is invalid. But if the principal instructs the agent to buy a roll of cloth to be made into clothes or some striped cloth of whatever nature or sort the agent may think fit, the agency is general and the agent may purchase whatever nature or sort he chooses.

- 1469. The nature of a thing is changed with any change in the substance of such thing, or the object for which it was intended, or the manufacture thereof.

Example:- Cotton cloth and linen cloth are of different nature, since the substance from which they are made is different. The wool and skin of a sheep are of a different nature since the object for which they are used is different, the skin being used to make bags, and the wool to make thread to weave carpets, two totally different things. Sharkot felt differs from shak felt, although both are made from wool, since there is a difference in their manufacture.

- 1470. If the agent acts in contravention of his instructions as to the nature of the thing to be purchased, that is to say, if the principal tells the agent to purchase something of a certain nature, and he buys the property of of some other nature, the principal is not bound thereby, however much more advantageous the thing may be which the agent has bought. That is to say, the agent is considered to have bought the property for himself and not for his principal.

- 1471. If the principal instructs the agent to purchase a ram, and he buys a sheep, the principal is not bound thereby, and the sheep belongs to the agent.

- 1472. If the principal instructs the agent to purchase a certain piece of land, and buildings are erected on such land, the agent cannot thereafter purchase such land on behalf of his principal. But if he instructs him to purchase a certain house, and such house is plastered, or another wall is added thereto, the agent may purchase such house of behalf of his principal.

- 1473. If the principal instructs the agent to purchase milk, without indicating what milk, the principal shall be understood to mean the milk which it is the custom to use in the district.

- 1474. If the principal instructs the agent to buy rice, the agent may purchase any sort of rice sold in the market.

- 1475. If any person intends to appoint some other person as agent to buy a house, he must state the district in which it is situated and the price thereof. If he does not do so, the agency is invalid.

- 1476. If any person intends to appoint some other person his agent to purchase a pearl or a red ruby, he must state the price he is prepared to pay. If he fails to do so, the agency is invalid.

- 1477. In the case of things estimated by quantity, the quantity or price of the subject matter of the agency must be stated.

Example:- A appoints B his agent to buy corn. A must state the number of Kiles, or the price thereof, by stating the amount of money to be expended on the corn. If he fails to do so, the agency is invalid.

- 1478. The subject matter of the agency need not be described.

Example:- It need not be stated whether of the best quality or of medium quality, or of the lowest quality.

The description of the subject matter of the agency must, however, correspond to the position of the principal.

Example:- A, who lets horses on hire, appoints B his agent to buy a horse. The agent may not purchase an Arab horse at twenty thousands piastres. If he does so, the principal is not bound thereby. That is to say, the horse is not bought for the principal, but becomes the property of the agent only.

- 1479. If the appointment as agent is made subject to a limitation, no act may be performed by the agent in contravention thereof. If he does so, the principal is not bound, and any property purchased belongs to the agent. But if the agent acts in contravention of his appointment in a way more advantageous to the principal, such act is not considered to amount to contravention. Examples:-

(1). A instructs his agent, B, to buy a certain house for ten thousand piastres. If B exceeds this price, A is not bound and the house becomes B's property. If B buys it for less than ten thousand piastres, it is considered to be bought for the principal.

(2). A instructs B, his agent, to buy on credit. B buys and pays cash. The property belongs to the agent. But if A instructs B to buy for ready money and the agent buys on credit, the property is considered to be bought for the principal.

- 1480. If a person buys half the thing he is appointed agent to purchase, such purchase is not binding upon the principal if such thing will be injured by being divided. If not, he is bound thereby.

Example:- A instructs B, his agent, to buy a roll of cloth. B buys half a roll. A is not bound thereby, and the cloth becomes the property of the agent. But if A tells B to buy six Kiles of corn, and B buys three kiles, the corn is presumed to have been bought for the principal.

- 1481. If the principal instructs his agent to buy him cloth to make a cloak, there is not sufficient cloth in that purchased by the agent to make the cloak, the principal is not bound thereby and the cloth belongs to the agent.

- 1482. If the price of a thing is not mentioned, the person who is appointed agent to purchase may buy such thing for the estimated value thereof, or at a price subject to minor misrepresentation. Things the price and value of which are fixed, however, such as meat and bread, may not be bought at even subject to minor misrepresentation. If the agent buys such things as a result of flagrant misrepresentation, however, the principal is in no case bound by the purchase, and the property belongs to the agent.

- 1483.Purchase outright is understood to be purchase for cash. Thus, if a person who has been appointed agent for the purchase of anything purchases such thing by exchanging other property therefor, the principal is not bound thereby, and such thing belongs to the agent.

- 1484. If a person appoints some other person his agent to purchase something which is necessary for some particular season it is considered to relate to that season.

Example:- A appoints B his agent to purchase a cloak made of goat hair in the spring season. B is considered to be appointed agent to purchase such a cloak for use in the summer season. If he buys after the season has passed or buys in the spring of next year, the principal is not bound by such purchase, and the cloak becomes the property of the agent.

- 1485. A person who is appointed agent to buy some specified thing cannot purchase such thing for himself. If when buying such thing he states that he has purchased it for himself, it nevertheless becomes the property of the principal. Nevertheless, if he buys such thing for a higher price than that fixed by the principal, or, if no price has been fixed and he buys as a result of flagrant misrepresentation, the property in that case belongs to the agent. Again, if the principal is present and the agent states that he has bought such thing for himself,the property belongs to the agent.

- 1486. If a person appoints some other person his agent to buy a horse,the horse becomes the property of his principal if at the time he made the purchase he stated that he has bought on behalf of his principal. If he states that he has bought for himself, the horse becomes his property. If he merely states that he has purchased the horse without stating, and later states that he has purchased on behalf of his principal, such statement is effective if made before the horse is destroyed or some defect appears. But if makes such statement after the horse is destroyed or after some defect appears, such statement is of no effect.

- 1487. If two persons separately appoint a person as agent to purchase a certain thing, the property belongs to the person whom the agent intended to effect the purchase.

- 1488. If an agent for purchase sells his own property to his principal such sale is invalid.

- 1489. If the agent becomes aware of a defect in the property purchased before delivering it to his principal, he may himself reject it. He may not reject it after delivery, however, without an order and authority from his principal to do so.

- 1490. If the agent buys property to be paid for at some future date, the same condition as to payment affects the principal, and the agent may not ask the principal to make payment forthwith. If the agent, however, purchases by an immediate cash payment, and the vendor thereafter adjourns the date for payment, the agent can demand payment forthwith from the principal.

- 1491. If an agent for purchase pays the price from his own property and takes delivery of property purchased, he can exercise a right of recourse against his principal, that is to say, he can recover from him the price which he has paid. If he has not already paid the price which he has paid. If he has not already paid the price of the property purchased to the vendor, he may claim the price from his principal, and may exercise a right of retention over the property until such time as the principal has paid.

- 1492. If the property purchased by an agent for purchase is accidentally destroyed or lost while in the possession of the agent, the loss must be borne by the principal, and no reduction is made in the price if the agent has exercised a right of retention over such property in order to obtain payment of the price, however, and such property is destroyed or lost, the price must be paid by the agent.

- 1493. An agent for purchase may not rescind a contract of sale without the permission of his principal.

SECTION III. AGENCY FOR SALE.

- 1494. An agent who has been granted an absolute power to conclude contracts of sale may sell his principal's property at any price he thinks fit, whether great or small.

- 1495. If the principal has fixed the price, that is to say, if he has instructed the agent to sell for so much, the agent may not sell for less than such price. If he does so, the sale is concluded subject to ratification by the principal. If the agent sells it on his own initiative for a price lower than that mentioned, and delivers the property to the purchaser, the principal may call upon him to make good the loss.

- 1496. If an agent for sale purchases his principal,s property for himself, such purchase is invalid.

- 1497. An agent for sale may not sell the property of his principal to persons whose evidence given on his behalf is invalid. If he sells for than the value of the property, however, the sale is valid. If the agent is appointed in virtue of a general power, the principal instructing him to sell to whomsoever he may think fit, the agent may validly sell to such persons for an estimated price.

- 1498. If an agent has been granted an absolute power of sale, he may sell his principal's property for cash or on credit for a period recognised by merchants in respect to such property. He may not, however, sell on credit for a longer period than that recognised by custom. If the agent has been appointed, either expressly or by implication, to sell for cash, he may not sell on credit.

  Example :- A principal instructs his agent to sell certain property for cash or to sell certain property for cash or to sell certain property and pay a debt of his with the proceeds. The agent may not sell on credit.

- 1499. If injury is caused by the separation of a thing, the agent cannot sell half thereof.

- 1500. An agent may take a pledge or a surety in respect to the price of property which he has sold on credit. If the pledge is destroyed or the surety becomes bankrupt, the agent is not liable to make good the loss.

- 1501. If a principal instructs his agent to take a pledge or a surety in respect to property sold, the agent may not sell such property without taking a pledge or a surety.

- 1502. If an agent for sale fails to obtain the price of the property sold from the purchaser, he cannot be forced to pay the price thereof to his principal out of his own property.

- 1503. The price of the thing sold may validly be received both by the agent and the principal.

- 1504. If the agent is working without remuneration, he is not obliged to obtain payment of the price of the property sold. If he does not do so of his own accord, however, he must appoint his principal to be his agent to obtain payment of the price. But persons such as brokers and auctioneers who are appointed as agents for sale subject to remuneration, are obliged to obtain payment of the price of the thing sold.

- 1505. An agent for sale may rescind the sale on his own initiative. The rescission, however, is not executory as regards the principal, and the agent must pay the price thereof to the principal.

SECTION IV. INSTRUCTIONS GIVEN BY ONE PERSON TO ANOTHER.

- 1506. If one person gives an instruction to another person to pay a sum of money owing by him to some third person, or to the State, and such person pays such sum of money from his own property, he may thereafter exercise a right of recourse against the person who gave the instruction, whether such right of recourse has been agreed upon or not. That is to say, whether he uses expressions which imply a right of recourse, as where he instructs a person to pay a sum of money owing by him and thereafter to recover such sum from him, or where he instructs him to pay and recover from him later, or whether he merely instructs him to pay a sum of money owing by him

- 1507. If one person instructs another to pay a sum of money owing by him from his own property in base coin and he pays in sound coin, base coin only can be recovered from the person who gave the instruction. If such person is instructed to pay in sound coin, but pays the debt in base coin, he can recover base coin only. If a person who has been instructed by some other person to pay a sum of money owing by him, sells his own property to the creditor and pays such person's debt therefrom, the person who pays the debt may recover the amount thereof from the person who gave the instruction, whatever that amount may be . If he sells his own property to the creditor for an amount greater than the value thereof the person who gave the instruction for the debt to be paid cannot deduct the balance from the debt.

- 1508. If any person instruct any other person to incur expenditure for himself or his relations and family, such person may recover a reasonable amount of expenses from the person who gave the instruction whether the latter has expressly authorised him to do so or not. Again, one person instructs another to have his house repaired and the latter does so. He may recover a reasonable sum from such person, even though no agreement has been made to that effect.

- 1509. If any person instructs any other person to make a loan of money, or to give him alms, stating that he will repay him later, and such person does so, He may recover such money from the person who gave the instruction. If the person giving the instruction, however, makes no stipulation as to recourse as by stating that he will give him money, or that the person paying the money may later recover it from him, but merely gives an instruction to pay, such person has no right of recourse. Nevertheless, if it is customary in such matters to have recourse against the person giving the instruction, as where the person to whom the instruction is given is a member of the family of the person giving the instruction, or is his partner, such person may exercise a right of recourse, even though no stipulation has been made therefor. (See Article 36).

- 1510. Any instruction given by any particular person is only effective in regard to that person's property.

  Example:- A instructs B to throw certain property into the sea. B does so knowing that the property in question belongs to some one else. The owner of the property can call upon B to make good the loss. The person who gave the instruction is not liable, unless he used compulsion.

- 1511. If any person instruct any other person to pay a debt owing to him, and amounting to a certain sum, from his own property and such person promises to do so, but fails to pay the sum in question, such person cannot be made to pay the debt by reason merely of having promised to do so.

- 1512. If the person to whom an instruction to pay a debt is given owes money to the person giving the instruction, or has money belonging to the latter deposited with him for safe keeping, such person is bound to pay the debt. But if the person giving the instruction orders certain of his property to be sold and the debt to be paid therefrom, the person to whom the instruction is given is not obliged to pay such debt even though he is unsalaried agent. If he is salaried agent, however, he is obliged to sell such property and pay the debt of the person who gave the instruction from the proceeds.

- 1513. If any person gives a sum of money to some other person instructing him to pay it to a creditor of his, the other creditors of the person giving the instruction have no right to claim a share therein and the person to whom the instruction has been given may only pay the money to the creditor mentioned in the instruction.

- 1514. If any person gives any other person a sum from which to pay a debt owing to some third person, and it is known that the person to whom the money belongs has died before such money has been made over to the creditor, the money is question must be paid to the estate of the person to whom the money belonged, and the creditor must have recourse against the estate.

- 1515. If any person gives a sum of money to pay to his creditor with instructions that the sum in question shall not be handed over unless an acknowledgement is endorsed on the bill or a receipt given therefor, and such person hands over the money without obtaining any acknowledgement or receipt, and the creditor later denies having received the money, and the debtor, being unable to prove payment, is obliged to pay the debt a second time, the latter may call upon the person to whom he gave the money to make good the loss.

SECTION V. AGENCY FOR LITIGATION.

- 1516. Both plaintiff and defendant may authorise any person they may wish to act as their agent for litigation. Neither party need obtain the consent of the other.

- 1517. Any admission made against his client by the person authorised to act as his agent for litigation is valid if made in Court. If made out of Court,it is invalid and the agent may be dismissed.

- 1518. Any person who appoints another his agent for litigation may validly forbid him to make any admission against him, in which case an admission made by the agent against his client is invalid. (See last paragraph of Article 1456). Again, if the agent makes an admission in Court, and is not authorised to do so, he shall be dismissed.

- 1519. An agency for litigation does not include an agency to take delivery. Consequently, if an advocate is not an agent to take delivery, he cannot act as agent to take delivery of the subject matter of the judgement.

- 1520. An agency to receive does not include an agency for litigation.

SECTION VI. DISMISSAL OF AGENTS.

- 1521. The principal may dismiss his agent from his agency. He may not do so, however, if the rights of third parties are affected. Thus, a person owing a sum of money gives his property as a pledge for the debt. At the time the contract of pledge was concluded, or at some later date, he appoints a person as his agent to sell the pledge when the debt falls due. The principal may not dismiss the agent without the consent of the pledgee. Similarly, at the request of the plaintiff, a defendant appoints a person his agent for litigation. He cannot dismiss him in the absence of the plaintiff.

- 1522. The agent himself may relinquish the agency, but, as stated above, he may not do so if the rights of third persons are affected, but must perform his duties.

- 1523. Upon a principal dismissing an agent from his agency, the dismissal does not becomes effective until information thereof has been given to the agent, and any disposition of property made by him up to that time is valid.

- 1524. Upon the agent giving up the agency, he must inform his principal thereof, and the agent is responsible for performing his duties as agent until the principal has been so informed.

- 1525. The principal may dismiss a person appointed as agent to receive a debt during the absence of the debtor. If the principal appointed him as agent in the presence of the debtor. Thus, if the debtor pays the debt to him while unaware of his dismissal, he is free from liability for the debt.

- 1526. The agency terminates upon the completion of the duties for which the agent was appointed, and, naturally, is discharged therefrom.

- 1527. The agent is discharged upon the death of the principal. He is not discharged, however, if the rights of any third party are affected thereby. (See Article 760.)

- 1528. Upon the death of the principal, any agent appointed by the agent is discharged from the agency. (See Article 1466.)

- 1529. Agency is not transmissible by way of inheritance. That is to say, if the agent dies, the validity of the agency expires and consequently the heir of the agent does not stand in his stead.

- 1530. If the principal or the agent are afflicted with madness, the agency is null and void.

Promulgated by Royal Iradah, 20th Jumudi-ul-Ula, 1291.

AL-MAJALLA AL AHKAM AL ADALIYYAH
(The Ottoman Courts Manual (Hanafi))

BOOK XII. SETTLEMENT AND RELEASE.

INTRODUCTION.

TERMS OF ISLAMIC JURISPRUDENCE.

- 1531. A settlement is a contract concluded by offer and acceptance, and consists of settling a dispute by mutual consent.
- 1532. A person making a settlement is called a settlor.
- 1533. The price of settlement is called the consideration.
- 1534. The subject matter of the settlement is the matter in dispute.
- 1535. A settlement is divided into three parts: The first part consists of a settlement by way of admission, that is, a settlement brought about by the admission of the defendant. The second part consists of a settlement by way of denial of the defendant. The third part consists of a settlement by way of silence, that is, a settlement brought about by the silence of the defendant consequent upon the absence of any admission or denial.
- 1536. Release consists of two parts: The first part consists of release by way of renunciation of a right. The second consists of release by admission of payment. Release by way of renunciation occurs where one person releases another person by relinquishing the whole of the claims he has against such person, or by subtracting or reducing a certain number of them. It is this form of release which is dealt with in this book. Release by admission of payment is in the nature of an admission and consists of the confession by one person that he has received what was due to him from another person.
- 1537. A special release is a release of a person from an action instituted in respect to a claim relating to some particular matter, such as a house, or farm, or some other matter.
- 1538. A general release is a release of a person from all actions.

CHAPTER I. CONCLUSION OF A CONTRACT OF SETTLEMENT AND RELEASE.

- 1539. A person making a settlement must be of sound mind. He need not have arrived at the age of puberty. Consequently, a settlement made by a lunatic, or an imbecile, or a minor of imperfect understanding is always invalid. A settlement made by a minor who has been authorised by his tutor is valid, provided that the settlement does not result in a clear loss. Thus, if a person brings an action against a minor who has been authorised, and such minor makes an admission thereto, the result is a valid settlement by way of admission. A minor who has been authorised may make a valid contract of settlement to the effect that he will give time for the satisfaction of his claim. If such minor agrees to a settlement in respect to part of his claim and is in possession of evidence to support the same, such settlement is invalid; if he is not in possession of such evidence, however, and his opponent is known to be ready to take an oath, such settlement is valid. If he brings an action to recover property from another, and makes a settlement in respect to the value of such claim, such settlement is valid. A settlement by him for an amount considerably smaller than the value of the property is invalid.

- 1540. A valid settlement of an action brought by a minor may be made by his tutor provided that such settlement does not result in clear loss to the minor. If there is a clear loss, the settlement is invalid. Consequently, if a person brings an action for the recovery of a certain amount of money from a minor and the father of such minor has made a settlement upon the terms that payment shall be made from the property of the minor, such settlement is valid, provided that the plaintiff is in possession of evidence in support of his claim. If the plaintiff is not in possession of such evidence, the settlement is invalid. Should money be due to a minor from another person and the father make a settlement by deducting a part thereof, such settlement is invalid if evidence exists in support of the sum due. If no such evidence exists, however, and the person is known to be willing to take an oath, the settlement is valid. A settlement made by a tutor in respect of a sum due to the minor, in consideration of property equivalent to the value of the claim, is valid. But if such consideration involves flagrant misrepresentation, the settlement is invalid.

- 1541. A release by a minor, a lunatic or an imbecile is absolutely invalid.

- 1542. A power of attorney to carry on litigation does not imply a power of attorney to make a settlement. Consequently, if a person is appointed agent to bring an action against another person and such person settles the action without obtaining the permission of his principal, such settlement is invalid.

- 1543. If any person appoints any other person his agent to settle an action and the agent accordingly makes a settlement, the principal is bound by such settlement. The agent is in no way responsible for any claim made in connection therewith, unless he has made himself a guarantor therefor, in which case he is liable. Moreover, if an agent makes a settlement by way of admission to the effect that he will give property for property, and makes such settlement in his own name, such agent becomes liable for any claim made in connection therewith, that is to say, the amount covered by the settlement may be recovered from the agent, the latter preserving the right of recourse against his principal.yvT Examples:-

(1). An agent, acting in accordance with the term of his power of attorney, makes a settlement for a certain amount of money. The principal and not the agent will be obliged to pay such sum. But if an agent arranges a settlement for a certain sum of money and he guarantees such sum, the money in that case is recoverable from the agent, who has a right of recourse against his principal.

(2). In the event of a settlement being made by way of admission upon the terms that property shall be exchanged for property, the agent inducing the other party to settle with him in respect to which the settlement is made may be recovered from the agent, who has a right of recourse against the principal, owing to the transaction being in the nature of a sale.

- 1544. If a third person who is not authorised thereunto, that is to say, who acts without permission,intervenes in an action between two persons and makes a settlement with one of them, such settlement is valid in the following cases, but the unauthorised person is held to have acted on his own initiative: if such person guarantees the sum covered by settlement; if he allows the sum covered by the settlement to attach to his own property; if he allows the sum covered by the settlement to attach to certain specific money or goods present at the time; or if he makes a settlement for a certain sum of money and delivers that sum of money. In the latter case, should such party intervening fail to deliver the sum of money covered by the settlement, such settlement is dependent upon the adoption of the transaction by the defendant. The settlement is valid if adopted by the defendant, who must then pay the sum covered by such settlement. If he does not do so, the settlement is null and void, the action remaining undisturbed.

CHAPTER II. THE CONSIDERATION AND SUBJECT MATTER OF THE SETTLEMENT.

- 1545. If the consideration of the settlement is some specific object, such object is considered as an article which has been sold. If it is a debt, it is considered to be the price. Consequently, anything which may be the subject of sale or the price thereof in a contract of sale, may also be the consideration for a settlement.

- 1546. The consideration of the settlement must be the property of the person making the settlement. Consequently, if the person making the settlement offers some other person's property as the considcration for the settlement, such settlement is invalid.

- 1547. If it is necessary to take and give delivery of either the consideration of the settlement or the subject matter thereof, such thing must be clearly defined. If not, it need not be clearly defined.yvT
  • Examples:-

(1). A brings an action against B with regard to a house in the possession of B. B brings an action against A with regard to a garden in the possession of A. Both agree to a settlement of their actions without defining the nature of the dispute.

(2). A brings an action against B with regard to a house without defining the nature of the dispute, and they come to a settlement on the terms that the defendant shall pay the plaintiff a certain sum of money and the plaintiff shall drop the action. The settlement is valid. But if a settlement is made whereby the plaintiff gives the defendant a certain sum of money and the defendant in consideration thereof gives up his claim, such settlement is invalid.

CHAPTER III. THE SUBJECT MATTER OF THE SETTLEMENT.

SECTION I: SETTLEMENT IN RESPECT TO SPECIFIC PROPERTY.

- 1548. If a settlement by way of admission is made with regard to property in an action relating to specific property, such settlement is in the nature of a sale, and there is an option for defect, an option of inspection, and a contractual option, and, in the event of either the subject matter or the consideration of the settlement being real property, a right of pre-emption attaches thereto. If the whole or part of the subject matter of the settlement is seized by someone who is entitled thereto, the plaintiff may recover the amount of the consideration from the defendant, that is to say, either the whole or a portion thereof. If the whole of the consideration of the settlement or part thereof is seized by someone who is entitled thereto, the plaintiff may recover from the defendant the subject matter of the settlement, that is to say, the whole or part thereof.yvT Example:- A brings an action against B claiming a house from him. B admits that the house belongs to A and the two partners agree to a settlement for a certain sum of money. The house is considered to have been sold to the defendant, and, as stated above, the transaction is treated as though it were a sale.

- 1549. If a settlement by way of admission is made in an action with regard to property in respect to the usufruct thereof, such settlement is in the nature of hire and is treated as though it were a contract of hire.yvT Example:- A brings an action against B claiming a garden from him. B makes a settlement with A on terms that A is to live in this house for a certain period. A is considered to have taken the house on hire in exchange for the garden in respect to such period.

- 1550. A settlement by way of denial or silence amounts to receiving satisfaction in the case of the plaintiff, and abstention from swearing the oath by the defendant, whereby the point at issue is decided. Consequently, a right of pre-emption attaches to real property which is the consideration for a settlement, but does not attach to real property which is the subject matter of the settlement. If any person who is entitled thereto seizes the whole or part of such real property, the plaintiff must return to the defendant the amount of the consideration for the settlement, that is to say, the whole or a portion thereof, and may bring an action against the person who claims to be so entitled. If either the whole or part of the consideration is seized by someone entitled thereto, the plaintiff may again bring an action in respect thereto.

- 1551. If any person brings an action to recover any specific property, as, for example, a garden, and agrees to a settlement in respect to a portion thereof and releases the defendant in respect to the remainder of the action, such person is considered to have received a part of his claim and to have foregone the rest, that is to say, to have relinquished his right to bring an action in respect of the remainder.

SECTION II. SETTLEMENT WITH REGARD TO DEBT AND OTHER MATTERS.

- 1552. If any person effects a settlement with any other person in respect to a portion of a claim that he has against such person, the person effecting the settlement is considered to have received payment of part of the claim and to have foregone his right to the balance, that is to say, to have released such person from the remainder.

- 1553. If any person effects a settlement whereby a debt repayable forthwith is converted into a debt repayable at some future date, he is considered to have relinquished his right to payment forthwith.

- 1554. If any person effects a settlement whereby a debt repayable in sound coin may be repaid in base coin, such person is considered to have relinquished his right to payment in sound coin.

- 1555. A settlement may validly be effected in actions relating to the right of taking water, the right of pre-emption and the right of way, whereby a payment is made in order to avoid swearing an oath.

CHAPTER IV. FUNDAMENTAL CONDITIONS GOVERNING SETTLEMENT AND RELEASE.

SECTION I. FUNDAMENTAL CONDITIONS GOVERNING SETTLEMENT.

- 1556. When the settlement is complete, one of the two parties may not go back therefrom. BY agreeing to the settlement, the plaintiff becomes entitled to the consideration for the settlement. He no longer possess any right to bring an action. The defendant may not claim the return of the consideration for the settlement from him.

- 1557. In the event of the death of one of the two contracting parties, the heirs may not cancel the settlement.

- 1558. If the settlement takes the form of giving something in satisfaction, the two parties thereto may cancel and rescind the settlement of their own accord. If the settlement does not take such form, but consists of giving up certain rights any cancellation thereof is invalid. (See Article 51.)

- 1559. If a contract of settlement is concluded whereby a payment is made in order to avoid swearing an oath, the plaintiff is considered to have relinquished his right of bringing an action, and he cannot have the defendant put on his oath.

- 1560. If the consideration for the settlement is destroyed in whole or part before it has been handed over to the plaintiff, and such consideration is a thing which is specified, it is considered to be in the nature of a thing seized by someone entitled thereto. That is to say, if a settlement is made by way of admission, the plaintiff may claim the whole or part of the subject matter of the settlement from the defendant. If the settlement is made by way of denial or silence, the plaintiff may proceed with his action. (See Articles 1548 and 1550.) If the consideration for the settlement is a debt that is to say, consists of things which are not specified, such as so many piastres, the settlement is not thereby affected, and the plaintiff is entitled to receive from the defendant an amount equivalent to the portion lost.

SECTION II. FUNDAMENTAL CONDITIONS GOVERNING RELEASE.

- 1561. If any person states that he has no claim against or dispute with some other person, or that he is not entitled to anything from him, or that he has finished or given up a claim he had against him, or that he is no longer entitled to anything from him, or that he has received complete satisfaction from him, he is considered to have released such person.

- 1562. If any person releases any other person from any obligation, such obligation ceases to exist and he can no longer make any claim in connection therewith. (See Article 51.)

- 1563. A release does not extend to anything happening in future. That is to say, if one person releases another, any rights antecedent to the release cease to exist. Such person may, however, bring an action with regard to rights which accrue after the release.

- 1564. If any person releases any other person from an action relating to a particular matter, such release is a special release and no action will be heard with regard to that matter. He may, however, bring an action with regard to any other matter.yvT Example:- A releases B from an action with regard to a house. No action will be heard concerning such house. An action, however, will be heard relating to a farm and similar matters.

- 1565. If any person states that he has released any other person from all actions or that he has no claim in respect to him, such release is general, and he may not bring an action in respect to any right which accrued prior to the release, to the extent that no action relating to a right accruing by reason of a contract of guarantee will be heard. Thus, if a person brings an action alleging that another person was surety for some third person, the action will not be heard. Nor may such person allege that some other person was surety for some person prior to that person's release. (See Article 662.)

- 1566. If a person sells property to some other person and receives the price and releases the purchaser from all actions relating to the thing sold, and the purchaser likewise releases the vendor from all actions with regard to the price and a document is drawn up between them on these lines, and the thing sold is seized by someone entitled thereto, the release ceases to be of any effect and the purchaser may claim the return of the price from the vendor. (See Article 52.)

- 1567. The persons who are released must be known and designated. Consequently, if any person states that he has released all persons who are in his debt or that he has no claim upon any person whatsoever,such release is invalid. But if he states that he has released the people of a certain place and people of such place and the number thereof are definitely known, the release is valid.

- 1568. A release is not dependent upon acceptance. but if the release is disclaimed it is of no effect. Thus, if one person releases another there is no need for the latter to accept. But if at the meeting where the release is made, such person states that he refuses to accept the release, such release is of no effect. If a person disclaims a release after having accepted it, it is of no effect. Again, if a person in whose favour a transfer of debt has been made releases the transferee, or a creditor releases a surety, or the transferee, or the surety disclaims the release, such release continues to be effective.

- 1569. A person who is dead may validly be released from his debts.

- 1570. If a person releases one of his heirs from his debts during the course of a mortal sickness, such release in not valid and executory. If he releases a person who is not his heir from his debts, however, such release is effective as regards a third of his property.

- 1571. If a person whose estate is overwhelmed by debts releases a person who is indebted to him during the course of a mortal sickness, such release is invalid and not executory.

PROMULGATED BY ROYAL IRADAH, 6TH SHUAL, 1291.

AL-MAJALLA AL AHKAM AL ADALIYYAH
(The Ottoman Courts Manual (Hanafi))

BOOK XIII. ADMISSIONS.

CHAPTER I. CONDITIONS GOVERNING ADMISSIONS.

- 1572. An admission is a statement by one person admitting the claim of some other person against him. The person making the admission is called an admittor. The person in whose favour the admission is made is called the admittee. The subject of the admission is called the thing admitted.

- 1573. In order to be able to make a valid admission, a person must be of sound mind and have arrived at the age of puberty. Consequently, an admission by a minor, or a lunatic or an imbecile, whether male or female, is invalid. An admission made against such persons by their tutors or guardians is equally invalid. A minor,however, who is of perfect understanding and has been authorised is regarded as a person who has reached the age of puberty in respect to all acts performed by him which he has been authorised to do.

- 1574. A person in whose favour an admission is made need not be of sound mind. Consequently, a person may make a valid admission concerning property in favour of a minor or imperfect understanding and such person will be obliged to give up such property.

- 1575. A person making an admission must do so of his own free will. Consequently, an admission made as a result of force or constraint is invalid.(See Article 1006).

- 1576. A person making an admission should not be under interdiction. (See Sections II, III and IV of the Book of Interdiction.)

- 1577. An admission must not be contrary to obvious facts. Consequently, if the body of a minor bears no signs of puberty, he cannot be heard to make an admission that he has arrived at the age of puberty.

- 1578. A person in whose favour an admission is made must not be absolutely unknown; mere imperfect knowledge of such person, however, does not invalidate an admission.

, Example:- If a person points to certain property in his possession and admits that it is the property of some indeterminate person, or if he admits that the property belongs to one of the inhabitants of a certain town, the inhabitants of such town being indeterminate in number, such person's admission is invalid. On the other hand, if he states that the property belongs to one of two definite persons or to one of the inhabitants of a certain quarter, and the inhabitants of such place are of a determinate number, the admission is valid. In the event of a person stating, as mentioned above, that certain property belongs to one of the two determinate persons, such persons may, if they agree to do so, take the property from the person making the admission and thereupon they become joint owners of such property. If they do not so agree, either of them may place the person making the admission upon his oath that such property is not his. If the person making the admission refuses to take the oath in respect to both persons, the property continues to be jointly owned between them. If the person making the admission refuses to take oath with regard to one of the persons only, the property goes absolutely to the person whose oath he refuses. If the person making the admission takes an oath with regard to both such persons, the former is not liable to any action on the part of the latter, the property belonging to him and remaining in his possession.

CHAPTER II. VALIDITY OF AN ADMISSION.

- 1579. A valid admission may be made with regard to a determinate and also with regard to an indeterminate object. The validity of an admission relating to contracts which can only be made with regard to determinate objects, however, such as sale and hire,depends upon the thing with regard to which the admission is made being determinate. Thus, a valid admission may be made by a person that a thing belonging to another person has been entrusted to his safe keeping, or that he has wrongfully appropriated or stolen the property of another and he shall be obliged to make known the nature of such property. But if a person admits that he has sold something to a certain person, or hired something from him such admission is invalid and he may not be called upon to say what thing he has sold or hired.

- 1580. The validity of an admission is not dependent upon the acceptance of such admission by the person in whose favour the admission is made. Should such person disclaim the admission, however, such admission is null and void. If the person in whose favour the admission is made disclaims part of such admission only, the admission is null and void in regard to that part only, and is valid in respect to the remainder.

- 1581. A difference as to the subject of the admission between the person making the admission and the person in whose favour it is made does not invalidate the admission. Thus, if a person brings an action for the recovery of one thousand piastres due under a loan, and the defendant admits one thousand piastres is due for the price of a thing sold, the difference in no way invalidates the admission.

- 1582. A request for a settlement with regard to any property is equivalent to an admission in respect thereto. Thus, if A requests B to repay a debt of one thousand piastres and request A to make a settlement for seven hundred piastres in respect to such debt, A admits the thousands piastres claimed. But if A states that he will settle the action in respect to the thousand piastres merely in order to avoid a dispute, there is no admission of the thousand piastres.

- 1583. If a person seeks to buy, hire or borrow property in the possession of another, or requests such person to bestow such property upon him by way of gift, or to give him such property for safe keeping, or the latter requests the former to take property into his safe keeping, and such person agrees to do so, there is an admission made by such person that the property is not his.

- 1584. An admission dependent on a condition is null and void. An admission dependent upon the arrival of a generally recognised period of time, however, is equivalent to an admission of a debt repayable at a future definite date.

  Example:- A informs B that he will pay him a certain sum of money if he reaches a certain place or if he undertakes a certain business. The admission is void and the sum of money need not be paid.

But if A states that he will repay B a certain sum of money on the first of a certain month, or on the twenty-sixth of October next, such statement is considered to be an admission of debt repayable at a future definite date, and upon the arrival of such date, payment of the sum in question must be made. (See Article 40.)

- 1585. An admission may validly be made that a thing is undivided jointly-owned property. Consequently, if one person admits to another that he is in possession of an undivided share of certain immovable property held in absolute ownership belonging to him, such as a half or a third, and the latter confirms such admission, and the person making admission dies before the division and delivery of such property, the fact that the subject matter of the admission is an undivided share in no way invalidates such admission.

- 1586. An admission may validly be made by a dumb person using the recognised signs of such persons. An admission by signs cannot validly be made by a person who is able to speak. Thus, if one person asks another who is able to speak whether he is owing some third person a certain sum of money and such person nods his head, there is no admission of the debt.

CHAPTER III. EFFECT OF AN ADMISSION.

SECTION I. GENERAL.

- 1587. A person is bound by his admission in accordance with the terms of Article 79, unless the admission is proved to be false by a judgement of the Court. Thus, a person is legally entitled to a thing in the possession of another, which the latter has obtained by purchase. AT the trial, the purchaser, in order to prove his case, states that the thing sold belong4d to the vendor and that he sold it to him. The person legally entitled to such thing proves his claim and judgement is given by the Court in his favour. The purchaser may thereupon take action against the vendor and recover from him the price of the thing sold, because although at the trial he opposed the person legally entitled to the thing by admitting that such thing was the property of the vendor, he is not bound by the admission, the Court having found such admission to be void of any foundation.

- 1588. No person may validly retract an admission made with regard to private rights. Thus, if a person admits owing a certain sum of money to another and later retracts his admission, the retraction is invalid and he is bound by his admission.

- 1589. Should a person allege that he has not been truthful in making an admission, the person in whose favour the admission is made shall swear an oath that such admission is true.

Example:- A gives a written acknowledgement that he has borrowed a certain sum of money from B. Later, A denies that he has borrowed such money in fact, in spite of his having given the acknowledgement, by reason of his not yet having received the money in question from B. The person in whose favour the admission is made shall then take an oath that such admission is not false.

- 1590. If one person admits to another that he is in such person's debt to the extent of a certain sum of money, and the latter states that the money to paid is not his, but belongs to another person, and such person confirms that statement, the money in question becomes the property of the second person in whose favour the admission is made, but the right of receiving it belongs to the first person in whose favour the admission is made. Consequently, if the second person in whose favour the admission is made claims the money from the debtor, the latter is not obliged to pay it to him. If the debtor, however, pays the debt of his own free will to the second person in whose favour the admission is made, he is released from his debt and the first person in whose favour the admission is made cannot claim it again from the debtor.

SECTION II. DENIAL OF OWNERSHIP AND THE TITLE TO A THING LENT.

- 1591. If a person making an admission makes it in such a manner as to show that the subject matter of the admission belongs to him, the result is a gift to the person in whose favour the admission is made, but such gift does not become absolute until it has been handed over and received. If he does not do so, the result is an admission that the subject matter of the admission was the property of the person in whose favour the admission is made, prior to such admission, which is tantamount to a denial of ownership.

Examples:-

(1). A states that all his property and things in his possession belong to B, and that he has no right to them at all. The result is a gift to B of all property and things in A's possession at that time and delivery and receipt thereof are essential.

(2). A states that all the property and things attributed to him, with the exception of the clothes he is wearing, belong to B and do not concern him in any way. The result is an admission by A that the property in question belongs to B. Such admission, however, does not include property acquired by A after the admission.

(3). A states that all his property and things in his shop belong to his eldest son and that he has no right thereto whatsoever. The result is a gift to his eldest son of all his property and things in the shop at that time, and such property must be delivered. But if A states that all property and things in a certain shop of his belongs to his eldest son and that he has no right thereto whatsoever, the result is an admission in favour of his son that the property in such shop is the property of his son and he has denied ownership thereof. This admission,however, does not include any property placed in the shop afterwards.

(4). A states that his shop situated in such and such a place belongs to his wife. The result is in the nature of a gift, of which delivery is necessary. But if A states that such and such a shop reputed to be his belongs to his wife, the result is an admission that the shop was his wife's property before such admission and not his own property.

- 1592. If a person states that the shop which he holds in absolute ownership and by title deed belongs to some other person, that he has no connection therewith of any sort, and that his name inscribed in the deed was lent for convenience only, the result is an admission that the shop belongs to that other person; or if a person states that a shop which he holds in absolute ownership bought by title deed from some other person was purchased on behalf of a third person, that the price was paid out of that person's property, and that the name of the first person was inscribed in the title deed for convenience only, the result is an admission that the shop was in fact the property of the third person.

- 1593. If a person is in possession of a written acknowledgement admitting a claim for a certain sum of money against some other person and states that such sum belongs to a third person, and that his name on the document has been inscribed for convenience only, the result is an admission that the sum in question belongs to such third person.

- 1594. If a person while in good health makes an admission disclaiming ownership as set out above, or admits that his name has been used for convenience only, his admission is valid and he is bound by it during his lifetime, and his heirs likewise after his death. The effect of an admission made as above while the person making the admission is suffering from a mortal sickness is governed by the terms of the following Chapter.

SECTION III. ADMISSION BY A PERSON SUFFERING FROM A MORTAL SICKNESS.

- 1595. A mortal sickness is a sickness where in the majority of cases death is imminent, and, in the case of a male, where such person is unable to deal with his affairs outside his home, and in the case of a female, where she is unable to deal with her domestic duties, death having occurred before the expiration of one year by reason of such illness, whether the sick person has been confined to bed or not. Should the sickness be of longer duration and the period of one year expire while in the same condition such person is regarded as being in good health and his transactions as valid, unless the illness increases, and his condition becomes changed for the worse. Should his illness increase, however, and his condition become worse resulting in death before the expiration of one year, he is considered from the time of the change up to his death, to have been suffering from a sickness.

- 1595. Should a person have no heir at all, or should a man have no heir other than his wife, or should a woman have no heir other than her husband, any admission made during the course of a mortal sickness is regarded as a bequest and will be upheld. Consequently, if a person having no heirs disclaims ownership of his property during a mortal sickness by making an admission that the whole thereof belongs to some other person, such admission is valid, and the estate of the deceased person may not be touched by the representative of the Treasury. Similarly, if a man having no heir other than his wife disclaims ownership of his property during a mortal sickness by making an admission that such property belongs to his wife, or a woman having no heir other than her husband disclaims ownership of all her property by making an admission that such property belongs to her husband, such admission is valid and the estate of neither of the deceased persons may be touched by the representative of the Treasury.

- 1597. An admission made by a person during an illness from which he recovers that property belongs to one of his heirs, is held to be valid.

- 1598. If a person after having made an admission during a mortal sickness that certain specific property, or a debt, belongs to one of his heirs, and then dies, the validity of such admission depends upon the ratification of the other heirs. If they agree, the admission is held to be good; if not, it is invalid. Provided that if the other heirs have agreed thereto during the lifetime of the person making the admission, they cannot withdraw their agreement and the admission is held to be valid. An admission with regard to something deposited for safe keeping, moreover, may always validly be made in favour of an heir. Thus, if a person during a mortal sickness admits that he has received property which he has deposited for safe keeping with his heir, or that he has consumed property belonging to his heir known to have been deposited with him for safe keeping, such admission is valid.

Examples:-

(1). A person admits that he has received property of his deposited for safe keeping with one of his sons. Such admission is valid and executory.

(2) A person admits that one of his sons has received, as agent, money due to him from a certain person and that he has handed it over to him. Such admission is valid.

(3). A person admits that he has sold the property of one his sons entrusted to him for safe keeping, or his diamond ring worth five thousand piastres lent to him for his use, and has spent the proceeds on his own business. Such admission is valid. The value of the ring must be made good from the estate.

- 1599. In this connection, by heir meant a person who was an heir at the of the sick person's death. Provided that if a right to inherit arises out of a new cause at the time of the death of the person making such admission and not previously, this shall in no way invalidate an admission made while that person was not an heir. Similarly, if a person during the course of a mortal sickness makes an admission in favour of a woman who is a stranger to him in respect to certain property, marries her and then dies, such admission is executory. If the right to inherit is not produced by such a new cause, however, but by an old one, the admission is not executory.

Example:- A has a son and makes an admission in favour of one of his brothers by the same father and mother. Should the son predecease the father, the admission does not becomes executory merely because the brother in whose favour the admission was made has become his heir.

- 1600. An admission made during a mortal sickness but relating to matters concerning a period during which the person making the admission was in good health, is considered to be an admission made during a sickness. Consequently, if a person admits during a mortal sickness that he has been paid a certain number of piastres due from one of his heirs while he was in a state of good health, such admission is not executory unless the other heirs confirm the same. Again, if a person admits during a mortal sickness that he has made a gift of certain property of his to one of his heirs while in a state of good health, and that he has delivered the same, such admission is not executory unless confirmed by the other heirs, or proved by evidence.

- 1601. An admission made by a person during a mortal sickness to another person who is not one of such person's own heirs is good, even though it includes the whole of his property, whether consisting of some specific object or of some debt. Should it appear that the admission is false, however, it being a matter of common knowledge that at the time the admission was made, the subject matter of such admission had become the property of the person making the admission by way of sale, gift, or transfer on inheritance, such facts must be duly examined. If the admission was made when drawing up a will, the result is a gift, and delivery of such gift is necessary. If made when drawing up a will, it is taken to be a bequest. In any case, the admission is only valid up to one third of the property of the person making the admission, whether a bequest or a gift.

- 1602. Debts contracted in good health take priority over debts contracted during ill health, that is to say, in the event of the death of a person whose estate is overwhelmed by debts contracted before his mortal sickness, such debts are paid in priority to those contracted by him by way of admission during his mortal sickness. Consequently, debts contracted while in a state of good health are paid first out of the sick person's estate. If there is any balance remaining over, debts contracted during sickness and arising out of clearly ascertained causes, such as purchase, loan, or destruction of property are considered to be debts contracted while in a state of good health. If the subject matter of an admission is some specific object, it is dealt with in the same manner. That is to say, if a person admits to some other person during the course of a mortal sickness that certain things are that person's property, such person has no right to the property with regard to which the admission has been made, unless the debts contracted during good health have been paid, or debts which are in the nature of debts contracted during good health and which for reasons as stated above, must be repaid.

- 1603. If a person admits during the course of a mortal sickness that he has been paid any sum due from any other person, not being a member of his family, such admission is receivable. If the debt was contracted by such person during the course of the illness, the admission is valid. Such admission, however, is not executory as regards persons who became creditors of the sick person while he was in a state of good health. If the debt was contracted by such person while in a state of good health, the admission is valid in any case and this whether there be debts which were contracted while in a state of good health or not.

  Example: - A while ill admits that he has sold certain property and received the price thereof while sick. Such admission is valid. Persons to whom he became indebted while in a state of good health, however, may refuse to be bound by such admission. If A, however, admits during the course of a mortal sickness that he has sold certain property while in a state of good health and has received the price thereof, such admission is valid in any case, and persons to whom he became indebted while in a state of good health are bound thereby.

- 1604. A person who pays a debt due to one of his creditors during the course of a mortal sickness may not thereby destroy the right of the other creditors. He may, however, repay a sum of money he borrowed and pay the price of property he bought while sick.

- 1605. In this connection, a guarantee of property is considered in the same light as the original debt. Consequently, if a person becomes surety for any debt contracted by his heirs or any sum due to him, during the course of a mortal sickness, it is not executory. If such person becomes surety for some other person, not being a member of his family, it is valid up to a third of his property. If such person admits during the course of a mortal sickness that he has become surety for a person, not being a member of his family, while in a state of good health, the admission is valid up to the whole extent of his property. Debts contracted during a state of good health, if any, however, are preferred.

CHAPTER IV. ADMISSIONS IN WRITING.

- 1606. An admission in writing is the same as an oral admission. (See Article 69).
- 1607. If a person causes his own admission to be written down by some other person, it has the force of an admission. Therefore if a person instructs a clerk to make out a document to the effect that he is owing another person a certain sum of money, and himself signs or seals such document, the document is regarded as though it were written in his own hand and is considered to be written admission.
- 1608. The entries made by a merchant in his books which are properly kept are in the nature of

written admissions.

Example:- A, a merchant, makes an entry in his own register that he owes B a certain sum of money. Such entry constitutes an admission of the debt, and, should the occasion arise, is considered as an oral admission.

- 1609. If a person himself writes or causes a clerk to write an acknowledgement of a debt, which he signs or seals and delivers to some other person, and if such acknowledgement is made out in due form, that is to say, in accordance with the usual practice, it constitutes an admission in writing and has the same force as an oral admission. Receipts which are normally given are of the same category.

- 1610. If any person as mentioned above writes or causes any other person to write, any acknowledgement of debt, which is signed or sealed, and which he admits to be his and then denies the debt contained therein, such denial is disregarded, and the debt must be paid.

Should he deny that the acknowledgement is his, the handwriting or seal being well known, the denial is disregarded, and action is taken in accordance with the acknowledgement.

If the handwriting and seal are not well known, such person shall be caused to write down specimens of his handwriting, which shall be submitted to experts. If they report that the hand writing in both cases is that of one and the same person, such person shall be ordered to pay debt in question.

Finally, if the acknowledgement is free from any taint of fraud or forgery, action shall be taken in accordance with the acknowledgement. If it is not free from suspicion, however, and should the debtor deny the original debt, he shall, if the plaintiff so demand, be made to swear an oath that neither the debt nor the acknowledgement is his.

- 1611. Should any person give an acknowledgement of a debt as mentioned above, and then die, and the heirs admit that the acknowledgement was made by the deceased, the debt must be paid out of the deceased's estate.

Should the heirs deny that the acknowledgement was made by the deceased, and should his handwriting and seal be well known, action shall be taken in accordance with such acknowledgement.

- 1612. If a purse full of money is found among the effects of a deceased person, and it is written thereon that the purse is the property of some particular person and has been given to the deceased on trust for safe keeping, the person in question has a right to take the purse from the estate of the deceased and there is no need for any further proof.

PROMULGATED BY ROYAL IRADAH, 9 JUMADI UL ULA, 1293.

AL-MAJALLA AL AHKAM AL ADALIYYAH
(The Ottoman Courts Manual (Hanafi))

BOOK XIV ACTIONS.

INTRODUCTION

TERMS OF ISLAMIC JURISPRUDENCE.

- 1613. An action consists of a claim made by one person against another in Court. The person making the claim is called the plaintiff. The person against whom the claim is made is called the defendant.

- 1614. The thing claimed is the thing about which the action is brought by the plaintiff. It is also called the subject matter of the action.

- 1615. Estoppel is some statement previously made by the plaintiff which conflicts with the action he has brought, and which causes such action to be declared null and void.

CHAPTER I. CONDITIONS AND FUNDAMENTAL RULES RELATING TO AN ACTION AND THE DEFENCE THERETO.

SECTION I. CONDITIONS FOR THE VALIDITY OF AN ACTION.

- 1616. The plaintiff and the defendant must be of sound mind. A lunatic and a minor of imperfect understanding may not validly bring an action. Their tutors and guardians may act on their behalf in their capacity of plaintiff and defendant.

- 1617. The defendant must be known. Consequently, if the plaintiff alleges that he is entitled to a certain sum of money from one or more persons who are specified, inhabiting a certain village, the claim is invalid, and the defendant must be specified.

- 1618. The defendant must be present when the action comes on in Court. If the defendant fails to come to the Court, or to send a representative, action shall be taken as is set forth in the Book on the Administration of Justice by the Court.

- 1619. The subject matter of the action must be known. If it is not known, the action is invalid.

- 1620. The subject matter of the action may be made known by pointing it out, or by mentioning its qualities or by describing it. Thus, in the case of some specific piece of movable property, if such property is present in Court, it is sufficient to point it out. If it is not so present, it may be made known by mentioning the qualities description and value thereof. If it is real property, it may be designated by mentioning the boundaries thereof. If it is a debt, the nature, variety, description and amount thereof must be stated. These matters will be dealt with in the following Articles.

- 1621. If the subject matter of the action is some specific movable property and is before the Court, The plaintiff may bring an action and point to the thing claimed, asking for it to be restored to him, since the defendant has wrongfully dispossessed him thereof. If the subject matter of the action is not before the Court, but it can be sent for and produced without expense, it shall be placed before the Court for the purpose of the trial of the action, the giving of evidence, or swearing the oath. If it cannot be brought before the Court without expense, the plaintiff shall give a description and state the value thereof. In actions relating to wrongful appropriation of property, and in the case of pledges, it is not necessary to state the value.

T Example:- An action may validly be brought in which the plaintiff states that his emerald ring has been wrongfully appropriated, but fails to state the value, or even states that he does not know the value thereof.

- 1622. If the subject matter of the action consists of specific pieces of property, the nature, sort and qualities of which are different the one from the other, it is sufficient if the total value of the whole of them is stated. There is no need to state the value of each of them separately.

- 1623. If the subject matter of the action is real property, the name of the town and village or quarter and of the street and the four or three boundaries thereof, and the names of the persons, if any, to whom such such boundaries belong, together with the names of their fathers and grandfathers must be stated when the action is brought and when giving evidence. In the case of a person who is well known, however, it is sufficient to state his name and description. There is no need to state the names of his father and grandfather. Similarly, if the description of the boundaries may be dispensed with owing to their being so well known, there is no need to state the boundaries wither when bringing the action or giving evidence in connection therewith. The plaintiff may also validly bring an action stating that the real property the boundaries of which are set forth in a document he produces to the Court is his property owned in absolute ownership.

- 1624. The fact that the plaintiff correctly states the boundaries, but incorrectly states the length or area thereof in no way affects the validity of the action.

- 1625. In an action for the price of real property, it is not essential to state the boundaries thereof.

- 1626. If the subject matter of the action is a debt, the plaintiff must state the nature, variety, description and amount thereof.

Example:- It must be stated as regards the nature of the debt whether it is of gold or silver or as regards the variety whether it consists of Ottoman or English coin and in respect to the description whether it consists of sound or base coin. The amount must also be stated. If it is stated in general terms, however, to consist of so many piastres, the action is valid, and the amount in dispute will be considered with reference to the custom prevailing in the locality. If there are two types of currency recognised, and the circulation and standard of one is greater than the other, the amount will be construed with reference to the inferior currency. Again, if a person brings an action claiming so many pieces of five, the money is taken to be the black pieces of five, that is base coin, in circulation at the present time.

- 1627. If the subject matter of the action is some specific piece of property, there is no need to state how the ownership thereof was acquired, but the action may validly be brought by stating that the property in question is owned in absolute ownership. If it consists of a debt, however, the origin thereof must be stated, that is to say, whether it is price of something sold, or rent, or arising from any other reason.

- 1628. The effect of an admission is that it bears upon the subject matter of the admission. It does not bear upon the origin thereof and therefore an admission is not a cause of ownership. Consequently, no person may bring an action claiming something merely by reason of admission of the defendant.

Examples:-

(1). A brings an action alleging that certain property belongs to him, and that B has dispossessed him thereof and in addition has admitted that such property belongs to A. The action will be heard. But if A brings an action alleging that certain property is his because B, who has taken possession thereof, has admitted that it belongs to A, the action will not be heard.

(2). A brings an action alleging that B is owing him a certain sum of money on account of a loan and that B has admitted the debt. The action will be heard. But if A brings an action alleging that has admitted that he owes A certain sum of money on account of a loan, and that he consequently claims this sum from him, the action will not heard.

- 1629. The subject matter of the action must be capable of proof. Consequently, no action may validly be brought with regard to anything the existence of which can be shown to be impossible either by a process of reasoning or by custom.

Example:- A alleges that B is his son, B being older than A, and the matter of his birth well known. The action will fail.

- 1630. If the action is proved, judgement must be given against the defendant in respect to some particular thing.

Examples:-

(1). A gives something to B as loan for use. C then comes forward and claims that he is a relative of A requesting that such thing shall be lent to him. The action will fail.

(2). A appoints B his agent for a certain purpose. C comes forward and alleges that he is A's neighbour and that he is a more suitable person to be appointed agent. The action will fail.

The reason for this is that every person may lend his property for use to whomsoever he pleases as his agent and even though the matters alleged by the plaintiffs may be true, no judgement can be issued in respect to the defendant.

SECTION II. THE DEFENCE TO AN ACTION.

- 1631. A defence consists of making an allegation by the defendant in reply to an action brought by the plaintiff.

Examples:-

(1). A brings an action claiming a certain sum of money from B on account of a loan. B replies that he has paid A, or that A has released him from the debt, or that they have come to a settlement, or that the sum in question is not a loan, but is the price of the property sold to A, or that he made a transfer to A of a sum of money due to him from C, and that the sum in question was paid by A to him in respect of such transfer. This is B's defence.

(2). A brings an action against B stating that B became surety for the payment of a sum of money due to him from C. B replies that C has paid the sum in question. This is B's defence.

(3). A brings an action against B stating that B is in possession of property belonging to him. B replies that some time ago C brought an action against him in respect to some property and that at the trial of the action A gave evidence in favour of C. This is B's defence.

(4). A brings an action against the heirs to the estate of a deceased person, claiming a certain sum of money, which the heirs deny. A proves his claim, and thereupon the heirs allege that the deceased paid the debt in his lifetime. This is the heirs' defence to the action.

- 1632. Upon the defendant proving his defence, the action brought by the plaintiff is dismissed. If he fails to prove his defence, he may call upon the plaintiff to take the oath. If the plaintiff refuses to take the oath, the defendant's defence is proved. If the plaintiff takes oath, the action brought by the plaintiff is maintained.

- 1633. If any person brings an action against some other person claiming a certain sum of money from him and the defendant replies by stating that he has transferred the payment of the debt to some third person and that both parties agreed to such transfer and proves such statement in the presence of the person to whom he transferred the debt, the claim of the plaintiff is rejected and the defendant freed therefrom. If the person to whom the debt has been transferred is not present, the defendant is considered to have answered the claim of the plaintiff pending the arrival of such person.

SECTION III. PARTIES TO AN ACTION.

- 1634. If any person brings an action in respect to any matter, and the defendant admits the claim, judgement is given on the admission. If he denies the claim, the action is heard, and evidence may be given. If judgement is not given on the admission of the defendant, he does not become a party to the action by reason of his denial.

Example:- A brings an action against B alleging that B sent a messenger of his to by certain property and claims the price. If B admits the claim, he is bound to pay and hand over the price of the thing sold. If he denies, he becomes the defendant to A's claim whose case is then heard and who may produce evidence. If A brings an action alleging that B's agent for purchase bought such property, and the defendant admits the claim, B must pay and hand over the price of the sale. If he denies however he does not become defendant to A. In that case the plaintiff's action will not be heard.

Tutors, guardians and trustees of the pious foundations are excepted from this rule. Thus, if any person brings an action stating that the property of an orphan or of a pious foundation is his, and the tutor or guardian or trustee admit the claim, the admission is of no effect and no judgement may be issued based thereon. They may,however, make a valid denial and an action brought by the plaintiff as a result of such denial, and the plaintiff's evidence, will be heard. If an action is brought as the result of an admission based upon contract concluded by a tutor, guardian or trustee of a pious foundation, the action will be heard.

Example:- A tutor sells property belonging to a minor, having legal justification for so doing. The purchaser brings an action in connection therewith. An admission made by tutor is valid.

- 1635. In an action relating to some specific piece of property, the person is possession must be made defendant.

Example:- A wrongfully appropriates B's horse and sells and delivers it to C. B wishes to get his horse back. He must bring his action against the person in possession of the horse. If he wishes to recover the value of the horse, however, he must bring his action against the person who has wrongfully appropriated the horse.

- 1636. If a person brings an action claiming that he is entitled to property which has been purchased, it must be ascertained whether the purchaser has taken delivery of such property. If so, the defendant at the trial of the action and hearing of the evidence will be the purchaser only. There is no need for the vendor to be present. If the purchaser has not yet taken delivery of the property from the vendor, both the purchaser of the property, and the vendor as the person in possession of the property, must be present at the trial of the action.

- 1637. In actions relating to a thing deposited for safe keeping brought against the person with whom it has been deposited, or to a thing lent against the person borrowing it, or a thing hired against the person hiring it, or a pledge against the pledgee, both parties must be present. But if property deposited for safe keeping, or lent, or hired, or pledged has been wrongfully appropriated, the person in possession of such property may bring the action against the person wrongfully appropriating and there is no need for the presence of the owner. If such persons are not present, the owner alone may not bring the action.

- 1638. A person to whom property has been entrusted for safe keeping may not be made defendant in an action against the purchaser.

Example:- A brings an action against B alleging that he is in possession of a house which he brought from C for a certain sum of money, claiming that the house be handed over to him. B replies that C handed the house over to him for safe keeping. The plaintiff's claim fails and B is not obliged to prove that C in fact handed the house over to him for safe keeping. If A admits that C handed the house to B for safe keeping, but adds that thereafter C sold it to him and made him his agent to receive it from C, and A proves the sale and his appointment as agent, he is entitled to take the house from the person to whom it has been entrusted for safe keeping.

- 1639. A person to whom a thing has been entrusted for safe keeping cannot be made defendant in an action brought by the creditor of the person depositing the thing for safe keeping with him. Consequently, if a creditor proves before a person to whom property has been entrusted for safe keeping that a debt is owing to him by the person depositing such property, he cannot satisfy his debt from such property but, as is set forth in Article 799, a person who is entitled to maintenance from some absent person may bring an action claiming that the sum necessary for his maintenance shall be paid to him from money deposited by the absent person for safe keeping.

- 1640. A creditor may not bring an action against a person in debt to the person owing him money. Consequently, if any person proves before a person in debt to a deceased person that he has a claim against such deceased person, he may not obtain payment from the debtor.

- 1641. A vendor may not bring an action against a person who purchased something which he has sold to some other person.

. Example:- A sells property to B. B takes delivery thereof and sells it to C. A may not bring an action against C alleging that B has bought the property from him and has taken delivery thereof without paying the price and that he claims the price from C, or that he claims the thing sold in order to exercise a right of retention over such thing until he has received payment of the price

- 1642. In the case of a deceased person, one of the heirs alone may become plaintiff, or act as defendant, in actions brought of behalf of or against such deceased person. In the case of an action brought to recover some specific piece of property from the estate, however, the heir in whose possession the property is, must be made defendant. The action may not be brought against an heir who is not in possession of such property.

Examples:-

(1). One of the heirs alone may bring an action to recover a debt owing to the deceased. After proving his claim judgement is given for all the heirs for the total amount of the claim. The heir acting as plaintiff can obtain his own part alone. He cannot obtain the shares of the other heirs.

(2). A person brings an action to recover a debt owing by the estate of a deceased person. He may bring the action in the presence of one of the heirs only, and this, whether such heir is in possession of property belonging to the estate or not. If the heir in question admits the debt in an action brought in this way, and this admission in no way binds the other heirs. If he does not admit the debt, and the plaintiff proves his case in his presence alone, judgement shall be given against the whole of the heirs. Upon the plaintiff proceeding to collect the amount of the debt from the estate, the other heirs may not call upon him to prove the debt again in their presence. They have the right, however, of defending the action brought by the plaintiff.

(3). If a person brings an action to recover a horse in the possession of one of the heirs only, prior to partition of the estate, and which he claims he deposited with the deceased for safe keeping, the heir in possession of the horse may be made defendant. No action will be heard against any other of the heirs. If the person in possession admits the claim, judgement should be given in accordance with such admission, which does not effect the other heirs. His admission is effective in respect to the amount of his own share only and the judgement shall state that his share is the horse belongs to the plaintiff proves his case, Judgement shall be given against the whole of the heirs. (See Art. 78).

- 1643. If an action is brought claiming some specific piece of property owned by several joint owners, the ownership arising out of some cause other than inheritance, one of the joint owners may not be made defendant in respect to the share of the other.

Example:- A brings an action claiming as his a house which has been purchased jointly by several persons, and proves his case in the presence of one of the joint purchasers only. If judgement is given in his favour, the judgement relates to such joint owner's share only and does not extend to the others.

- 1644. In an action brought in respect to places affecting the public interest, such as the public highway, where one member of the public only is plaintiff, the action shall be heard and judgement given against the defendant.

- 1645. In an action relating to things the benefit of which is jointly owned by two villages, as in the case of a river or grazing ground, the inhabitants of which are indeterminate in number, the presence of a certain number of them is sufficient. If they are determinate in number, however, it is not enough for some of them to be present, but the whole of them must be present either personally, or through their representative.

- 1646. The inhabitants of a village which are more than a hundred in number are considered to be indeterminate in number.

SECTION IV. ESTOPPEL.

- 1647. A statement contradicting a statement previously made with regard to the same matter invalidates an action for ownership.

Examples:-

(1). If a person arranges to purchase a piece of property, but before completing the purchase brings an action claiming that such property is his own absolutely, such action will not be heard.

(2). If a person states that he has no right to any particular thing, but, nevertheless, brings an action claiming that such property is his own absolutely, such action will not be heard.

(3). A brings an action against B asserting that he gave a certain amount of money to B to hand to C. A further states that B retained the money instead of giving it to C as directed, and that he instructed B to fetch the money and pay it over to C. The plaintiff establishes his case by evidence. If the defendant denies such statements but later, while admitting having received the sum of money for delivery to C, states that he has in fact delivered it to C, and seeks to bring an action in rebuttal of the plaintiff's claim, such action cannot be heard.

(4). A brings an action alleging that a certain shop in the possession of B is his property. B admits that the shop was formerly A's property, but asserts that A sold it to him on a certain date. A completely denies this statement, stating that they had never concluded a contract of sale and purchase. If B, the person in the possession of the shop, proves his case, the plaintiff cannot later be heard to say that he did in fact sell the shop to B, but the sale was a sale subject to redemption, or subject to a condition making the contract voidable.

- 1648. If a person admits that certain property belongs to another, he may not later bring an action claiming that such property is his, nor may he bring an action on behalf of any other person, such as his agent or guardian.

- 1649. If a person releases another from all actions, he may not later bring an action against such person claiming from him property which he asserts to be his own. This, however, will not prevent him from bringing an action on behalf of another person, in the capacity of such person's agent or guardian.

- 1650. A person who has brought an action claiming property on behalf of another person may not later bring an action claiming such property as his own. But after bringing an action on his own behalf he may bring an action on behalf of some other person in the capacity of such person's agent, the reason being that an advocate sometimes claims property in his own name, but a person who is himself a party to an action does not assert that the property belongs to another.

- 1651. One claim cannot be paid separately by two persons. Similarly, a claim arising from a single cause cannot be demanded from two persons.

- 1652. Estoppel operates to prevent two persons claiming the same thing, as in the case of an agent and the person appointing him and an heir and the person from whom he inherits, if estoppel would operate to invalidate a claim in an action by one person. Thus, if in an action an agent introduces a claim in conflict with an action previously instituted by his principal, such claim is invalid.

- 1653. If one of the parties admits the claim, the estoppel ceases to be operative.

Example:- A brings an action claiming that he has lent a certain sum of money to B. A later brings an action asserting that the sum of money was by way of guarantee. The defendant admits this, whereupon the estoppel ceases to be operative.

- 1654. If the Court finds a statement to be false, the estoppel ceases to be operative.

Example:- A brings an action claiming certain property in the possession of B. The defendant disputes the claim, alleging that the property belongs to C from whom he bought it. If the plaintiff proves his case, he gets judgement. The person against whom judgement is given has a right of recourse against the vendor for the price of the property, because B was estopped from having recourse against the vendor by reason of his admission that such property belonged to the vendor. The estoppel ceases to be operative, since the judgement of the Court has disregarded the admission.

- 1655. If the matter is subject to doubt, and the plaintiff can offer a satisfactory explanation, the estoppel is removed.

Example:-

(1). A hires a house, and later brings an action against the lessor asserting that his father bought the house from him when he was a child, adding that at the time he hired the housed he was not aware of the facts of the case. If A can produce documentary evidence of the title the case will be heard.

(2). A hires a house and later brings an action against the lessor claiming that he had ascertained that such house had devolved upon him some time previously by way of inheritance from his father. The case will be heard.

- 1656. The commencement of the division of an estate is an admission that the property divided has been held in common. Consequently, a plaintiff is estopped from bringing an action after the division of the property, alleging that the property divided belongs to him.

Example:- A, an heir, brings an action after the division of the estate asserting that he bought one of the things divided from the deceased person, or that the deceased person while in good health bestowed such thing upon him by way of gift and gave delivery thereof. Such action will not be heard. But if A asserts that the deceased person gave him the property in question while he was an infant and that at the time of the division of the property he was unaware of such fact, this is regarded as a valid excuse and the case will be heard.

- 1657. If it is possible to reconcile two apparently contradictory statements, and if the plaintiff does in fact explain away any apparent contradiction, there can be no estoppel.

Example:-

(1). A admits that he is the lessee of a house. Later, he brings an action alleging that he is the owner of the house. The case will not be heard. But if explains away the contradiction by stating that he bought the house from the owner after he had hired such house, the case will be heard.

(2). A brings an action claiming the return of a sum of money advanced by way of loan. The defendant by his reply states that he has received nothing from him, or that the two parties had no business transaction together of any sort, or that he does not know the plaintiff. A proves his case. If the defendant later brings an action against A asserting that he has repaid the sum in question, or that A released him from repayment thereof, the defendant is estopped from bringing such action by reason of the contradiction. But if, upon the case being brought by A, the defendant replies that he owes nothing and when the plaintiff proves his case admits owing the sum, but asserts that he has since repaid it, or has been released from repayment thereof by the plaintiff, and proves his case, there is no estoppel.

(3). A brings an action against B alleging that he has deposited something with B for safe keeping and claiming the return thereof. The defendant replies denying the allegation and stating that no such thing was ever deposited with him for safe keeping. A proves his case by evidence and the defendant then seeks to defeat A by alleging that he has returned the thing to A and given delivery thereof. B is estopped from making such defence. If the thing entrusted to B for safe keeping is in the possession of B, the plaintiff takes the thing itself. If it is no longer in existence, however, B must pay A the price thereof. But if A brings an action and B replies alleging that no such thing belonging to the plaintiff has ever been deposited with him for safe keeping, and A then proves his case by evidence, and B admits that A deposited the thing with him for safe keeping, but that he has returned such thing to A and given A delivery thereof, B is not estopped.

- 1658. A person who admits being a party to an unconditional and perfectly valid contract, his admission being reduced to writing, is estopped from alleging later that the contract was entered into subject to a condition as to redemption, or is voidable. (See Art. 100).

Examples:-

(1). A sells and delivers his house owned in absolute ownership to B for an agreed price. A then goes into Court and makes an admission to the effect that he has sold his house to B, the boundaries whereof are as stated, such sale being unconditional and perfectly valid, for a certain sum of money. If a later, after his admission has been reduced to writing, brings an action stating that the sale was subject to a condition as to redemption, or that it was made subject to a condition rendering it voidable, such action will not be heard.

(2). If A settles an action which he has brought against B, and makes an admission in Court that the settlement has been validly made, and after such admission has been reduced to writing brings an action alleging that the settlement was made subject to a condition making it voidable, such action will not be heard.

- 1659. If A in the presence of B sells property held in absolute ownership, which he asserts is his own, to C, and gives delivery thereof to him, and B later brings an action alleging that such property is his or that he has a share therein, although he was present when the sale took place and kept silence without any valid excuse for so doing, it must be ascertained whether B is a relative of the vendor, or his or her husband or wife. If so, the action will not be heard in any case. If he is a stranger, the fact that he was present at the time the sale was concluded, does not of itself prevent the hearing of the action. On the other hand, if, in addition to being present when the sale took place, he keeps silence without any valid excuse for so doing while the purchaser deals with the property as though it were his own, such as by erecting buildings or pulling them down, or planting trees thereon, and then brings an action claiming that such property is his own, or that he has a share therein, such action will not heard.

CHAPTER II. LIMITATION.

- 1660. Actions relating to a debt, a property deposited for safe-keeping, or real property held in absolute ownership, or inheritance, or actions not relating to the fundamental constitution of a pious foundation, such as actions relating to real property dedicated to pious purposes leased for a single or double rent, or to pious foundations with a condition as to the appointment of a trustee, or the revenue of a pious foundation, or actions not relating to the public, shall not be heard after the expiration of a period of fifteen years since action was last taken in connection therewith.

- 1661. Actions brought by a trustee of a pious foundation relating to the fundamental constitution thereof or by persons maintained by such foundation may be heard upto a period of thirty-six years. They shall not be heard in any event, however, after the period of thirty-six years has expired.

  Example:- A has held a piece of real property in absolute ownership for a period of thirty-six years. The trustee of a pious foundation thereupon brings an action claiming that the piece of real property in question is part of the land belonging to his pious foundation. The action will not be heard.

- 1662. Actions relating to a private road, to a right of flow and to a right of taking water, when relating to real property held in absolute ownership, shall not be heard after the expiration of a period of fifteen years. If they relate to real property which has been dedicated to pious purposes, however, the trustees thereof is entitled to bring an action relating thereto up to a period of thirty-six years. Actions relating to the government land and actions relating to private roads, to a right of flow and to a right of taking water, if they concern government land, shall not be heard after the expiration of a period of ten years since action was last taken in connection therewith.

- 1663. Limitation which is effective in this connection, that is to say, which prevents an action being heard, relates only to a period of time which has been allowed to elapse without any excuse. The effluxion of time which has occurred by reason of some lawful excuse,such as cases where the plaintiff is a minor,or a lunatic,or an imbecile,and that whether he has a guardian or not,or where the plaintiff has gone to some other country for the period of a journey, or where the plaintiff has gone to some other country for a period of a journey, or where the plaintiff has been in fear of the power of his opponent, is disregarded. Consequently, limitation begins to run from the time of the cessation or removal of the excuse.

  Examples:-

  (1) No attention is paid to time which has elapsed while a person was a minor. The period of limitation only begins as from the time he reaches the age of puberty.

  (2) A has an action against B, a person in authority of whom he stands in fear. If time has elapsed by reason of A's not being able to bring an action against B while in authority, this fact shall not prevent an action being brought. the period of limitation only begins to run from the date of the

cessation of the power of B.

- 1664. The period of a journey is three days at a moderate speed, that is a distance of eighteen hours.

- 1665. If one of two persons living in places which are separated from each other by the period of a journey, meets the other person in one of such places once during a certain number of years, so that an action pending between them can be brought to trial, but neither of them takes any steps in the matter, no action may be brought by one against the other in respect to any matter which arose before the period of limitation began to run.

- 1666. If any person brings an action in Court against any other person in respect to some particular matter once in a certain number of years, without the case being finally decided, and in this way fifteen years pass by, the hearing of the action is not barred. But any claim made out of Court does not cause the period of limitation to cease to run. Consequently, if any person makes a claim in respect to any particular matter elsewhere than in Court, and in this way the period of limitation elapses, the hearing of an action by the plaintiff is barred.

- 1667. The period of limitation begins to run as from the date at which the plaintiff had the right to bring an action in respect to the subject matter of his claim. Consequently, in an action in respect to a debt repayable at some future definite date, the period of limitation only begins to run as from the date on which the debt fell due for payment, since the plaintiff has no right to bring an action in respect to the debt before the due date has arrived.

Examples:-

(1). A brings an action against B claiming from him the price of a thing sold to him fifteen years ago, subject to a period of three years for payment of the price. The action may be heard, since only twelve years have passed since the date of payment arrived.

(2). An action is brought in regard to property dedicated to pious purposes limited to children from generation to generation. The period for limitation is respect to an action brought by children of the second generation begins to run as from the date of the extinction of the children of the first generation, since the children of the second generation have no right to bring an action while the children of the first generation are alive.

(3). In actions relating to a marriage portion payable at a future date, the period of limitation begins to run from the date of the divorce or death of one of the spouses, since a marriage portion payable at a future date only falls due for payment on divorce or death.

- 1668. Limitation in respect to a person who is bankrupt only begins to run as from the date of the cessation of the bankruptcy.

Example:- A brings an action against B, who has been insolvent for fifteen years, and who recently has come into funds, in respect to a debt owing for a period of fifteen years, having refrained from bringing the action previously owing to B's being bankrupt. The action will be heard.

- 1669. If any person as mentioned above fails to bring an action without any excuse, such action is barred by effluxion of time and will not be heard during his lifetime, nor, on his death, will an action by his heirs be heard.

- 1670. If a person entitled to bring an action fails during a certain period to do so and on his death his heir likewise fails to do so for a certain period and the total of both periods amounts to the period of limitation, such action will not be heard.

- 1671. A vendor and purchaser, a person making and a person receiving a gift are like a person leaving property and a person inheriting property.

Examples :-

(1). A owns a piece of land for a period of fifteen years. B who owns a house abutting on to A's land takes no action during this period, and thereafter sells the house to a third person. The purchaser then brings an action against A alleging that A's land comprises a private road leading to his house. The action will not be heard.

(2). The vendor remains silent for a period and the purchaser similarly remains silent for a period, if the total amount of both periods amounts to the period of limitation, an action brought by the purchaser will not be heard.

- 1672. If some of a number of heirs in an action brought in respect to property of the deceased in the possession of some third person are barred owing to the period of limitation having elapsed, and others, by reason of some valid excuse, such as that they are minors, are not, and such action is successful, judgement shall be given in their favour for their share of the property, but such judgement shall be given in their share of the property, but such judgement shall not include the others.

- 1673. If any person admits that he has taken certain real property on hire, he may not claim to have become the owner of such property by reason of a period of more than fifteen years having elapsed. But if denies that he has taken it on hire and the owner states that the real property in question belongs to him absolutely, that he gave it on hire to him a certain number of years ago, and that he has always received the rent, the question will be examined as to whether the lease is generally known among the people, and if so, the action will be heard, but not otherwise.

- 1674. A right is not destroyed by the effluxion of time. Consequently, if the defendant explicitly admits and confesses in Court in a case in which the period of limitation has elapsed that the plaintiff is entitled to bring his action, the limitation is of no effect and the judgement will be given in accordance with the admission of the defendant. If the defendant, however, makes no admission in Court and the plaintiff alleges that he made the admission else where, the plaintiff will fail both on the original action and on the admission. But if the admission which is the subject of the action was reduced to writing at some previous date in a document known to contain the seal or handwriting of the defendant, and the period between the date on which such document was drawn up and the date of bringing the action is less than the period of limitation, an action on the admission will be heard.

- 1675. No period of limitation applies to actions concerning places appropriated to the use of the public such as the public highway, rivers and pasturing grounds.

Example :- A has appropriated and held a pasture ground belonging to a particular village for a period of fifty years without his right thereto being disputed. Thereafter the inhabitants of the village bring an action against A in respect to the pasture ground. The action will be heard.

PROMULGATED BY ROYAL IRADAH, 9 JUMADI UL UKHRA, 1293.

AL-MAJALLA AL AHKAM AL ADALIYYAH
(The Ottoman Courts Manual (Hanafi))

BOOK XV. EVIDENCE AND ADMINISTRATION OF OATH.

INTRODUCTION

TERMS OF ISLAMIC JURISPRUDENCE.

- 1676. Evidence consists of the adduction of reliable testimony.
- 1677. Conclusively substantiated evidence consists of statements made by a number of persons where it would be contrary to reason to conclude that they had agreed to tell a lie.
- 1678. Property owned in absolute ownership is property the ownership of which is not limited by a restrictive cause of ownership, such as inheritance or purchase. Ownership which is limited by any such cause is also called indirect ownership.
- 1679. A person in possession is a person who effectively possesses a specific piece of property, or a person acting as owner of and disposing of property held in absolute ownership.
- 1680. An outsider is a person who does not exercise possession over or dispose of property as mentioned above.
- 1681. Tendering the oath consists of administering the oath to one of the parties.
- 1682. Administration of the oath to both parties consists of putting both parties on oath.
- 1683. By maintaining an existing state of affairs is meant giving judgement for matters to continue as they are. It is in the nature of confirmation. Confirmation also means giving judgement for the continuation of a well ascertained matter, the non- existence of which is not suspected, by which is meant maintaining matters as they were.

CHAPTER 1. NATURE OF EVIDENCE.

SECTION 1. DEFINITION OF EVIDENCE AND NUMBER OF WITNESSES.

- 1684. Evidence consists of the giving of information by a person in Court and in the presence of the parties by employing the word "evidence", that is to say, by saying formally; "I give evidence", in order to prove the existence of a right which one person seeks to establish against another. * *(The translation of certain technical terms has been omitted, as having no meaning for the English reader.)

- 1685. In civil cases, evidence is only valid when given by two males, or one male and two females: but in places where males cannot be possessed of necessary information, the evidence of females alone will be accepted in respect to property.

- 1686. Evidence of the dumb and the blind is not receivable.

SECTION II. THE MANNER OF GIVING EVIDENCE.

- 1687. Evidence not given at the trial is invalid.

- 1688. Witnesses must personally have seen the thing with regard to which they give evidence and must testify accordingly. The giving of hearsay evidence that is to say, evidence of what the witness has heard other people say, is inadmissible. But if a witness has heard other people say, is inadmissible. But if a witness states that he has heard from a reliable source that a certain place has been dedicated to pious purposes, or that a certain person is dead, that is to say, if he gives evidence of such fact because he heard it from a reliable source, such evidence is accepted. In matters of state administration, death and paternity, a person may give hearsay evidence without stating that he is giving hearsay evidence, that is to say, without stating that he is saying what he has heard.yvT j Example:- A states that he he knows that B was governor or judge of the town at a certain date or period, or that B died at a certain time, or that B is the son of C. If A gives such evidence definitely without stating that it is hearsay, even though he has not investigated such matters and his age is such that he could not examined them, his evidence is accepted. Similarly, if A fails to state he is giving hearsay evidence and although such evidence has not been the subject of investigation by him, nevertheless, such evidence shall be accepted, if A states that such a thing is common knowledge with the people.

- 1689. If the witness fails to employ the formula: "I give evidence" and contents himself with saying that he knows a thing to be so, or if he states that he gives information, such statement is not considered to be evidence. Should the Court, however, thereupon ask the witness whether that is his manner of giving evidence and the witness replies in the affirmative, the statement becomes good evidence. Should it be necessary merely to verify or ascertain certain things, as for example in the case of reports furnished by experts, the word "evidence" need not be mentioned, since such reports merely contain information and not legal evidence.

- 1690. If the person in whose favour or against whom evidence is being given, and the thing about which evidence is being given, are present and if the witness points to the three of them, this shall be considered to be sufficient identification. There is no necessity to state the names of the father and grandfather of the persons for or against whom evidence is given. If the evidence relates to a deceased person, however, or an absent principal, the witness must state the names of such person's father or grandfather. But in the case of a person who is of high repute and well known, it is sufficient for the witness to state such person's name and description, since the real object is to describe him in such a way as to distinguish him from other persons.

- 1691. When giving evidence as to real property, the boundaries of such property must be stated. If the witness is unable to mention the boundaries of the real property with regard to which evidence is given, but states that he could indicate them on the spot, he shall proceed to the spot and there indicate the boundaries.

- 1692. Should the plaintiff bring an action based upon the boundaries set forth in his title deed, in accordance with the terms of Article 1623, witnesses may validly give evidence that such a person is the owner of the property, the boundaries of which are set forth in the title-deed.

- 1693. If a person brings an action to recover a sum of money owing to the person from whom he has inherited by some other person, it is sufficient if the witnesses give evidence that the sum of money is question was owing to the deceased by such person. There is no necessity to state that such sum has been inherited by the heirs. Should some specific thing be the subject of the claim and not the debt, that is to say, should a definite piece of property belonging to the testator be claimed, which is in the possession to the testator be claimed, which is in the possession of such person, the case will be decided in the same manner.

- 1694. If a person brings an action to recover a sum of money from the estate of a deceased person, witnesses may validly give evidence that such a sum of money is due to that person by the deceased. There is no necessity to state that the money was owing up to the time of his death. The same rule applies if an action is brought to recover certain property and not a debt, that is to say, when the plaintiff brings an action to recover property of his own in the possession of the deceased.

- 1695. If a person brings an action to recover a sum of money due from some other person, witnesses may validly give evidence that such a sum is owing by the latter to the plaintiff. If, however, the defendant puts in issue the question as to whether the debt is still due, witnesses may not validly state that they have no information as to whether the debt is still due or not.

SECTION III. FUNDAMENTAL CONDITIONS AS TO THE GIVING OF EVIDENCE.

- 1696. A condition precedent to giving evidence in civil cases is the institution of an action.

- 1697. Evidence which is contrary to obvious facts is inadmissible. Example:- If A has been seen alive, or a house has been seen to be in good condition, evidence that such person is dead, or that such house has fallen into disrepair is not admissible.

- 1698. Evidence of facts contrary to what is proved by conclusively substantiated evidence is inadmissible.

- 1699. The legal object of evidence is to prove a right. consequently, purely negative evidence is inadmissible,as where someone states that a certain person did not belong to a certain person, or that someone is not in debt to a certain person.

Conclusively substantiated evidence of a purely negative character, however, is admissible.yvT u Example:- A brings an action to recover a sum of money advanced as a loan, alleging that he lent a certain sum of money,at a certain time, and at a certain place, to a certain person. If conclusively substantiated evidence is given proving that A was not in that place at that time, but was elsewhere, such evidence is admissible and the plaintiff's case will be dismissed.

- 1700. It is a condition precedent to giving evidence that the witness should be entirely impartial. Consequently, evidence by an ascendant on behalf of a descendant or of a descendant on behalf of an descendant, that is to say, the evidence of a father and a grandfather and of a mother and a grandmother on behalf of their children and grandchildren and of children and grandchildren on behalf of their father and grandfather and mother and grandmother, and one of the spouses on behalf of the other, is not admissible. Subject to these exceptions, however, the evidence of relations on behalf of one another is admissible. The evidence of a man who is maintained at some other person's expense, and that of a person in the salaried employment of another on behalf of such person, is inadmissible. The evidence of fellow servants on behalf of one another, however, is admissible. Again, the evidence of partners on behalf of each other in respect to the partnership property, and of a surety in respect to payment by the principal of the sum for which he stood surety, is inadmissible. In other matters, however, the evidence of such persons on behalf of one another is admissible.

- 1701. The evidence of a person on behalf of his friend is admissible. But if the bonds of friendship uniting them are such that they use each other's property, such evidence is inadmissible.

- 1702. It is a condition precedent to the validity of the evidence that there should be no enmity of a temporal nature between the witness and the person against whom he gives evidence. Enmity of a temporal nature is ascertained by reference to custom.

- 1703. A person cannot be both plaintiff and witness. Consequently, the evidence of a guardian on behalf of an orphan and of an agent on behalf of his principal is inadmissible.

- 1704. A person may not give evidence of his own acts. Consequently, agents and brokers may not give evidence as to any sales effected by them. Similarly, if the judge of a town who has retired gives evidence as to a judgement delivered by him before his retirement, such evidence is inadmissible. But if he gives evidence after his retirement as to an admission made before him prior to his retirement, such evidence is valid.

- 1705. A witness must be an upright person. An upright person is one whose good qualities are greater than his bad qualities. Consequently, the evidence of persons who habitually behave in a manner inconsistent with honour and dignity, such as dancers and comedians, and persons who are known to be liars, is inadmissible.

SECTION IV. RELEVANCY OF EVIDENCE TO THE POINT AT ISSUE IN THE ACTION.

- 1706. Evidence is admissible if it agrees with the nature of the claim and not otherwise. There is no necessity, however, for mere conformity as to the language employed. It is enough if there is conformity in fact. yvT
Examples:-
(1). The action concerns an object deposited for safekeeping and witnesses give evidence that the defendant has admitted the deposit; or the action concerns wrongful appropriation of property and witnesses give evidence that the defendant has admitted the wrongful appropriation. The evidence is admissible.
(2). A debtor alleges in Court that he has paid his debt. Witnesses give evidence that the creditor released the debtor from payment. The evidence is admissible.

- 1707. The evidence must agree with the claim, whether such evidence goes to the whole or to part only of such claim.yvT x Examples:-
(1). A brings an action alleging that certain property has belonged to him for the last two years. Witnesses give evidence that such property has belonged to A for the last two years. Such evidence is admissible. It is also admissible if they give evidence that such has belonged to A for one year.
(2). The plaintiff's claim is for one thousand piastres. Witnesses give evidence as to five hundred.

Their evidence in regard to the five hundred is valid.

- 1708. Evidence in respect to more than is claimed is inadmissible. If, however, the divergence between the claim and the evidence is in fact capable of explanation and the plaintiff does so explain such divergence, the evidence is admissible. Examples:-

  (1). A brings an action alleging that certain property has been his for the last two years. Witnesses give evidence that such property has belonged to him for the last three years. The evidence is inadmissible.

  (2). The plaintiff's claim is for five hundred piastres. Witnesses give evidence as to one thousand piastres. The evidence is inadmissible. But if the plaintiff, by explaining that at one time one thousand piastres were in fact due to him from the defendant, but that five hundred piastres of that amount have since been repaid,of which the witnesses were unaware, shows that the action is in conformity with the evidence of the witnesses, the evidence of such witnesses is admissible.

- 1709. If the plaintiff brings an action for absolute ownership without stating how he became possessed of the property, alleging, for example, that a vineyard belongs to him, and witnesses give evidence as to the origin of the ownership, stating from whom the plaintiff bought the vineyard, the evidence is admissible. Thus, if the witnesses give evidence as to ownership arising from a definite cause and the Court asks the plaintiff as to whether his claim to the property arises from that cause or from some other, and the plaintiff replies that he does in fact claim the property by reason of such cause, the Court shall accept the evidence given by the witnesses. If, however, the plaintiff states that his claim is based upon some other cause, or that it is not based on that cause, the Court shall reject the evidence of the witnesses.

- 1710. A plaintiff may validly bring an action claiming ownership arising out of some definite cause, as for example, in the case of a vineyard. If the plaintiff, without mentioning the vendor, states that he has purchased such vineyard, or without stating the details, merely alleges that he has bought such a vineyard from a certain person, such action shall be considered to be an action for absolute ownership; and if the witnesses give evidence that the vineyard in question us the plaintiff's absolute property, such evidence is admissible. If the witnesses, however, give evidence as to absolute ownership of property, stating that the plaintiff bought such property from a certain person and describe the vendor, such evidence is inadmissible. The reason for this is that once an absolute right of ownership is established, the effect thereof is retrospective and will extend to matters incidental to such thing. For example, the fruit formerly produced by the vineyard also becomes the property of the plaintiff. If the right of ownership arises out of some definite cause, however, it can only be effective as from the date upon which such right arose, for example, as from the date of the sale. Consequently, a right of absolute ownership is more extensive than a right of ownership arising out of some definite cause and thus the witnesses have given evidence for more than the plaintiff has demanded.

- 1711. Evidence given in an action with regard to debt which is contrary to the claim is inadmissible.yvT Examples:-

  (1). The plaintiff claims payment of one thousand piastres alleged to be due to him as the price of a sale. If the witnesses give evidence to the effect that the defendant owes such sum in respect to a loan, their evidence is inadmissible.

  (2). The plaintiff claims that certain property has devolved upon him by way of inheritance from his father. Witnesses give evidence that the property has devolved upon him by way of inheritance from his mother. The evidence is inadmissible.

SECTION V. CONTRADICTORY EVIDENCE.

- 1712. The evidence of witnesses which is contradictory in respect to the matter regarding which the evidence is given, is inadmissible. yvT Example:- One witness gives evidence in respect to a thousand piastres gold; another witness gives evidence as to one thousand piastres in silver MEDJIDIES. Their evidence is inadmissible.

- 1713. If there is a contradiction in the evidence given by witnesses regarding matters incidental to the subject matter of their evidence and such contradiction extends to the subject matter of the evidence itself, such evidence is inadmissible. If the contradiction with regard to the incidental matter does not affect the subject matter of the evidence, however, the evidence is admissible. Consequently, if the evidence is given with regard to a mere fact, such as wrongful appropriation, or payment of a debt, and one witness gives evidence that the thing was done at another time or another place, such evidence is admissible, since the conflict of evidence shows a discrepancy to exist concerning the subject matter of the action. As regards matters, however, which are placed on record, such as sale, purchase, hire, suretyship, transfer of debt, gift, pledge, debt, loan, release and testamentary disposition, any contradiction of witnesses as to circumstances of time or place will not affect the validity of the evidence, since such contradiction does not affect the subject matter of the evidence.yvT z Example:- A asserts that he has paid a debt due. One witness gives evidence that A paid such debt in his house. Another witness gives evidence that A paid the debt in his shop. The evidence of the witnesses is inadmissible.
But if a person brings an action in Court claiming property in possession of some third person, asserting that such person sold him the property for a certain sum of money and claims delivery thereof, and one witness gives evidence that such property was sold in a certain house and the other that it was sold in a shop, such evidence is admissible, since an act once performed cannot be repeated, but a matter put on record can be repeated.

- 1714. Should witnesses contradict each other as regards the colour of property wrongfully appropriated, or whether it is of the male or female sex, their evidence is inadmissible.yvT r Example:- Wrongfully appropriation of an animal. A witness gives evidence to the effect that the animal is a grey horse. Another witness states that the animal is a dark-brown horse. Another witness states that it is a chestnut horse. Another witness states that it is a horse, while yet another states that it is a mare. The evidence of these witnesses is inadmissible.

- 1715. Contradictions as to the amount of the price in the evidence of witnesses in an action on a contract renders such evidence inadmissible.yvT ' Example:- One witness gives evidence stating that certain property was sold for five hundred piastres and another witness that it was sold for three hundred piastres. Their evidence is inadmissible.

SECTION VI. INQUIRY INTO THE CREDIBILITY OF WITNESSES.

- 1716. When witnesses have given evidence, the Court shall ask the person against whom evidence has been given whether he considers that the witnesses told the truth when giving their evidence. If such person states that he considers the witnesses are truthful or straight-forward as regards the evidence they have given, he has taken to have admitted the matter in issue, and judgement is given on his admission. If, however, he states that the witnesses have given false evidence, or that, while being upright persons, they are mistaken in regard to such matters or have forgotten the matter, or while admitting that the witnesses are upright persons, at the same time denies the matter in issue, judgement shall not be given =, but the Court shall take steps to ascertain, both publicly and privately, whether the witnesses are upright or not.

- 1717. The inquiry as to the credibility of witnesses shall be addressed either publicly or privately to the person having authority over such witnesses.
Thus, if the witnesses are students, the inquiry shall be addressed to the teacher of the school in which they are carrying on their studies, as well as from reliable inhabitants. If they are soldiers, from the officers and clerks of their battalion. If the witness is a clerk, from his superiors and from his fellow clerks in the office. If a merchant, from reliable persons who are also merchants. If a member of a guild, from the warden of such a guild and the members of the committee thereof. If he belongs to any other class, then from reliable inhabitants of the district or village.

- 1718. A private inquiry as to the credibility of a witness is called in technical legal language a sealed writing. The Court shall insert in the document the name of the plaintiff and defendant, the subject matter of the action, the names and descriptions of the witnesses, their profession, their identity,their place of residence, the names of their fathers and their grandfathers, or their names only it they are persons of note, together with their description, adding finally anything which will differentiate the witnesses from any other persons. The document shall then be sealed and placed in an envelope and sent to the persons selected to give information as to the credibility of the witnesses. If such persons, after perusal of the document, consider that the witnesses whose names are written therein are trustworthy, they shall state in writing under the names of the witnesses in question that they consider them to be trustworthy. They shall then sign the document and return it to the Court, sealing the envelope without allowing the person who has brought the document, or any other person, to ascertain the contents thereof.

- 1719. If the persons to whom the document is addressed for the purpose of giving the information fail to certify in writing that the witnesses are upright and that their evidence is admissible, or if in fact they state that they are not upright, or that they do not know them, or that they know nothing of the condition of such persons, or that it is matter beyond their knowledge, or make some similar statement either directly or by implication, the effect of which is that they are unable to certify the uprightness of the witnesses, or if they return the documents to the Court duly sealed, but without having written anything thereon, the Court shall not accept such evidence.
Upon the occurrence of such an event, the Court shall not tell the plaintiff that his witnesses are disqualified for giving evidence, but shall merely instruct him to produce other witnesses if he has any. If the document states, however, that the witnesses are trustworthy and that their evidence is admissible, a public enquiry shall thereupon be instituted as to the credibility of the witnesses.

- 1720. The public inquiry as to the credibility of witnesses is conducted as follows: the persons called upon to give the information are brought before the Court and the inquiry is made in the presence of the two parties; or the two parties, accompanied by a person specially deputed for that purpose, proceed to the place where the persons called upon to give the information reside, and the inquiry takes place publicly in their presence.

- 1721. Although in the case of a private inquiry one person may validly be selected to give information as to the credibility of witnesses, at least two should be appointed out of consideration of prudence.

- 1722. A public inquiry is in the nature of evidence. Consequently, the rules relating to evidence and the number of witnesses are applicable in this case also. It is unnecessary, however, for the persons selected to give informations to the credibility of the witnesses, to use the word evidence.

- 1723. If, in the opinion of the Court, the credibility of the witnesses has been proved in one particular case, the Court need not again inquire into the credibility of the same witnesses, if they give evidence with regard to some other matter before the expiration of a period of six months from the date on which they last gave evidence. If more than six months have have passed, however, the Court must again proceed to the enquiry.

- 1724. If either before or after the inquiry into the credibility of witnesses, the person against whom the evidence is given attacks the witnesses, alleging that they are giving their evidence for some ulterior motive, such as avoiding a loss or realising a gain, the Court shall call upon him to furnish proof of his allegations. If such person is able to prove his case by evidence, the Court shall reject the evidence of such witnesses. If not, the Court shall hold an inquiry into the credibility of the witnesses, if this has not already been done. If an inquiry has in fact been held, the Court shall give judgement in accordance with the evidence.

- 1725. In the event of some of the persons selected to give information as to the credibility of witnesses reporting against them and of others reporting in their favour, the Court shall give preference to the hostile report and shall refrain from giving judgement thereon.

- 1726. In the event of the decease of disappearance of witnesses who have given evidence in civil matters, the Court may still hold an inquiry into the credibility of their evidence and give judgement accordingly.

APPENDIX. SWEARING WITNESSES.

- 1727. Should the person against whom evidence is given ask the Court, before giving judgement, to put the witnesses on their oath that their evidence is not false, the Court may, If it deems it necessary, strengthen their evidence by administering the oath. The Court may inform the witnesses that their evidence will not be accepted unless they swear the oath.

SECTION VII. WITHDRAWAL OF EVIDENCE.

- 1728. Should witnesses who have given evidence in Court, such evidence is considered not to have been given and the witnesses shall be reprimanded.

- 1729. Should witnesses who have given evidence in Court withdraw such evidence after judgement has been delivered, the judgement stands, but the witnesses must pay the value of the subject matter of the action to the party against whom judgement has been given. (See Article 80).

- 1730. Should any of the witnesses withdraw their evidence as mentioned above, the evidence required being given by the others, those who withdraw need not pay the value of the subject matter of the action, but shall be reprimanded only. If the number of witnesses, however, is not enough to give the evidence required, half the value of the subject matter of the action must be paid by the witness who has withdrawn, if there is one only, or if there are more than one, then by them all in equal shares.

- 1731. A withdrawal of evidence, to be valid, must be made in Court. Any withdrawal made elsewhere is invalid. Consequently, a person against whom evidence is given will not be heard to allege that the witnesses have withdrawn their evidence out of Court. A witness who has given evidence in one Court may validly withdraw his evidence in another Court.

SECTION VIII. CONCLUSIVELY SUBSTANTIATED EVIDENCE.

- 1732. No importance is paid to the mere number of witnesses; that is to say, that if one of the parties has more witnesses than the other, he will not be preferred for that reason alone. If the number of witnesses, however, is so large that they conclusively substantiate the evidence, they will be preferred.

- 1733. Conclusively substantiated evidence is tantamount to positive knowledge.

- 1734. There is no necessity for the word "evidence" to be used in cases of conclusively substantiated evidence and there is also no need to insist that the witnesses should be of upright character. Consequently, there is no need for an inquiry as to the credibility of such persons.

- 1735. No definite number of persons is necessary to constitute conclusively substantiated evidence. There number must be so considerable, however, that it would be contrary to reason to conclude that they had agreed to tell a lie.

CHAPTER II. DOCUMENTARY EVIDENCE AND PRESUMPTIVE EVIDENCE.

SECTION I. DOCUMENTARY EVIDENCE.

- 1736. No action may be taken on writing or a seal alone. If such writing or seal is free from any taint of fraud or forgery, however, it becomes a valid ground for action, that is to say, judgement may be given thereon. No proof is required in any other way.

- 1737. The Sultan's rescript, and entries in the land registers are considered to be conclusive, since they are not tainted by fraud.

- 1738. As is set forth hereinafter in the Book relating to the Administration of justice by the Courts, registers kept by the Courts in such a way as to be free from any irregular practice or deception are considered to be conclusive.

- 1739. Documents instituting a pious foundation are not in themselves considered to be conclusive. If registered, however, in Court registers which are reliable as stated above, they are then considered to be conclusive.

SECTION II. PRESUMPTIVE EVIDENCE.

- 1740. A presumption is also a ground for judgement.

- 1741. A presumption is an inference which amounts to positive knowledge.yvT C Example:- A is seen leaving an empty house precipitately with a blood-stained knife in his hand. B thereupon enters the house and find C, who had just had his throat cut. It is certain that A is the murdered of C. No attention is paid to any mere possibility such as the possibility that C killed himself. (See Article 74).

CHAPTER III. ADMINISTERING THE OATH.

- 1742. One ground of judgement is taking or refusing to take the oath. Thus, should the plaintiff be unable to prove his case, the defendant shall take an oath at the instance of the plaintiff. If A, however, brings an action against B asserting that B is the agent of some third person, and B joins issue, it is not essential for B to be put on oath. Similarly, should two persons bring an action both asserting that they have bought from C property in the possession of C, and C later admits that he has sold the property of one of them but joins issue with the other, the oath shall not be administered to him. In this connection,hire, and receiving a pledge or a gift, are assimilated to purchase.

- 1743. Should it be intended to put one of the parties on his oath, he shall be caused to take the oath in the name of Allah.

- 1744. The oath may be sworn only before the Court or before some person representing the Court. A refusal to take oath before any other person is of no effect.

- 1745. A representative may validly be employed to place a person upon oath, but no substitution is permissible in swearing an oath. Consequently, the advocate of a party in an action may place the other party upon his oath, but when his client is put upon his oath, such client must swear the oath personally and not through his advocate.

- 1746. The oath is only administered upon the application of the opposite party. In four cases, however, the oath is administered by the Court without any application:-
(1).When a person lays claim to and proves that he has an interest in the estate of a deceased person, the Court shall require the plaintiff to swear an oath that he has not received anything in any way whatsoever in satisfaction of his interest from such deceased person, either directly or indirectly, nor that he has given a release thereof, nor transferred it to any other person, nor received anything in satisfaction thereof from any other person, nor received any pledge by way of security for his interest from the deceased person. Such form of oath is known as ISTIZHAR.
(2). When a person appears claiming to be entitled to certain property and proves his case, the Court shall require an oath to be taken by such person that he has not sold such property, nor disposed of it by way of gift, nor divested himself in any way of the property therein.
(3). When a person wishes to return a thing purchased on account of defect, the Court shall require him to take an oath that he did not, either expressly or impliedly, by reason of any disposition of such a thing as if it were his own property-- as is set forth in Article 344-- assent to the defect in the thing purchased.
(4). When the Court is about to give judgement in a case of pre-emption, the Court shall require the person claiming the right of pre-emption to swear an oath that he has not waived the right of pre-emption in any way whatsoever.

- 1747. If the defendant swears the oath at the instance of the plaintiff without the oath being administered by the Court, such oath is of no effect and must again be administered by the Court.

- 1748. When a person is about to swear an oath concerning his own act, he must swear such oath positively, stating that the matter is so, or is not so. But when a person is about to swear an oath concerning the act of some other person, he must be made to swear that he has no knowledge of such matter, that is to say, that he does not know such thing.

- 1749. The oath has reference either to cause or to effect. Thus, an oath that a certain thing has or has not happened is an oath as to cause; and an oath as to whether a thing is still continuing or not is an oath as to effect.yvT _ Example:- An oath in an action for sale and purchase to the effect that the contract of sale was never made at all is an oath as to cause; but an oath as to whether the contract is still continuing is an oath as to effect.

- 1750. When different action are joined together, one oath is sufficient. there is no necessity for a separate oath in each case.

- 1751. When in a civil action the oath is duly tendered to a person who is called upon to take the oath and such person refuses to take the oath, either expressly by refusing to swear, or impliedly by keeping silence without excuse, the Court shall give judgement on such refusal. If such person seeks to swear an oath after judgement has been delivered, the Court shall pay no attention thereto, and the judgement shall remain intact.

- 1752. A dumb man may validly take or refuse to take the oath by use of general recognised signs.

SUPPLEMENT.

- 1753. A plaintiff who has stated that he has no witnesses will not be heard to say that he intends to call witnesses. And if he has stated that he intends to call a certain witness and no other, he will not be allowed to call any other witness.

CHAPTER IV. PREFERRED EVIDENCE AND ADMINISTRATION OF THE OATH TO BOTH PARTIES.

SECTION I. ACTIONS REGARDING POSSESSION.

- 1754.In the case of a dispute relating to real property, possession thereof must be proved by evidence. Judgement will not be given that the defendant is in possession merely as the result of the affirmation of the two parties, that is, an admission made by the defendant in reply to the plaintiff,s claim. If the plaintiff, however, brings an action alleging that he has brought certain real property from a certain person, or that a certain person has wrongfully deprived the plaintiff of possession thereof, there is no need for the defendant to prove by evidence that he is in possession of such property. Again, if movable property is in the possession of a person, he is the possessor thereof, and there is no need for proof of that fact by evidence as stated above. The statement of the two parties on this point is sufficient.

- 1755. In the event of a dispute arising between two persons in respect to real property, each alleging that he is in possession of such property, the parties shall first of all be required to prove by evidence which of them is in possession. Should both parties produce evidence proving that they are in possession, such proof is taken to mean that they are in joint possession. Should one of the parties be unable to prove that he is in possession, while the other produces satisfactory proof thereof, judgement is given for possession in favour of the latter, and the former is considered to be out of possession. If neither party is able to prove that he is in possession, either may demand that the oath be administered to his opponent to the effect that he is not in possession of such real property. If both refuse to take the oath, they are taken to be jointly in possession of such property. If one person takes an oath, the other refusing to do so, judgement shall be given that the person taking the oath is in sole possession of such property and the other is considered to be out of possession. If both persons take oath, judgement shall be given that neither is in possession, and the real property in question shall be seized until such time as the true facts are established.

SECTION II. PREFERRED EVIDENCE.

- 1756. If two persons are joint owners of certain property, that is to say, if the two are in joint possession thereof, and bring an action, one party alleging that such property belongs to him alone, the other alleging that he is joint owner thereof, the evidence given of sole ownership shall be preferred. That is to say, if the two parties produce evidence in support of their case, the evidence of the person claiming absolute ownership is preferred to that of the person claiming joint ownership. If both of them claim to be absolute owners and produce evidence in support thereof, judgement shall be given that they are joint owners thereof. If one of the parties can produce no evidence and the other proves his case, judgement shall be given that the latter is sole owner of such property.

- 1757. In an action for absolute ownership, the evidence of the person not in possession is preferred if no date is mentioned.yvT | Example:- A brings an action with regard to a house in the possession of B, alleging that the house is his property and that B is wrongfully in possession thereof and asking that B should be evicted and the house restored to him. If B alleges that the house is his property and that consequently he is lawfully in possession thereof, the evidence of A will be preferred and heard.

- 1758. Actions relating to ownership arising from causes which are capable of repetition, as for example purchase, are regarded as identical with actions arising out of absolute ownership, if the date is not mentioned. In such cases, also the evidence of the person who is not in possession is preferred to that of the person in possession. Should both parties, however, claim that their right of ownership is held from one and the same person, the evidence of the person in possession is preferred.yvT L Example:- A brings an action claiming a shop in the possession of B, alleging that he bought such shop from one Veli Agha, and that B in this connection wrongfully took possession of the shop. B comes into Court and alleges that he bought the shop from one Bakir Effendi, or that he inherited it from his father, which is the reason for his being in possession. The evidence of A, the person not in possession, is preferred and heard. But if B, the person in possession, alleges that he bought the shop from Veli Agha, B's evidence is preferred to that of A, the person not in possession.

- 1759. In actions relating to ownership arising out of a cause which is incapable of repetition, as in the case of an animal giving birth to young, evidence of the person in possession is preferred. Consequently, in the event of a dispute relating to a colt between a person not in possession and one who is, and each party alleges that the colt is his property born from his own mare, the evidence of the person in possession is preferred.

- 1760. in a claim for ownership dependent on date, the evidence of the person giving the earliest date will be preferred.yvT U Example:- A brings an action relating to a plot of land in the possession of B, alleging that he bought such land a year ago from C. B by his answer states that the land developed upon him by way of inheritance from his father, who died five years ago. The evidence of the person in possession is preferred. But if B states that he inherited the land from his father who died six months ago, the evidence of the person not in possession is preferred. If each of the two parties alleges that he has bought the subject matter of the action from different persons, and each gives the date at which the person selling to them acquired the thing in question, the evidence given by the person giving the earliest dates will be preferred.

- 1761. In actions relating to the young of animals, no attention is paid to date, the evidence of the person in possession being preferred, as stated above. But if there is a discrepancy between the age of the animal which is the subject of the action and the date given by the person who is not in possession, the evidence of the latter is preferred. If the age of the animal is unknown, however, or if it is different from either date given, the evidence of neither is accepted, and the animal shall not be taken away from the person in possession.

- 1762. The greater claim is preferred.yvT - Example:- Vendor and purchaser disagree as to the quality or price of the thing sold. The evidence given by the party claiming most will be preferred.

- 1763. Evidence as to ownership is preferred to evidence as to loan for use.yvT
Example:- A claims the return of property in the possession of B, alleging that he lent the property to B for B's use. B by his reply alleges that A sold the property to him or bestowed it upon him by way of gift. The evidence as to the sale of the gift is preferred.

- 1764. Evidence as to sale is preferred to evidence as to gift, or pledge, or hire, and the evidence of hire to the evidence of pledge.yvT
Example:- A demands payment for certain property from B, which A alleges he sold B. B replies that A made a gift of such property to him and gave delivery thereof. The evidence of sale id preferred.

- 1765. In cases of a loan for use, the evidence in favour of a general loan is preferred.yvT Example :- A lends his horse to B to use. The horse dies while in the possession of B. A sues B for the value of the horse, alleging that he lent B the horse for a period of four days and on the fifth day it died without having been returned. B by his reply alleges that A did not limit the loan of the horse to a period of four days, but made the loan in general terms. The evidence of the person to whom the horse was lent is preferred.

- 1766.Evidence given as to good health is preferred to evidence given as to a mortal sickness.yvT 8
Example:- A makes a gift to one of his heirs and dies. Another heir alleges that the gift was made during the course of a mortal sickness. the person in whose favour the gift was made alleges that the gift was made while in good health. The evidence of the person in whose favour the gift was made is preferred.

- 1767. Evidence of soundness of mind is preferred to evidence of madness of imbecility.

- 1768. In the event of evidence being given concurrently as regards new and old things the evidence as to the new things is preferred.yvT
Example:- A possesses a right of flow upon the lands of B held in absolute ownership. A difference of opinion arises between them as to whether such right is of ancient or recent origin. The owner of the house alleges that it is of recent origin and demands the extinction of the right. The owner of the right of flow claims that such right is of ancient origin. The evidence of the owner of house is preferred.

- 1769. In the event of the person whose evidence is preferred being unable to prove his case by production of evidence, evidence is asked for from the person whose evidence has not been preferred. If he proves his case, his evidence shall be accepted; if he fails to do so, the oath shall be administered to him.

- 1770. In the event of the person whose evidence is preferred being unable to prove his case by the production of evidence as stated above, and if the party whose evidence is not preferred produces evidence, judgement shall be given in his favour. If the person whose evidence has been preferred wishes to produce evidence thereafter, such evidence shall not be heard.

SECTION III. PERSONS WHOSE EVIDENCE IS PREFERRED. JUDGEMENT BASED ON CIRCUMSTANTIAL EVIDENCE.

- 1771. If a husband and wife disagree as to the things in the house in which they dwell, the nature of the things must be examined. In the case of things suitable for the husband only, such as gun or a sword, or of things suitable for both, such as domestic utensils and furniture, the evidence of the wife is preferred. If both are unable to advance any proof, the husband may make a statement on oath. That is to say, if he states on oath that the things in question do not belong to his wife, judgement shall be given in his favour.
The evidence of the husband is preferred as regards things suitable for women only, such as clothing and jewellery. If both are unable to advance any proof, the wife may make a statement on oath. If one of the two makes and sells things which are suitable for the other, that person in any case may make a statement on oath.yvT , Example :- An earring is a piece of jewellery suitable for a woman. If the husband is a jeweller, he may make a statement on oath.

- 1772. Upon the death of one of the spouses, the heir stands in the place of the person from whom he inherits. If the two parties, as stated above, are unable to produce any proof as regards things suitable for both, the surviving spouse may make a statement on oath. Should both spouses have died at the same time, the heir of the husband may make a statement on oath as regards things suitable for both of them.

- 1773. Should a donor wish to revoke a gift and the beneficiary alleges at the trial of the action that the subject matter of the gift has been destroyed, the beneficiary may make statement not on oath.

- 1774. A person to whom a thing has been entrusted for safekeeping shall make a statement on oath as regards any question of his release from liability. Thus,if a person who has entrusted his property to another for safekeeping, brings an action against such person, and the latter by his reply alleges that he has returned the thing entrusted to him for safekeeping, such person shall make a statement on oath. But if he wishes to bring evidence in order not to swear an oath, such evidence shall be heard.

- 1775. If a person is indebted to another in respect to various sums of money and such person makes a payment to the creditor and an action is brought to determine in respect to which particular debt the payment has been made, the debtor shall make a statement.

- 1776. If a lessee of a mill seeks to deduct a portion of the rent of such mill after the expiration of the term of the lease by reason of the water having been cut off for a certain period during the currency of the lease and the lessor and lessee disagree thereon, and there be no evidence available, the nature of the case must be examined.
If the point at issue is the period of time during which the water was cut off, for example, if the lessee claims that it was ten days and the lessor five only, the lessee may make a statement on oath.
If the point at issue is as to whether the water has been cut-off at all, that is to say, if the lessor

absolutely denies that the water was cut off, judgement shall be given based on the circumstantial evidence of the case. Thus, if the water is running at the time the action is instituted and heard, the lessor shall make a statement on oath. If the water is not running at the time, the lessee shall make a statement on oath.

- 1777. If a dispute arises as to whether the channel along which water is flowing to a person's house is old or new, and the owner of the house alleges that it is new and wishes to remove it neither party can produce any evidence, the nature of the case must be examined. If the water is flowing at the time the case is instituted, or if it is a well-known fact that the water was flowing there formerly, no change shall be made in such channel. The owner of the channel may make a statement on oath, that is to say, he shall be caused to take an oath that the channel is not new. If at the time the case was instituted there was no water running in the channel and it is not known whether water flowed there formerly, the owner of the house may make a statement on oath.

SECTION IV. ADMINISTRATION OF THE OATH TO BOTH PARTIES.

- 1778. If a dispute occurs between vendor and purchaser as to the amount of the price, or the amount of the thing sold, or both, or as to the description or type thereof, judgement is given in favour of whichever of the two produces evidence. If both of them produce evidence, judgement is given in favour of the party who produces evidence for the greater amount.
If neither of the parties can prove their case, they shall be informed that either one party must admit the claim of the other, or the sale will be declared void. If neither party admits the claim of the other, the Court shall put each party upon his oath as to the claims of the other party, beginning with the purchaser. If either party refuses to take the oath, the other is taken to have proved his case. If both parties swear an oath, the Court shall declare the sale void.

- 1779. If a person taking a thing on hire has a dispute with a person giving a thing on hire with regard to the amount of the rent before taking possession of the thing hired, and an action is instituted in Court in connection therewith, judgement shall be given in favour of the person who produces evidence, as, for example, where the person taking the thing on hire alleges that the rent is so much and the person giving the thing on hire alleges that the rent is so much.
If both produce evidence, judgement shall be given in favour of the person giving the thing on hire.
If neither of the parties can prove their case, both of them are put on oath, beginning with the person taking the thing on hire, judgement being given against the person who refuses to take the oath.
If both parties take the oath, the Court shall declare the contract of hire to be void.
Should a dispute arises as to any question of time or distance, the matter shall be dealt with in the same manner. Provided, however, that if both parties produce evidence, judgement shall be given on the evidence of the person taking the thing on hire. If the oath is administered to both parties, the person giving the thing on hire shall first be put on oath.

- 1780. In the event of a dispute arising between the person giving and the person taking a thing on hire, as is set forth in the preceding Article, after the period of the contract of hire has expired, the oath is not administered to both parties. The person taking the thing on hire alone may make a statement on oath.

- 1781. If the person giving a thing on hire and the person taking a thing on hire have a dispute as to the amount of the rent during the period of the contract of hire, both parties shall be put on oath, and the contract cancelled as regards the remainder of the period. The person taking the thing on hire may make a statement as to the portion relating to the period which has elapsed.

- 1782. If a dispute arises between vendor and purchaser as to a thing sold which has been destroyed while in the possession of the purchaser, or if a defect of recent origin has been revealed which prevents such thing being returned, the oath is not administered to both parties, but to the purchaser only.

- 1783. If an action is brought with regard to the due date of any particular thing, that is to say, whether the time for the performance of such thing has arrived or not, or with regard to a right of option, or as to whether the whole amount or part only of the price has been received, the oath is not administered to both parties, but in these three cases only to the person who denies.

PROMULGATED BY ROYAL IRADAH, 26TH SHAABAN, 1293.

AL-MAJALLA AL AHKAM AL ADALIYYAH
(The Ottoman Courts Manual (Hanafi))

BOOK XVI. ADMINISTRATION OF JUSTICE BY THE COURT.

INTRODUCTION

TERMS OF ISLAMIC JURISPRUDENCE.

- 1784. The phrase administration of justice embrace the judgement and the duties of the judge.

- 1785. The judge is a person appointed by the Sovereign for the purpose of dealing with and settling actions and disputes arising between the people in accordance with the terms of law.

- 1786. The judgement consists of the stopping and settlement of disputes by the judge. Judgements are of two classes.
  The first class consists of the Court giving judgement whereby the person against whom the judgement has been given is forced to give up the subject matter of the action as where he orders the thing claimed to be given. This class of judgement is called an obligatory judgement, or a judgement for something which is due.
  The second class consists of the Court forbidding the plaintiff to bring an action as where it informs the plaintiff that he has no right to bring an action, and that he is forbidden to do so. This class of judgement is called a judgement by way of dismissal.

- 1787. The subject matter of the judgement consists of the obligation imposed by the Court upon the party against whom judgement is given. Thus, an obligatory judgement consists of recognising the right of the plaintiff, and in an action by way of dismissal consists of obliging the plaintiff to give up his action.

- 1788. The losing party is the person against who judgement is given.

- 1789. The successful party is the person in whose favour judgement is given.

- 1790. Arbitration consists of the parties to an action agreeing together to select some third person to settle the question at issue between them, who is called an arbitrator.

- 1791. A deputy defendant is an agent appointed by the Court to represent a defendant who fails to appear in Court.

CHAPTER I. JUDGES.

SECTION I. QUALITIES REQUISITE IN A JUDGE.

- 1792. The judge must be intelligent, upright, reliable and firm.
- 1793. The judge must have a knowledge of Islamic Law and jurisprudence and of the rules of procedure, and must be able to decide and settle actions in accordance therewith.
- 1794. The judge must be of perfect understanding. Consequently, any judicial act performed by a minor or an imbecile or a blind man or a person so deaf that he cannot hear the statements of the parties when speaking loudly, is invalid.

SECTION II. CONDUCT OF JUDGES.

- 1795. The judge must abstain from any act or deed of a mature injurious to the dignity of the Court, such as engaging or selling, or making jokes while in Court.
- 1796. The judge may not accept a present from either of the parties.
- 1797. The judge may not accept the hospitality of either of the parties.
- 1798. The judge must abstain from any act during the trial likely to arouse suspicion or cause misunderstanding, such as receiving one of the parties alone in his house, or retiring with one of them with his hand or his eye or his head, or speaking to one of them secretly or in a language not understood by the other.
- 1799. The judge must be impartial towards the two parties. Consequently, the judge must observe complete impartiality and equality towards the two parties in everything relating to the trial of the action, such as causing them to sit down during the course of the trial, and when looking towards or addressing them and this whether one of the parties is a person of high rank and the other of low estate.

SECTION III. DUTIES OF JUDGES.

- 1800. The judge is the representative of the Sovereign for the purpose of carrying of the trial giving judgement.
- 1801. The jurisdiction and powers of the judge are limited by time and place and certain matters of exception.yvT
  Examples:-
  (1). A judge appointed for a period of one year may only give judgement during that year. He may not give judgement before the year commences or after the expiration thereof.
  (2). A judge appointed for a certain district may give judgement in any place in such district. He may not, however, give judgement elsewhere. A judge appointed to give judgement in a particular Court may only give judgement in that Court. He may not give judgement elsewhere.
  (3). If an order is issued by the sovereign authority that actions relating to a particular matter shall not be heard in the public interest, the judge may not try such action. Action, the judge may be authorised to hear certain matters only in a particular Court and no other. The judge may only try those cases he is authorised to hear and give judgement thereon.

(4). An order is issued by sovereign authority to the effect that in a certain matter the opinion of a certain jurist is most in the interest of the people, and most suited to the needs of the moment, and that action should be taken in accordance therewith. The judge may not act in such a matter in accordance with the opinion of a jurist which is in conflict with that of the jurist in question. If he does so, the judgement will not be executory.

- 1802. If two judges are appointed jointly to hear and give judgement in an action, one of them alone may not try such action and deliver judgement. If he does so, the judgement is not executory. (See Article 1465).

- 1803. If there are various judges in one particular place, and one of the parties desires the case to be tried by one judge and the other wishes the case to be tried by another, and a difference of opinion occurs between them in the matter, the judge selected by the defendant shall be preferred.

- 1804. If a judge is removed from his post, but the news of his removal is not communicated to him for some time, any cases heard and decided by him during that period are valid. A judgement issued by him after the news of his removal has been communicated to him is invalid.

- 1805. A judge who is duly authorised may appoint a person as deputy judge and may dismiss him. He may not do so, if he is not duly authorised. If he himself is dismissed or dies, his deputy is not likewise dismissed. (See Article 1466). Consequently, if a judge in a certain district dies, the action in that district dies, the action in that district shall be tried by the deputy of the deceased judge, until the arrival of a new judge.

- 1806. The judge may decide a case on evidence heard by the judge. Thus, if the judge has heard evidence in an action and communicates it to his deputy, the latter may give judgement without rehearing the evidence. Similarly, if the deputy of a judge is authorised to give judgement, he may hear evidence on a certain matter and refer it to the judge, and the latter may give judgement thereon without rehearing the evidence. If a person who is not authorised to give judgement, however, but only to hear evidence for the purpose of investigating and inquiring into a matter, refers a question to the judge the latter may not give judgement, but must hear the evidence himself.

- 1807. A judge of the district may hear actions relating to land situated in another district. But as stated in the Book on Actions, the boundaries thereof must be set forth as required by law.

- 1808. The person in whose favour judgement is given must not be an ascendant or descendant or the wife of the judge, nor his partner, nor a private employee in respect to the property which is the subject matter of the judgement, nor a person who lives at the expense of the judge. Consequently, the judge may not hear a case relating to one of such persons, nor give judgement in his favour.

- 1809. If the judge of a town or the persons connected with him as stated in the preceding Article, are concerned in an action with any of the inhabitants of such town, the case shall be heard by some other judge in the town, if one is to be found there. If there is no other judge in the town, the case may be tried by an arbitrator to be appointed by the parties, or, if the judge is authorised to appoint a representative the case shall be heard by him or in the case may be tried by the judge of an adjoining district. If the parties do not agree to settle the matter in any one of the ways mentioned above, they may ask the sovereign authority to delegate some person empowered to deal with the question.

- 1810. In the hearing of actions, the Court shall deal with them in order of priority. The Court may, however, expedite the hearing of an action when it is in the interests of justice to do so.

- 1811. A judge may, when necessary, ask the opinion of some other person on a point of law.

- 1812. A judge may not give judgement when in such a condition that he cannot think clearly, as where he is in trouble, or suffering from hunger or sleeplessness.

- 1813. A Judge may not delay a case unduly by reason of investigations as to the facts.

- 1814. The judge is responsible for keeping a register in Court and recording therein all judgements given and documents issued in such a manner as to be free from any irregularity. In the event of the judge being removed, he must hand over such register to his successor either personally or through some person in whom he has confidence.

SECTION IV. THE HEARING OF AN ACTION.

- 1815. the judge must hold the trial in public. He may not, however, reveal the nature of the judgement before it is pronounced.

- 1816. When the parties are present in Court for the purposes of the trial, the judge shall first of all call upon the plaintiff to state his case. If he has previously reduced his claim to writing it shall be read over and confirmed by the plaintiff. He shall then call upon the defendant to answer. Thus, he shall inform the defendant that the plaintiff makes such and such claim against him, and shall ask the defendant to reply

- 1817. If the defendant admits the claim, the judge shall give judgement on the admission. If he denies, the judge shall call upon the plaintiff for his evidence.

- 1818. If the plaintiff proves his case by evidence, the judge shall give judgement accordingly. if he cannot prove it, he has a right to the oath, and if he asks to exercise such right, the judge shall accordingly tender the oath to the defendant.

- 1819. If the defendant swears the oath, or if the plaintiff does not ask for the oath to be administered, the judge shall order the plaintiff to give up his claim upon the defendant.

- 1820. If the defendant refuses to take the oath, the judge shall deliver judgement based upon such refusal. If the defendant states that he is prepared to swear an oath, after judgement has been so delivered, the judgement shall remain undisturbed.

- 1821. The content of a judgement or of a document issued by the judge of a Court in the ordinary way and which is free from any taint of forgery or fraud, may be acted upon and judgement given thereon, without the necessity for any proof by evidence.

- 1822. If the defendant persists in keeping silence and refuses to answer either in the affirmative or negative, after being questioned as stated above, his silence in considered to amount to a denial. If he states that he neither confesses nor denies, his answer is considered to amount to a denial. In both cases the plaintiff shall be called upon to produce evidence.

- 1823. If the defendant instead of admitting or denying the plaintiff's claim, puts forward a counter claim, action shall be taken in accordance with the matter mentioned in the Book on Actions and book on Evidence.

- 1824. Neither party may interrupt the other while he is making a statement. If he does so, he shall be prohibited therefrom by the Court.

- 1825. The Court shall provide a competent and reliable interpreter for the translation of statements made by any person who does not know the language of the parties.

- 1826. In the case of actions brought by relatives or in cases where there is a possibility of the parties coming to a settlement, the judge shall advise the parties one or twice to come to a settlement. If they agree, a settlement shall be drawn up in accordance with the terms of the Book on Settlements. If they do not so agree, the case shall be tried out.

- 1827. After the judge has concluded the trial, he shall give judgement and make it known to the parties. He Shall then draw up a formal judgement containing full reasons for the decision and orders given. A copy thereof shall be given to the successful party and, if necessary, a copy to the party losing the action.

- 1828. Once the judge is fully in possession of the facts and reasons for the judgement, he may not delay promulgation thereof.

CHAPTER II. JUDGEMENTS

SECTION I. CONDITIONS ATTACHING TO A JUDGEMENT.

- 1829. No judgement may be issued unless an action has been instituted. Thus, for a judge to give a judgement in any matter where the rights of the public are affected, an action must have been brought by one person against another in respect to that matter. Any judgement issued which is not based upon an action is invalid.

- 1830. The parties must be present when judgement is given. That is to say, the parties having been present during the hearing of the action, must be present also when judgement is given. But if any person brings an action against some other person and the defendant admits the claim, and leaves the Court before judgement is pronounced, the judge may pronounce judgement in his absence, based upon the admission. Again, if the defendant denies the plaintiff's action, and the plaintiff comes into Court and brings evidence to prove his claim, and the defendant leaves the Court before the enquiry as to the credibility of the witness is commenced and before judgement is given, the judge may proceed to the enquiry as to the credibility of the witness, and pronounce judgement in his absence.

- 1831. If the defendant is personally present in Court after evidence has been given in the presence of his representative, the judge may give judgement against him on such evidence. On the other hand, if the representative of the defendant is present and evidence has been given in the presence of the defendant, the judge may give judgement against the representative after hearing the evidence.

- 1832. If an action is brought against the whole of the heirs of a deceased person, and the evidence has been given in the presence of one of them, and such heir leaves before judgement is pronounced, the judge may give judgement against any other heir who may be summoned to be present on such evidence. There is no need for the evidence to be repeated.

SECTION II. JUDGEMENT BY DEFAULT.

- 1833. The defendant shall be summoned to appear before the Court by the judge upon the application of the plaintiff. If he fails to appear, either personally or through a representative, in the absence of any valid excuse, he may be forced to appear.

- 1834. If the defendant fails to appear, either personally, or through a representative, and it is not possible to bring him into Court, the Court shall, on the application of the plaintiff, issue a summons to him on three separate occasions to appear in Court, and, upon his failing to appear, the judge shall inform him that a representative will be appointed for him, and that the case for the plaintiff together with his evidence, will be heard. If the defendant persists in his refusal to appear, either personally or through a representative, the judge shall appoint a person as his representative in order to safeguard his interests. The case for the plaintiff, together with his evidence, shall then be heard in the presence of the representative, and, if proved, judgement shall be issued accordingly.

- 1835. A judgement issued by default as mentioned above shall be served upon the defendant.

- 1836. If a person against whom a judgement has been issued by default appears in Court and shows that he has a defence to the plaintiff's claim, his defence shall be heard and action taken as may be necessary. If he has no defence to the claim, or if he brings a defence which fails, the judgement given shall be put into execution.

CHAPTER III. RETRIAL.

- 1837. An action in respect to which a judgement has validly been given, that is to say, a judgement which contains the reasons and grounds therefor, may not be heard again.

- 1838. If any person against whom judgement has been given alleges that such judgement is contrary to the rules of law and gives the reasons therefor, asking for the case to be heard in appeal, the judgement, if found to be in accordance with law, shall be confirmed. If not, the case will be heard in appeal.

- 1839. If the person against whom judgement has been given is dissatisfied with such judgement, and asks for the rectification thereof, such judgement shall be examined, and, if it is found to be in accordance with law, shall be confirmed. If not, it shall be reversed.

- 1840. A defence may be valid before judgement and after judgement. Consequently, if any person against whom judgement has been given, shows that he has a sound defence thereto, and asks for retrial of the action, his defence shall be heard in the presence of the person in whose favour judgement has been given, and the matter tried out.yvT " Example :- A brings an action against B alleging that a house in B's possession belongs to him, and that he inherited it from his father and proves his case. Judgement is given in his favour. B then sets up the defence that A's father sold the house to his father and produces a valid title-deed. B's defence will be heard, and if proved, the original judgement will be reversed and his action dismissed.

CHAPTER IV. ARBITRATION.

- 1841. Actions relating to rights concerning property may be settled by arbitration.

- 1842. The decision of an arbitrator is valid and executory only in respect to the persons who have appointed him, and the matters he has been appointed to decide. He may not have reference to any person or deal with any matters other than those included in the terms of reference.

- 1843. More than one arbitrator may be appointed, that is to say, two or more persons may be appointed to give a decision in respect to one matter. Both plaintiff and defendant may each validly appoint an arbitrator.

- 1844. In the event of several arbitrators being appointed as above, their decision must be unanimous. One alone may not give a decision.

- 1845. The arbitrators may, if they are duly authorised thereunto by the parties, appoint another person to act as arbitrator. They may not do so otherwise.

- 1846. If the arbitration is limited as to time it ceases to be of effect after the expiration of such time.yvT Example:- An arbitrator appointed to decide a matter within a period of one month as from a certain date, may only decide such matter within that period. He cannot give a decision after the expiration of that month. If he does so, the judgement will not be executory.

- 1847. Either of the parties may dismiss the arbitrator before he has given his decision. If the parties have appointed an arbitrator, however, and such appointment has been confirmed by a Court duly authorised thereunto, the arbitrator is considered to be a representative of the Court and cannot be dismissed.

- 1848. All decisions by arbitrators as regards the persons and matter in respect to which they have been appointed are binding and executory to the same extent as the decisions by the Courts concerning persons within their jurisdiction. Consequently, a decision validly given by the arbitrators in accordance with the rules of law is binding on all parties.

- 1849. A decision by an arbitrator, upon submission to a properly constituted Court, shall be accepted and confirmed, if given in accordance with law. Otherwise, it shall not be so confirmed.

- 1850. The parties appointing the arbitrators may authorise the arbitrators, if they think fit, to make a settlement, and such arbitrators may then make a valid settlement. Thus, if each of the parties appoint a person to act as arbitrator with power to dispose of the matter in dispute by way of settlement, and such arbitrators duly arrive at a settlement in conformity with the terms of the Book on Settlements, such settlement and arrangement is binding on both parties.

- 1851. Should an authorised person act as arbitrator in a dispute and give a decision and the parties later agree to adopt his decision, such decision is executory. (See Article 1453).

PROMULGATED BY ROYAL IRADAH, 26 SHAABAN, 1293.

www.ingramcontent.com/pod-product-compliance
Lightning Source LLC
Chambersburg PA
CBHW080241180526

45167CB00006B/2366